"Roy S. Whitehurst's *Teaching Media i*
Media News is exceptional in the media literacy field.
Leveraging his CIA expertise, it offers educators a well-researched toolkit with practical techniques, real-world examples, and engaging lesson plans. This indispensable guide empowers teachers to help students excel in our complex digital world, fostering critical thinking about contemporary media."

  —**Tim Jones**, *Library Media Specialist and K–12 Media Literacy Teacher of the Year 2023 (NAMLE)*

"In a complex information environment, learning how to evaluate different kinds of information is essential for tweens and teens in and beyond the classroom. The excellent help and advice in *Teaching Media Literacy with Social Media News* will be a boon to teachers and students. A wide variety of lesson plans, exercises and information will help teachers develop their students' critical thinking skills. Exercises using popular social media platforms will help make the lessons relevant to students."

  —**Joanna Burkhardt**, *Faculty Librarian, University of Rhode Island*

"If ever there was a time for this book, this is it. Forces are at work overtime to fool media illiterate students. Roy S. Whitehurst is uniquely qualified to provide educators with a critically important tool for their toolbox. You'll be pleased to have this one on the shelf for teachers."

  —**Frank W Baker**, *Media Literacy Clearinghouse, 2019 UNESCO Honoree*

Teaching Media Literacy with Social Media News

Featuring tools, activities, and insightful stories from a CIA analyst and instructor with 30+ years of experience, this practical and engaging book supports busy educators to teach the lifelong skills of news and media literacy to their students.

Based on existing curriculum and teaching standards, this guidebook shows how social studies and English language arts (ELA) teachers can build students' confidence with social media evaluation skills, which are critical to engaging in civic discourse and building a stronger democracy. In Part I, Whitehurst gives an overview of the media evaluation techniques based on those you would learn as a CIA analyst, including understanding how our biases and mindset make us vulnerable to disinformation, learning how media tries to persuade us, checking facts, and spotting disinformation. Part II dives deeper by showing teachers how learners can check if an argument on social media is valid and how fallacies and manipulation tactics in online arguments can complicate this important skill. It is illustrated by examples from social media and contemporary popular culture in different mediums, including videos, photos, memes, and AI-generated content. You can also find fresh and updated social media examples on the author's website, Media Literacy Sleuth.

Packed with practical classroom resources, examples from popular culture, and engaging insights into the CIA analyst role, this book is designed to support middle and high school teachers in teaching news and media literacy in social studies, civic education, and ELA.

Roy S. Whitehurst is a retired Media Analyst Instructor for the CIA. Roy spent 30+ years evaluating written information, photos, videos, and other media collected by the CIA before becoming an instructor, teaching media literacy skills to new CIA analysts.

Teaching Media Literacy with Social Media News

Practical Techniques for Middle and High School Classrooms

Roy S. Whitehurst

Routledge
Taylor & Francis Group

NEW YORK AND LONDON

Designed cover image: © Shutterstock

First published 2025
by Routledge
605 Third Avenue, New York, NY 10158

and by Routledge
4 Park Square, Milton Park, Abingdon, Oxon, OX14 4RN

Routledge is an imprint of the Taylor & Francis Group, an informa business

Library of Congress Cataloging-in-Publication Data
Names: Whitehurst, Roy S., author.
Title: Teaching media literacy with social media news : practical techniques for middle and high school classrooms / Roy S. Whitehurst.
Description: New York, NY : Routledge, 2025. | Includes bibliographical references.
Identifiers: LCCN 2024013048 (print) | LCCN 2024013049 (ebook) | ISBN 9781032748603 (hardback) | ISBN 9781032740577 (paperback) | ISBN 9781003471301 (ebook)
Subjects: LCSH: Media literacy--Study and teaching (Middle school) | Media literacy--Study and teaching (Secondary) | Social media in education.
Classification: LCC P96.M4 W47 2025 (print) | LCC P96.M4 (ebook) | DDC 302.23071/2--dc23/eng/20240621
LC record available at https://lccn.loc.gov/2024013048
LC ebook record available at https://lccn.loc.gov/2024013049

ISBN: 978-1-032-74860-3 (hbk)
ISBN: 978-1-032-74057-7 (pbk)
ISBN: 978-1-003-47130-1 (ebk)

DOI: 10.4324/9781003471301

Typeset in Warnock Pro
by SPi Technologies India Pvt Ltd (Straive)

To God, for giving me the capacity and opportunity to write this book; to my wife and daughter, who supported me every step of the way; and to my parents, who sparked my curiosity to think critically about the world.

Contents

Meet the Author

Roy S. Whitehurst grew up just outside Washington, DC. Its free museums, think tanks, and foreign embassies made him curious about the world. After earning a bachelor's degree in international relations from the College of William & Mary and a master's in international affairs from George Washington University, he acted on his curiosity by joining the Central Intelligence Agency (CIA) as an intelligence analyst. Roy spent most of the next 35 years evaluating written reports, photos, videos, and other media about foreign countries and producing analytic products for senior US policymakers.

In the later years of his career, Roy developed a passion for teaching these media literacy skills to new CIA analysts, most of whom were in their 20s and 30s. As the United States became increasingly polarized over media reports about the 2016 US presidential election, he realized there was a critical need to teach news literacy to middle and high school students. Roy wrote this book to do just that.

Roy maintains a website, **www.medialiteracysleuth.com**, where he periodically evaluates the credibility of media supporting middle and high school social studies, and, to keep students engaged, trending pop culture (art, media, and ideas preferred by ordinary people rather than the educated elite.[1] Unlike high culture, popular culture is known and accessible to most people).

In his spare time, Roy enjoys fishing, where he has become good at figuring out which fish tales are true and which are, well, "fishy."

▶ **NOTE**

1 Pop culture—Definition, Meaning & Synonyms | Vocabulary.com.

Preface

Our democracy is scarred. When protesters stormed the Capitol on January 6, 2021—an image vivid even now to most Americans and foreign observers—they were motivated largely by fear that the election was "stolen." The causes of the violence were many, but anxiety about growing diversity in the United States, a perception of "losing out" to other parties not aligned with their interests, and a feeling of being cheated by those in power and the political system were key drivers.[1,2,3]

The move was the denouement of years of disinformation—usually false or misleading information that is deliberately created to harm a person, social group, organization, or country.[4] The protesters and their supporters fell for the distorted media that played on their biases. They were mostly white men, but several teens were among the protesters,[5,6] revealing that teens are also vulnerable to believing and acting on disinformation.

It is reasonable to assume that many of the protesters and their supporters lacked the skills to properly evaluate information surrounding the election. They preferred information from people they trusted: their in-group. They searched for and were led astray by information that confirmed their preexisting views.

All of us are vulnerable to inaccurate information and many of us lack the skills to evaluate it. Our biases are products of our evolutionary past, and for tens of thousands of years, they served us well. People who behaved according to their biases—for example, by staying away from the overgrown riverbank where someone said there was a viper—were more likely to survive than those who did not.

Modern technologies are amplifying our biases. Search engine algorithms prioritize information in our social media feeds that we are predisposed to agree with—no matter how fringe—and shield us from information that might change our minds. They direct us to sites that inflame our suspicions, and social media connects us with like-minded people, feeding our fears. This makes us easy targets for polarization.

Bots—automated social media accounts that impersonate humans—enable ill-informed or malicious actors to take advantage of our vulnerabilities. Making matters worse, artificial intelligence and machine-learning algorithms allow malicious actors to create realistic digital representations of people's voices and images—so-called deepfakes—and associate them with anything the actor wants, essentially creating disinformation that can be hard to detect.

The proliferation of misleading and false information on social media is making things worse. Producing blogs, videos, tweets, and units of information called memes has become so cheap and easy that the information marketplace is inundated. Unable to process all this information, we let our cognitive biases decide what we should pay attention to. These mental shortcuts influence which information we search for, accept, remember, and repeat.

Tools are constantly developed to help us fight back. Yet no tool can make us, especially preteens (those aged 9—12 years) and teens, immune from misleading and false information. We need critical thinking to do that.

When I taught intelligence analysis to new CIA analysts, I saw how many of them had difficulty evaluating the credibility of media, including text, photos, videos, and charts. I realized that if many of these young CIA recruits have a hard time doing it, most preteens and teens, with less life experience, have an even tougher time. Motivated in part by the disinformation that emerged around the 2016 US presidential election—and the concern I felt when my wife's niece, echoing her peers, said she got a lot of her "news" from TikTok—I decided to write this book.

In this book, I provide methods for middle and high school teachers to help students learn and apply fact-checking and logic-checking to information. I do so by meeting students where they are—on social media—where they are exposed to so much false and misleading information and opinions unsupported by facts. I try to "hook" students by showing them how to evaluate news about pop culture they are already interested in. I also show them how to apply their skills to more traditional, recurring social studies, civics, and ELA topics connected to standards of learning. With this dual approach, I hope students will actually enjoy evaluating social media. The skills are critical for students to carry out civic duties and strengthen democracy. By learning them, students will enter the world ready to engage news, not avoid news because they distrust it.

▶ **NOTES**

1 January 6 Insurrection: One Year Later, Families Are Still Divided | Teen Vogue.

2 Racism's Prominent Role in January 6 US Capitol Attack, Human Rights Watch, Racism's Prominent Role in January 6 US Capitol Attack | Human Rights Watch (hrw.org), January 5, 2023.

3 Heading 'into a Buzzsaw': Why Extremism Experts Fear the Capitol Attack Is Just the Beginning," CNN, Capitol riots unleashed long—term danger, experts warn | CNN, January 18, 2021.

4 *Mis, Dis, and Malinformation*, Cybersecurity & Infrastructure Security Agency, https://www.cisa.gov/mdm.

5 "What We Know about the "Unprecedented" Capitol Riot Arrests," Clare Hymes, Cassidy McDonald, Eleanor Watson, August 11, 2021.

6 "Lawyer Argues 19—Year—Old Capitol Rioter's Brain Isn't Fully Matured in Bid to Avoid Jail," Newsweek, Jenni Fink, January 3, 2022.

Acknowledgments

I could not have written this book without the support of many people. I'm sure I will leave out some who deserve mention, for which I take full responsibility. With that said, I would like to call out several individuals in particular. Chris Sperry from Project Look Sharp encouraged me at the very start of my project by referring me to Frank Baker, media literacy consultant. Frank was enthusiastic from the start about my interest in media literacy and suggested I write a book synthesizing my knowledge and experience from my time at the CIA. I also owe a debt of gratitude to the team at Routledge, particularly my editor Emmie Shand, who gave me the support I needed to publish and market the book. Finally, I could not have written the book without my wife, whose patience and support allowed me to carve out time every day to research and write, and my daughter, who encouraged me to keep going.

Relevant Learning Standards

The information and lessons in this book support the following learning standards:

Core State Standards for English Language Arts and Literacy in History/Social Studies, Science, and Technical Subjects:[1]

- "Delineate and evaluate the argument and specific claims in a text, including the validity of the reasoning as well as the relevance and sufficiency of the evidence."
- "Distinguish among facts, reasoned judgment based on research findings, and speculation in a text."
- Distinguish among fact, opinion, and reasoned judgment in a text.
- Identify aspects of a text that reveal an author's point of view or purpose (e.g., loaded language, inclusion or avoidance of particular facts).
- Determine the meaning of words and phrases as they are used in a text, including figurative, connotative, and technical meanings; analyze the cumulative impact of specific word choices on meaning and tone (e.g., how the language of a court opinion differs from that of a newspaper).
- "Assess how point of view or purpose shapes the content and style of a text."
- "Integrate visual information (e.g., in charts, graphs, photographs, videos, or maps) with other information in print and digital texts."
- "Integrate and evaluate content presented in diverse formats and media, including visually and quantitatively, as well as in words."
- Introduce claim(s) about a topic or issue, acknowledge and distinguish the claim(s) from alternate or opposing claims, and organize the reasons and evidence logically.

- Support claim(s) with logical reasoning and relevant, accurate data and evidence that demonstrate an understanding of the topic or text, using credible sources.
- Use words, phrases, and clauses to create cohesion and clarify the relationships among claim(s), counterclaims, reasons, and evidence.
- Provide a concluding statement or section that follows from and supports the argument presented.
- Gather relevant information from multiple print and digital sources, using search terms effectively; assess the credibility and accuracy of each source; and quote or paraphrase the data and conclusions of others while avoiding plagiarism and following a standard format for citation.
- Draw evidence from informational texts to support analysis, reflection, and research.

Some US states have modified the Common Core State Standards or created their own standards that resemble those above.

ISTE Learning Standards for Students: 1.3—Knowledge Constructor, developed by the International Society for Technology in Education (ISTE).[2] Where needed, I have added information in brackets to clarify how each standard ties in with the book.
- 1.3a—Students plan and employ effective research strategies to locate information and other resources for their intellectual or creative pursuits.
- 1.3b—Students evaluate the accuracy, perspective, credibility and relevance of information, media, data or other resources.
- 1.3d—Students build knowledge by actively exploring real-world issues and problems [discussed in social media posts], developing ideas and theories [about social media posts], and pursuing answers and solutions [overall evaluation of the social media post].

ISTE Learning Standards for Educators: 2.3—Citizen, 2.6—Facilitator, and 2.7—Analyst.[3] Where needed, I have added information in brackets to clarify how each standard ties in with the book.

- 2.3a—Create experiences for learners to make positive, socially responsible contributions and exhibit empathetic behavior online [understanding the point of view and bias of a social media post] that build relationships and community.
- 2.3b—Establish a learning culture that promotes curiosity and critical examination of online resources and fosters digital literacy and media fluency.
- 2.6a—Foster a culture where students take ownership of their learning goals and outcomes in both independent and group settings [solo and group learning activities and lesson plans included in most chapters of the book].
- 2.7b—Use technology to design and implement a variety of formative [learning activities at the end of most book chapters] and summative assessments [game-based learning activity at the end of the book's Part I] that accommodate learner needs, provide timely feedback to students and inform instruction.

▶ NOTES

1 "Common Core State Standards for English Language Arts & Literacy in History/Social Studies, Science, and Technical Subjects," June 2, 2010, CCSSI_ELA Standards.indd (ccsso.org).
2 "ISTE Standards: Students," ISTE.
3 "ISTE Standards: Educators," ISTE.

A Note about Lesson Plans

The learning activities in this book include suggestions for lower and higher achieving students based on Bloom's Taxonomy (revised). They require higher achieving students to engage in more self-directed learning by reflecting on and critiquing their news consumption.

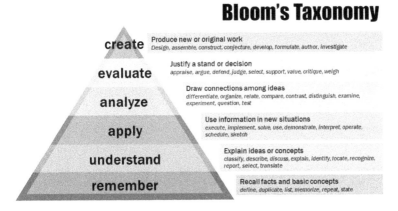

Figure 0.1 Bloom's Revised Taxonomy.[1]

I recognize that some teachers may be hesitant to have students evaluate controversial news topics included in the book for fear of backlash from parents, school administrators, and even other educators. I remind teachers that the examples in the book are just that—examples. I include them for the news literacy lessons they hold—although I try to include a mix of content from across the political spectrum—to convey to students that people from across that spectrum need to improve their news literacy skills. Wrestling with these issues, including those that may be controversial, is part of becoming news literate. It is my opinion that teachers should use these examples as a guide, finding fresh examples as appropriate.

▶ NOTE

1 https://commons.wikimedia.org/wiki/File:Bloom%27s_Revised_Taxonomy.jpg.

Introduction

And Ye Shall Know The Truth and The Truth Shall Make You Free.—John VIII—XXXII.[1] I was a newly hired CIA analyst when I nervously entered the lobby of CIA's Original Headquarters Building for the first time in the mid 1980s and saw this quote engraved on the wall. At first, I could only think that it must apply to CIA's brave officers overseas risking their lives to collect secrets to defend our freedom. But it didn't take me long to realize that the inscription applied to everyone at CIA. If we can find the truth, we can be truly free.

I spent the next 30-plus years evaluating written documents, photos, videos, and other media for the "truth" about what the United States' foreign adversaries were doing and planning to do. It was a tremendously rewarding experience.

Fast-forward. During most of 2016–2022, I taught new analysts these skills, including how to detect fake and misleading media. But I quickly remembered how hard this was for me starting out and how hard it was for many of the new hires I was teaching. I wondered, if evaluating the credibility of media was hard for many new CIA analysts, how hard was it for middle and high school students to evaluate posts in their social media feeds, where they spend so much of their time?

The answer, I found out, is that it's *very* hard. Many fact-checking sites have been established in the last few years, but most do not focus on media saturating preteens' and teens' social media feeds. Logic-checking is even less prevalent, but it goes hand in hand with fact-checking.

To help fill the void, I share in this book some media evaluation techniques I learned as a CIA analyst and apply them to news posts on social media. Part I, covering Chapters 1–14, provides an overview of the skills, including understanding how our biases and mindset make us vulnerable to disinformation, learning how media tries to persuade us, checking facts, and spotting disinformation. This part uses trending pop culture

DOI: 10.4324/9781003471301-1

media to pique students' interest, and it also helps students learn about recurring social studies, civics, and ELA topics.

Part II, covering Chapters 15–18, dives deeper. The first chapters show how students can check how "good" an argument is on social media and how fallacies and manipulation tactics in often "bad" arguments complicate this important skill. This section also uses a mix of trending pop culture media and recurring social studies, civics, and ELA topics to keep students engaged while learning the curriculum.

I recommend that teachers use the first part of the school year, typically from September to December, to weave in the skills covered in Parts I and II. For most school calendars, that works out to about 14 weeks, accounting for holidays and other breaks. Most chapters include one or two suggested lesson plans, with brief notes about how teachers can help lower and higher achieving students make the most of the lesson. I recommend teachers use pop culture media during the first few weeks to pique students' interest in learning the skills, gradually mixing in relevant media related to social studies, civics, and ELA in later weeks.

Finally, in Part III, Chapter 19, I show how to apply the skills learned in Parts I and II to civics, ELA, and social studies topics on social media that recur throughout the school year. I also continue to use pop culture topics to maintain student interest.

The book includes links to my website, www.medialiteracysleuth. com, where I periodically post evaluations of trending pop culture media and media appropriate for use in civics, ELA, and social studies curricula.

Note: Given the speed of the Internet, fact-checkers and other watchdogs have already identified some of the news examples from social media in this book as disinformation, removed them from social media platforms, and even reported on them. In fact, in some cases, that is how I was able to identify these examples. Nonetheless, I include them because they are good examples that students can use to practice identifying possible signs of disinformation, including nefarious bot accounts and artificial intelligence content.

I encourage teachers to search online to see if an example has already been evaluated before deciding whether to use it. Students need to practice identifying and evaluating news versus simply Googling to find evaluations and letting the evaluations do the work for them. The skills they learn will help them when they encounter news reports in real time that have not yet been evaluated and allow them to make better decisions on whether to believe and share the reports.

▶ DEFINITIONS

Disinformation: Media that is usually false or misleading and is deliberately created to harm a person, social group, organization, or country.[2] It is usually spread to make money, gain political influence, or cause confusion or doubt about what is true. It is often spread by bots. Foreign governments are known to use bots to conduct many of these operations in an attempt to hide their identities.

Misinformation: Media that is usually false or misleading but not created or shared to harm a person, social group, organization, or country.[3] It is spread because the spreader thinks it is true. Bots are sometimes used to spread it quickly and more efficiently than a human can.

Malinformation: Media that is based on fact but used out of context to mislead, harm, or manipulate. An example of malinformation is editing a video to remove important context to harm or mislead.[4] Malinformation may be the hardest to detect and potentially the most damaging of the three types.

I use the term **disinformation** for all three types to streamline the discussion and because the evaluation steps discussed in this book can uncover all three.

▶ NOTES

1 Bible Quote Carving—CIA.
2 *Mis, Dis, and Malinformation*, Cybersecurity & Infrastructure Security Agency, https://www.cisa.gov/mdm.
3 *Mis, Dis, and Malinformation*, Cybersecurity & Infrastructure Security Agency, https://www.cisa.gov/mdm.
4 *Mis, Dis, and Malinformation*, Cybersecurity & Infrastructure Security Agency, https://www.cisa.gov/mdm.

How Young People Consume News

Chapter 1

▶ **LESSON PLAN**

This lesson helps teachers collect qualitative data from students about their news consumption. It asks each student to carefully consider their news consumption habits. It requires all students to identify, list, and understand how they consume news on social media. It requires higher achieving students to also critique and draw conclusions about their news consumption, asking, "How can I uncover new information and perspectives about my news consumption?" It consists of a homework assignment to be completed before the in-class activity. Teachers of middle school students may want to ask their students how much they think the teen-focused surveys apply to them.

Homework assignment: Ask each student to reflect on and develop their answers to the following questions.

- What do you consider news?
- What is your view of news?
- What types of news do you prefer consuming? Why?
- What types of news do you prefer to avoid? Why?
- Where do you get your news?
- How often do you seek to consume news?
- How well can you distinguish between fact and opinion while reading news?

DOI: 10.4324/9781003471301-2

- What sources do you trust the most for your news? The least? Why?

I suggest giving students a week to complete the assignment. You might consider asking them to take an inventory of their social media news consumption over the week and incorporate their findings into their output.

In-class activity: Display and ask the questions again. Ask for volunteers to share their output with the class.

▶ SHARE THE FOLLOWING INFORMATION WITH STUDENTS

News consumption is always changing, especially among pre-teens and teens, according to recent surveys. Pew Research Center surveyed 1,316 US teens aged 13 to 17 in 2022 to better understand their use of digital devices and online platforms,[1] and Common Sense.org surveyed 1,005 US teens aged 13 to 17 in 2019 to understand how they get their news.[2] Reuters surveyed 20 young adults aged 18 – 35 from the United Kingdom and the United States in 2019[3] and 72 young adults from the United Kingdom, United States, and Brazil in 2022; its findings should generally apply to preteens and teens.[4] The surveys, though relatively small in sample size, offer insights into how middle and high school students consume news today.

Teens, and presumably preteens, are getting the majority of their news online, and they often turn to online influencers and celebrities on YouTube and other social media sites rather than traditional news media to learn about current events, according to the Common Sense poll.[5] Preteens and teens still need and want news to connect their world to the larger world, but they don't necessarily see traditional media as the best or only way to do so.

Preteens' and teens' skepticism about information on social media is growing. It is reasonable to assume preteens and teens make a distinction between 'the news' as the narrow, traditional agenda of politics and current affairs and 'news' as a wider umbrella including sports, entertainment, celebrity gossip, culture, and science,[6] because this is the case for those aged 18–35, according to the 2022 Reuters poll.

YouTube, used by 95% of teens, topped their list among online platforms covered in Pew's survey (Figure 1.1). TikTok is next (67%), followed by Instagram and Snapchat, which are both used by about 60% of teens. Facebook is next with 32%; smaller shares use Twitter (now X), Twitch, WhatsApp, Reddit, and Tumblr.[7] It is reasonable to assume that similar percentages apply to preteens.

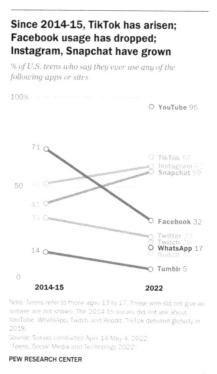

Since 2014-15, TikTok has arisen; Facebook usage has dropped; Instagram, Snapchat have grown

% of U.S. teens who say they ever use any of the following apps or sites

Figure 1.1 Since 2014–2015, TikTok has arisen; Facebook usage has dropped; Instagram and Snapchat have grown.

Pew Research Center, August 2022, "Teens, Social Media and Technology 2022."

YouTube and TikTok are the most popular sites among teens. About three-quarters of teens use YouTube at least daily, and 19% say they use the site or app almost constantly (Figure 1.2). Just over half of the teens (58%) visit TikTok daily, and about half use Snapchat and Instagram daily. Some 35% of all US teens say they are on at least one of these five platforms almost constantly.[8] Again, preteens should have similar usage patterns.

Figure 1.2 About one in five teens visit or use YouTube 'almost constantly.'

Pew Research Center, August 2022, "Teens, Social Media and Technology 2022."

▶ **ASK STUDENTS WHAT THEY THINK ABOUT THESE FINDINGS**

News media are now competing for attention with other distractions. There is a lot of 'background' or 'indirect' exposure to news through social media, other online conversations, documentaries, and TV shows, etc. Teens don't need to seek it out; the news often comes integrated with entertainment, interests, and personal life. Many teens are drawn to and more excited about infotainment; lifestyle, cultural, and grassroots issues; bloggers; and vloggers than traditional news.[9] These findings should generally apply to preteens as well.

▶ **ASK STUDENTS WHAT THEY THINK ABOUT THESE FINDINGS**

Traditional news brands see news as what you should know, while young adults and presumably preteens and teens see news as what you should know and what is useful, interesting, and fun to know.[10] More specifically, young adults, and perhaps to some extent preteens and teens, see 'the news' as a narrow focus on traditional party politics, international relations, economics and finance, and current affairs. 'News,' more broadly, is anything new that is happening in any walk of life: sports, entertainment, celebrity gossip, current affairs, culture, arts, technology, etc.[11] Rather than being curious, some young adults, and presumably some preteens and teens, try to avoid consuming news they consider irrelevant, negative, depressing, or a threat to their mental health.[12]

▶ **ASK STUDENTS WHAT THEY THINK ABOUT THESE FINDINGS**

The Reuters survey suggests that preteens and teens seek news they consider

1. is useful in their life,
2. helps their personal development,
3. contributes to their status and identity,

4. can act as social glue,
5. is enjoyable and engaging to consume,
6. has high entertainment value,
7. has fun content and delivery,
8. has a point of view (a position or perspective that the author or media outlet wants the viewer to adopt) or an angle on a story,
9. is clearly informed by facts (rather than prejudice or agenda),
10. helps them develop their own point of view, and
11. is different from predictable/politicized/extreme opinion and ideology.[13]

▶ ASK STUDENTS WHAT THEY THINK ABOUT THESE FINDINGS

It is encouraging that these younger audiences seek news informed by facts (#9) and in principle—though perhaps less so for preteens and teens—are clear that information is put in the public realm for a reason and is not to be taken at face value.[14]

But it is concerning that preteens and teens may not have the nuances of thought about news that young adults do. It is also worrying that the boundaries between fact, opinion, persuasion, etc., may be much more difficult for preteens and teens to identify, given their desire that news, including opinion and ideology, contributes to their status and identity. As a result, preteens and teens may be especially vulnerable to news "silos" that may restrict the types of news they are exposed to.[15]

It is also concerning that news is often consumed with non-news content in a fragmented, decontextualized format.[16] Young adults, and almost certainly preteens and teens, do not always or often consciously seek news or make active brand choices. Chance characterizes much of their news consumption as algorithms and people recommend news and third parties aggregate it.[17]

Social media apps on which teens and preteens spend so much time offer opportunities to control and curate their own unique news experiences. But young people, like the rest of us, are often in a hurry to consume news along with entertainment, etc., and may not take time to ensure they are consuming news from a variety of viewpoints. It is worrisome that some young adults, and presumably preteens and teens, avoid consuming news they consider irrelevant to their lives or negative, depressing, and a threat to their mental health.[18]

To deal with the problem, in May 2023, the US Surgeon General issued an advisory[19]—a public statement calling attention to an urgent public health issue—on concerns about the effects of social media on youth mental health. Among other recommendations, the advisory urges the "development, implementation, and evaluation of digital and media literacy curricula in schools and within academic standards...[to give]... children and educators the digital skills to strengthen their...ability to recognize, manage, and recover from online risks." It urges preteens and teens to learn and use digital media literacy skills to help tell fact from opinion unsupported by facts. Armed with such skills, preteens and teens can consume news on social media in a healthy way, which is critical to participate effectively and responsibly in civic discourse.

▶ ASK STUDENTS WHAT THEY THINK ABOUT THESE FINDINGS

Young adults, and presumably preteens and teens, are looking for online platforms that allow them to move across the media landscape easily. That's why they are heavy users of social media, especially on their phones; it is convenient to have all your entertainment, information, and social connections in one online space.[20]

The 20 young adults that Reuters surveyed—which we can reasonably assume applies to most middle and high school students—preferred getting a wide swath of news on social media apps vice specific news apps. News apps appeared on fewer phones, and the young adults used them less when they did appear.[21]

The following apps and topics (Figure 1.3) are in order of the average amount of time the survey participant spent on them as of 2019. The numbers on each app icon indicate how many phones that app was found on.[22]

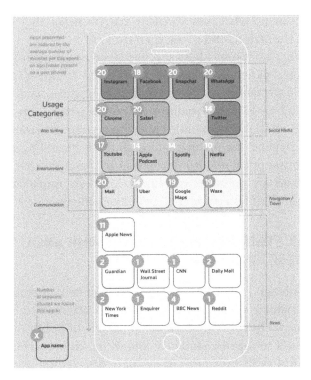

Figure 1.3 Apps presented are ordered by the average number of minutes per day spent on each app (when present on a user's phone).

How Young People Consume News and the Implications for Mainstream Media, https://reutersinstitute.politics.ox.ac.uk/our—research/how—young—people—consume—news—and—implications—mainstream—media, Reuters Institute for the Study of Journalism, September 2, 2019.

Although not included in the Reuters survey, TikTok is hosting more and more reputable news brands, increasing the platform's credibility as a source of news.[23] TikTok is no longer thought of solely as the place to watch ice bucket challenges and influencers hawking gadgets.[24] My wife's niece, who said she gets at least some news from the platform, may be on to something.

But being digital natives does not mean preteens and teens are news savvy.[25] They don't always prioritize impartiality when judging a news source's value.[26] And many teens and presumably preteens avoid what they consider 'narrow news' they perceive to be at the serious end of the spectrum.[27]

In sum, the young adults surveyed, and presumably preteens and teens, generally consume news from a longer menu of sports, entertainment, celebrity gossip, culture, and science, with a lighter focus on traditional news of party politics, international relations, economics and finance, and current affairs. Brands beyond the mainstream grab their attention and time. They are skeptical about information to the point that they do not inherently value news brands for their impartiality but rather for their entertainment and engagement value.[28]

▶ ASK STUDENTS WHAT THEY THINK ABOUT THESE FINDINGS

The challenge is to meet middle and high school students on their territory: social media.[29] This book attempts to do that, using media beyond the traditional agenda of politics and current affairs to capture students' attention, while teaching them the critical skills they need to evaluate the credibility of media in general. These are skills that will serve them well as their news preferences and consumption habits evolve.

▶ NOTES

1 "Teens, Social Media and Technology 2022," Pew Research Center, Washington, DC (August 2022), Teens, Social Media and Technology 2022 | Pew Research Center.

2 New Survey Reveals Teens Get Their News from Social Media and YouTube, CommonSense.org, August 13, 2019.

3 How Young People Consume News and the Implications for Mainstream Media, https://reutersinstitute.politics.ox.ac.uk/our-research/how-young-people-consume-news-and-implications-mainstream-media, Reuters Institute for the Study of Journalism, September 2, 2019.

4 "The Kaleidoscope: Tracking Young People's Relationships With News," Reuters Institute for the Study of Journalism, September 13, 2022.

5 New Survey Reveals Teens Get Their News from Social Media and YouTube, CommonSense.org, August 13, 2019.

6 "The Kaleidoscope: Tracking Young People's Relationships With News," Reuters Institute for the Study of Journalism, September 13, 2022.

7 "Teens, Social Media and Technology 2022," Pew Research Center, Washington, DC (August 2022), Teens, Social Media and Technology 2022 | Pew Research Center.

8 "Teens, Social Media and Technology 2022," Pew Research Center, Washington, DC (August 2022), Teens, Social Media and Technology 2022 | Pew Research Center.

9 How Young People Consume News and the Implications for Mainstream Media, https://reutersinstitute.politics.ox.ac.uk/our-research/how-young-people-consume-news-and-implications-mainstream-media, Reuters Institute for the Study of Journalism, September 2, 2019.

10 How Young People Consume News and the Implications for Mainstream Media, https://reutersinstitute.politics.ox.ac.uk/our-research/how-young-people-consume-news-and-implications-mainstream-media, Reuters Institute for the Study of Journalism, September 2, 2019.

11 "The Kaleidoscope: Tracking Young People's Relationships with News," Reuters Institute for the Study of Journalism, September 13, 2022.

12 "The Kaleidoscope: Tracking Young People's Relationships with News," Reuters Institute for the Study of Journalism, September 13, 2022.

13 How Young People Consume News and the Implications for Mainstream Media, https://reutersinstitute.politics.ox.ac.uk/our-research/how-young-people-consume-news-and-implications-mainstream-media, Reuters Institute for the Study of Journalism, September 2, 2019.

14 "The Kaleidoscope: Tracking Young People's Relationships with News," Reuters Institute for the Study of Journalism, September 13, 2022.

15 "The Kaleidoscope: Tracking Young People's Relationships with News," Reuters Institute for the Study of Journalism, September 13, 2022.

16 "The Kaleidoscope: Tracking Young People's Relationships with News," Reuters Institute for the Study of Journalism, September 13, 2022.

17 "The Kaleidoscope: Tracking Young People's Relationships with News," Reuters Institute for the Study of Journalism, September 13, 2022.

18 "The Kaleidoscope: Tracking Young People's Relationships with News," Reuters Institute for the Study of Journalism, September 13, 2022.

19 United States. Office of the Surgeon General. (2023). Social Media and Youth Mental Health: The US Surgeon General's Advisory. Department of Health and Human Services, Washington, DC.

20 How Young People Consume News and the Implications for Mainstream Media, https://reutersinstitute.politics.ox.ac.uk/our-research/how-young-people-consume-news-and-implications-mainstream-media, Reuters Institute for the Study of Journalism, September 2, 2019.

21 How Young People Consume News and the Implications for Mainstream Media, https://reutersinstitute.politics.ox.ac.uk/our-research/how-young-people-consume-news-and-implications-mainstream-media, Reuters Institute for the Study of Journalism, September 2, 2019.

22 How Young People Consume News and the Implications for Mainstream Media, https://reutersinstitute.politics.ox.ac.uk/our-research/how-young-people-consume-news-and-implications-mainstream-media, Reuters Institute for the Study of Journalism, September 2, 2019.

23 "The Kaleidoscope: Tracking Young People's Relationships with News," Reuters Institute for the Study of Journalism, September 13, 2022.

24 "The Kaleidoscope: Tracking Young People's Relationships with News," Reuters Institute for the Study of Journalism, September 13, 2022.

25 "The Kaleidoscope: Tracking Young People's Relationships with News," Reuters Institute for the Study of Journalism, September 13, 2022.

26 "The Kaleidoscope: Tracking Young People's Relationships with News," Reuters Institute for the Study of Journalism, September 13, 2022.

27 "The Kaleidoscope: Tracking Young People's Relationships with News," Reuters Institute for the Study of Journalism, September 13, 2022.

28 "The Kaleidoscope: Tracking Young People's Relationships with News," Reuters Institute for the Study of Journalism, September 13, 2022.

29 "The Kaleidoscope: Tracking Young People's Relationships with News," Reuters Institute for the Study of Journalism, September 13, 2022.

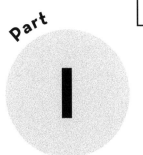

Learn the Skills

Chapter 2

Playing on Our Emotions, Mindset, and Biases

I had been out of grad school for several years and busy working a steady job, but something was missing. I figured I needed companionship and that dating would bring it. I started viewing ads about dating services, which showed happy young men and women seemingly finding their perfect mate. I signed up, paying something north of $1,000 to have the company 'match' me with 'compatible' women near my home. I joined despite reading a lot of data from dissatisfied customers.

The flashy ads that persuaded me to join the dating service were consistent with my **mindset**—a mental attitude, disposition, inclination, or habit based on our education, experience, biases, and assumptions; this lens affects how we interpret and respond to situations and events.[1] More specifically, the ads appealed to my **fixed mindset**—a cognitive strategy that activates our biases and narrows our vision of the range of possibilities. My fixed mindset told me that a dating service would be the only way to find a mate. A **flexible mindset**, on the other hand, is a cognitive strategy that can help us overcome our biases by expanding our vision of the range of possibilities.[2]

My mindset activated my **cognitive bias**—a systematic error in thinking that occurs when people are processing and interpreting information in the world around them; it affects the

DOI: 10.4324/9781003471301-4

decisions and judgments they make.[3] It is mental—a shortcut people take in order to process the mass of information they receive daily.[4] More specifically, it activated my **vividness bias**, by which I gave greater weight to vivid or dramatic pictures and stories in the ads of people finding mates, discounting the mountain of data saying otherwise. Needless to say, I stayed pretty lonely for a few more years.

Here is a list of some common cognitive biases that make us vulnerable to media persuasion:

▶ COMMON COGNITIVE BIASES

- **Anchoring bias**: Overly influenced by the first piece of information we encounter, keeping us from finding new information, much like an anchor keeps a boat from drifting. Example: You rush to buy that new app because the first influencer you saw on TikTok recommended it, even though many other reviewers panned it. You might show students the following illustration (Figure 2.1) to help them understand this bias:

Figure 2.1 Effect of the anchoring bias.

Roy Whitehurst, www.canva.com, November 20, 2023. Background image: Mote Oo Education on Pixabay.com.

- **Confirmation bias**: Seeking or favoring evidence to confirm theories and ignoring or discounting evidence that could disprove them. You might show a clip from the movie *The Messenger: The Story of Joan of Arc* to illustrate this bias.[5] Joan believes that a sword lying in a field is a sign from divine powers, but the Conscience insists that it wasn't a sign; it was just a sword in a field. The Conscience describes several ways that a sword may have been in a field to illustrate to Joan that she dismissed all other possibilities in order to support her beliefs.
  Video (https://www.youtube.com/watch?v=9oSJdSL8YOE) QR Code 2.1

- **Groupthink/bandwagon effect**: Fear of being "left out," or a drive for consensus, prompts an uncritical acceptance of a popular viewpoint. The more people (especially those we already like or care about) believe something, the more likely we are to climb on the bandwagon. Examples: Everyone seems to be taking the TikTok challenge, so I did too! Everyone I know claims they use artificial intelligence to do their homework without getting caught, so I do too.

- **Mirror imaging**: Assuming a person or group of people will "act like us," judging from our values and perception of interests.

- **Resistance bias**: A tendency to maintain our current, often long-standing judgments, even in the face of new evidence. Example: In 1543, Nicolaus Copernicus detailed his radical theory of the universe, in which the earth and the other planets rotated around the sun. But humans held onto their belief that the sun revolved around the earth for more than a century after his discovery.

- **Vividness bias**: Giving greater weight to vivid or dramatic examples. Example: We might fear airplane crashes even though we are thousands of times more likely to die in a car crash.

Humans are hard-wired with cognitive biases, and many have a fixed mindset toward certain topics and people that magnify their biases. Yet often, those biases can be erroneous, emotionally driven, and fail to take in the nuance, research, and patience needed to make truly accurate conclusions based on critical thinking. Cognitive biases can be particularly troublesome when people are pressed for time, under stress, feeling impulsive, or otherwise emotional.

Even a high ability to analyze and reason, when mixed with prior partisan affiliations or highly charged emotion, can deepen cognitive bias, according to Wilhelm and colleagues.[6] For example, people who are normally good at science literacy and technical reasoning can, for some polarizing issues such as climate change, convince themselves of what they want to be true rather than trying to actually find the truth, according to a study by Kahan and colleagues in the journal *Nature*.[7] In other words, we are all vulnerable, including middle and high school students.

We think we have good judgment—be it about adopting a political belief or buying a product that a celebrity we like is hawking on social media. But retailers and marketers have nearly perfected using our cognitive biases against us to drive sales and increase profits.

In his book *Thinking Fast and Slow*, behavioral psychologist Daniel Kahneman discusses how the human brain is wired to make decisions in two ways: via a fast, automatic, emotional system and via a thoughtful, calculating system.[8] We tend to use the fast system (enabled by a fixed mindset) when viewing social media, especially posts with an emotional appeal, and the more methodical process (enabled by a flexible mindset) when making decisions involving less emotion, such as deciding which cell phone to buy.

Many of the social media we encounter seek to exploit our tendency to use fast thinking to persuade us to believe a point of view or act a certain way. Media makers do this by appealing to our emotions and cognitive biases, making us less able to determine the credibility of the media.

Helen Lee Bouygues, president of the Reboot Foundation that promotes critical thinking in daily life, points out that one way retailers and influencers on social media play on our biases is through our **anchoring bias**. With this bias, we tend to make judgments and decisions using facts easily recalled but often irrelevant.[9] For example, the first price we see for an item often determines whether we think it is a "good deal."[10] A "TikTok made me buy it" item trending as I write this is a sleep mask that doubles as a pair of Bluetooth headphones with a built-in microphone for calls; one can comfortably listen to music while falling asleep. Marketing, word of mouth, and viral campaigns on social media tout the must-have features of the product and suggest the product should normally cost $23–$36. When a shopper sees the product "on sale" for $15, they are more likely to believe it is a good deal, even though there is no reason the product should have been priced at $23–$36 to start with.[11]

Bouygues reminds us that another way retailers tap into our cognitive biases is by using the **bandwagon effect**. This is when marketers convince us that we need to jump on a trend or movement. For example, companies and influencers promoting pickleball—a game popular with all ages—will create sales or promotions on social media for pickleball products and services that combine the anchoring bias and the bandwagon effect to spur an emotional, snap decision. Marketers will say things like, "All your friends are using the new pickleball racket. Get yours today for a discount!"[12] Middle and high school students are especially vulnerable to the **halo effect**—a cognitive bias that occurs when we let positive traits we associate with our friends and celebrity influencers affect how we perceive a product or service.[13] Marketers on social media will also try to use the **scarcity bias** and false deadlines to press you into buying or doing something quickly, says Bouygues.[14]

In situations where we don't have strong preexisting biases toward something or someone, our fixed or flexible mindset often steps in to either strengthen or weaken them, respectively. For example, a middle school student newly arrived from another country who says she will ace the test about the US Constitution in her US government class is demonstrating a flexibility mindset and minimizing the influence on her thinking of biases she may have about the document. **In this book, I focus more on cognitive biases than mindset, with the assumption that a fixed-thinking mindset that inflames biases is operating in the background**.

The quest to ride trends and be popular on social media can cause many of us, and particularly middle and high school students, to let our cognitive biases short-circuit our critical thinking skills.[15] Students who understand how social media want to use our emotions, fixed mindset, and cognitive biases to persuade us will have taken the first step toward improving their ability to evaluate the credibility of media, in and out of the classroom.

▶ LESSON PLAN

This lesson requires all students to identify, list, and explain their mindset and biases and apply them to new information. It requires higher achieving students to also draw conclusions and critique how their mindset and biases influence how they evaluate the information.

Direct students to an electronic or hardcopy list of cognitive biases that make us vulnerable to media persuasion. Direct each student to the same electronic chart, photo, video, and article from social media. The chart should include the title but not the caption, the photo should have its caption removed, the video should have its audio muted, and the article should have key words removed. Each piece of media demonstrates a different bias. I include an example of each in the following sections. I recommend using examples related to a pop culture topic to pique students' interest early in the school year.

Have each student examine the media and identify the bias(es) they think each piece demonstrates. I recommend having students work individually so they realize how each person in the class can see different biases. Ask for volunteers to report their findings.

▶ CHART

Students examine a chart like this one (Figure 2.2) from UNICEF, based on data Gallup collected, with the title and a word from each label removed:

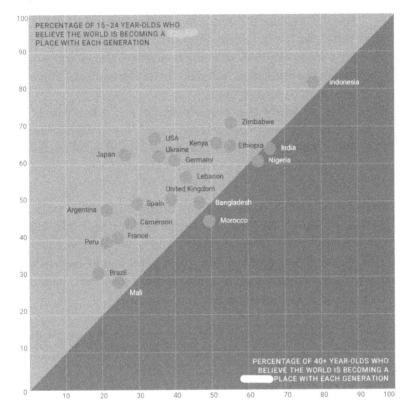

Figure 2.2 Captions left off and revealed in second graph: "Percentage of 15- to 24-year-olds who say the world is getting better with each generation" and "Percentage of 40+-year-olds who say the world is getting better."

UNICEF (2021), "The Changing Childhood Project," UNICEF, New York.

Round one: Ask students to work individually and silently to study the chart and consider the following questions. They should identify what they think is the chart's title and the same missing word for the label in the upper left and lower right. Students should not research the chart, just give their thoughts by looking at it.

Here are some questions students could ask themselves:

- *How does the chart make me feel upon first look?* Students should consider their mindset, biases, and emotions.
- *What do I see?* Because the title and part of each label have been omitted, they must examine the chart closely and make inferences based on their observations. Encourage them to make a list.
- *What do I think the chart maker was trying to capture?*
- *What is the "story" behind the chart? How can I find out?*
- *What can I infer from the chart beyond what it shows directly?*

Round two: When most students finish, have them work in pairs or groups. This time, they need to interrogate the chart together using the same questions and agree on the missing word in the labels and the title they think would best fit the chart. Again, students should not research the chart, just give their thoughts by looking at it.

- As students begin to find differences in the words they choose to describe the chart, they will try to convince each other why their words are better.
- The students will start to see that their choice of words for the chart's labels and title indicates subtle and even unconscious beliefs about the chart. Classmates whom they may have thought viewed the world just as they did may have different points of view, and things they had thought were facts might be opinions.

Round three: Now ask one group to share their agreed labels and title and how they agreed on it. Have classmates ask questions to clarify their observations.

Round four: Show the chart with the full title and labels revealed (Figure 2.3):

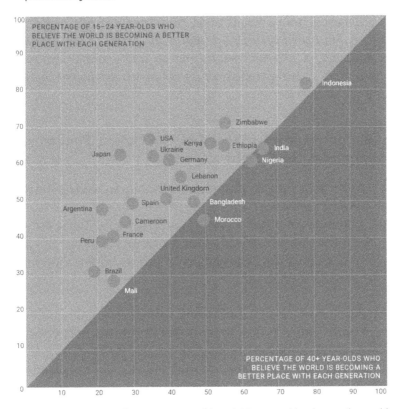

THE BEST IS YET TO COME

Percentage who believe the world is becoming a better place with each generation

- COUNTRY
- 15–24   YEAR-OLDS
- 40+   YEAR-OLDS

PERCENTAGE OF 15–24 YEAR-OLDS WHO BELIEVE THE WORLD IS BECOMING A BETTER PLACE WITH EACH GENERATION

Indonesia
Zimbabwe
USA
Kenya
Ukraine   Ethiopia   India
Japan   Germany   Nigeria
Lebanon
United Kingdom
Spain   Bangladesh
Argentina
Cameroon   Morocco
France
Peru
Brazil
Mali

PERCENTAGE OF 40+ YEAR-OLDS WHO BELIEVE THE WORLD IS BECOMING A BETTER PLACE WITH EACH GENERATION

Figure 2.3 Percentage of 15- to 24-year-olds and 40+-year-olds who say the world is getting better with each generation.

UNICEF (2021), "The Changing Childhood Project," UNICEF, New York.

Have students compare their labels and titles with the actual labels and title. Ask them why and how their labels and titles may differ from the actual ones. This should generate a substantive and meaningful discussion of mindset and implicit bias.

Fixed and flexible mindset, confirmation bias, selection bias, and historical bias are common biases that may come up in discussion.

Details about the Chart You May Want to Share with the Students

This chart is from a report titled *The Changing Childhood Project: A Multigenerational, International Survey of 21st Century Childhood*. It reflects results from an international survey of more than 21,000 people from 21 countries conducted by Gallup for UNICEF.

Ask Your Students: What Did You Notice, Ponder, and Learn from This Graph?

After they answer, you might follow up by asking the following questions
- Which countries' statistics surprised you? What do you think about the statistics for the United States?
- What personal biases might be influencing your interpretation of the graph?

 Students examine a photo like this, with the caption removed:
Photo (https://solent.photoshelter.com/image/I0000pcrn84 U4G4Y) QR Code 2.2
Round one: Ask students to work individually and silently to study the photo, ask the following questions about it, and come up with a caption they think should go with it. Students should not research the photo, just give their thoughts by looking at it.
Here are some questions students should ask:

- *How does the image make me feel upon first look?* Students should list their mindset and emotions.
- *What do I see?* Because the caption has been omitted, they must examine the photo closely and make inferences based on their observations. Encourage them to make a list.
- *What do I think the photographer was trying to capture?*
- *If there are people in the image (there are for this one), what might their expressions communicate?*
- *What is the "story" behind the image? How can I find out?*
- *What can you infer from this photo beyond what it shows directly? What's the deeper story that comes from this photo?*

Round two: When most students finish, have them work in pairs or groups to interrogate the photo using the same questions. They should agree on the caption they think would best fit the photo. Students should not research the photo, just give their thoughts by looking at it.

- As students begin to find differences in the words they choose to describe the image, they will try to convince each other why their words are better.
- The students will start to see that images impact meaning and that their choice of words for the photo's caption indicates subtle and even unconscious beliefs about the photo. Classmates they may have presumed viewed the world just as they did may have different points of view, and things they thought were facts might be opinions.

Round three: Now ask one group to share their agreed caption and how they agreed on it. Have classmates ask questions to clarify their observations.

Round four: Show the photo with the actual caption. Have the student groups compare their captions with the actual caption. Ask them why and how their captions differ from the actual one. This should generate a substantive and meaningful discussion of mindset and implicit bias.

Actual caption: *A humpback whale is spotted by tourists near the Haʻapai islands in Tonga on June 21, 2022.* (Erez Beatus/Solent News/Shutterstock)[16]

Learning point: If we consider the images we use to tell our history, and we choose to use different words to describe the images, we invite different points of view into our understanding of the world. We broaden our perspective and gain empathy with diverse people.

   Video[17] (https://www.youtube.com/watch?v=0JMkzakXgIY) QR Code 2.3

   This activity is also effective with videos.

Round one: Tell the students you are going to **play a short video with the audio muted and closed captions removed**

and that you will **stop the video at 0:35 seconds**. Have each student ask the following questions about the video as you play it. They should work individually and silently, asking the same questions they would of a photo. They should not research the video, just give their thoughts by looking at it.

- *How does the clip make me feel?* Students should list their mindset and emotions.
- *What do you see?* Because the dialogue and close captions have been omitted, students must examine the video closely and make inferences based on their observations. Encourage them to make a list.
- *What do you think the videographer was trying to capture?*
- *If there are people in the video* (there are for this one), *what might their expressions communicate?*
- *What's the "story" behind the video? What do you think the dialogue is saying? How can I find out?*
- *What can you infer from the video beyond what it shows directly? What's the deeper story that comes from the video?*

Round two: When most students finish, have them work in pairs or groups. This time, they need to agree on what they think is happening in the video. Students should not research the video, just give their thoughts by looking at it.

- As students begin to find differences in their interpretations, they try to convince each other why their interpretation is better.
- The students start to see that images impact meaning and that their interpretations of the video indicate their own subtle and even unconscious beliefs. Classmates whom they may have presumed viewed the world just as they did may have different points of view.

Round three: Ask the student groups to share what they think is happening in the video and why.

Round four: Play the video again, this time to the end (4:11 min) and with the sound and closed captions turned on.

Now ask the students to compare their interpretations with what the reporter describes. You could ask the students to explain why and how their interpretations may differ from the reporter's. This should generate a substantive and meaningful discussion of mindset and cognitive bias.

Learning point: Stress to the students that if we consider the video images we use to tell our history, and we choose to use different words to describe those videos, we invite different points of view into our understanding of the world. We broaden our perspective and gain empathy with diverse people.

▶ ARTICLE

Have students do a Mad Lib—a fill-in-the-blank game where a reader comes up with words to finish a story without knowing the storyline. They will use an article to help them see their mindset and biases.

This activity is based on one described by Jacqueline Whiting of EdSurge.[18,19] You could choose to do this activity with a short article trending in students' social media feeds to pique their interest.

The activity uses excerpts from paragraphs one and two in the article "Inequality in Teaching and Schooling: How Opportunity Is Rationed to Students of Color in America" by Linda Darling-Hammond at the Stanford University School of Education. The article appeared in the book *The Right Thing to Do, The Smart Thing to Do: Enhancing Diversity in the Health Professions: Summary of the Symposium on Diversity in Health Professions in Honor of Herbert W. Nickens, M.D.* published in 2001 by National Academies Press.[20]

▶ ARTICLE EXCERPTS[21]

"[T]he school experiences of African-American and other 'minority' students in the United States continue to be substantially separate and unequal. Few Americans realize that the US

educational system is one of the most unequal in the industrialized world, and that students routinely receive dramatically different learning opportunities based on their social status. ...
Poor and minority students are concentrated in the least well-
funded schools, most of which are...funded at levels substantially below those of neighboring suburban districts...policies
associated with school funding, resource allocations, and tracking leave minority students with fewer and lower-quality books,
curriculum materials, laboratories, and computers; significantly
larger class sizes; less qualified and experienced teachers; and
less access to high-quality curriculum."[22]

I've removed some of the words and replaced them with
blanks, Mad Lib style:

"Few Americans realize that the US educational system is one of
the most _ _ _ _ _ _ _in the industrialized world, and that students
routinely receive dramatically _ _ _ _ _ _ _ _ _ learning opportunities based on their _ _ _ _ _ _ _ _ _ _ _ _ ...policies associated with
school funding, resource allocations, and tracking leave _ _ _ _ _
_ _ _ students with _ _ _ _ _ and _ _ _ _ _ - _ _ _ _ _ _ _ books, curriculum materials, laboratories, and computers; significantly _ _
_ _ _ _ class sizes; less _ _ _ _ _ _ _ _ _ and _ _ _ _ _ _ _ _ _ _ _ _
teachers; and _ _ _ _ access to high-quality curriculum."[23]

▶ HAVE THE STUDENTS DO THIS ACTIVITY IN ROUNDS

Round one: Students work alone and without talking, choosing
words they think work in context and getting the paragraph to
make sense. They should not try to guess what the author really
said. Students should not research the article, just give their
thoughts after reading it.

Round two: When most students are finished, have them work
in pairs or groups. Group members need to agree on the words
that fill each blank. Students should not research the article, just
give their thoughts after reading it.

- Students will begin to find differences in the words they
  used in round one and will try to persuade each other why
  their words are better.

- In the past running cited by Jacqueline Whiting, the students—many of whom lived in similar neighborhoods and had been classmates for years—realized that language affects meaning and that their word choices indicate subtle, unconscious beliefs. They discovered that classmates who they thought viewed the world like they did had a different mindset and points of view, and things they thought were facts might be opinions.[24]

Round three: Ask the student pairs or groups to focus on one sentence from the excerpt and share how they completed it.

Ask, "What do these words imply? What do they say about the people doing the action?"

Round four: In the final round, compare the word choice each group used with the original author's. Ask the students to explain why there is a difference.

Some students may be struck by the need to read completely—not just skim a headline or snippet in a media feed. Others may notice how limiting it is to describe an issue as binary, as in having only two sides. Still others may realize that mindset and bias, based on our upbringing, background, and prior media exposure, are inherent in all of us and contribute to our worldviews. For all students, what resonates is the implicit weight of words.[25]

Learning point: At the end of the activity, drive home the point that many of us have a fixed mindset toward some things, and we all have emotion-driven biases. Unless we recognize our mindset and biases, we cannot minimize their effects. One way to do this is to consider the language we use to tell our history and choose different words. By doing so, we invite different points of view into our understanding of the world, broaden our perspective, and gain empathy with diverse people.

▶ NEXT STEPS

- In the first semester, have your students practice identifying their mindset and emotion-driven biases when they view pop culture media. Go to my website, www.medialiteracysleuth.com, for some examples.

- In the second semester, have your students use their insights to evaluate media supporting your social studies curriculum and the learning standards. Go to my website for some examples.

▶ NOTES

1 The American Heritage Stedman's Medical Dictionary, 2002 Houghton Mifflin Company.
2 Kai Sassenberg, Kevin Winter, Daniela Becker, Lara Ditrich, Annika Scholl & Gordon B. Moskowitz (2022) Flexibility mindsets: Reducing biases that result from spontaneous processing, *European Review of Social Psychology*, 33:1, 171—213, DOI: 10.1080/10463283.2021.1959124.
3 What Is Cognitive Bias? (verywellmind.com).
4 Cognitive Bias Is the Loose Screw in Critical Thinking | Psychology Today.
5 ClassHook | A Sword in a Field.
6 "Fighting Fake News: Teaching Students to Identify and Interrogate Information Pollution, Copyright 2023, Corwin Press.
7 Kahan, D., Peters, E., Wittlin, M. et al. (2012) The polarizing impact of science literacy and numeracy on perceived climate change risks. *Nature Climate Change*, 2, 732–735, DOI: 10.1038/nclimate1547.
8 "Thinking, Fast and Slow," Daniel Kahneman, New York: Farrar, Straus & Giroux, 2011.
9 "How Instagram Ads (and My Cognitive Bias) Convinced Me to Buy $100 Leggings," Helen Lee Bouygues, December 16, 2022, Forbes.com.
10 "How Instagram Ads (and My Cognitive Bias) Convinced Me to Buy $100 Leggings," Helen Lee Bouygues, December 16, 2022, Forbes.com.
11 "How Instagram Ads (and My Cognitive Bias) Convinced Me to Buy $100 Leggings," Helen Lee Bouygues, December 16, 2022, Forbes.com.
12 "How Instagram Ads (and My Cognitive Bias) Convinced Me to Buy $100 Leggings," Helen Lee Bouygues, December 16, 2022, Forbes.com.
13 "How Instagram Ads (and My Cognitive Bias) Convinced Me to Buy $100 Leggings," Helen Lee Bouygues, December 16, 2022, Forbes.com.

14 "How Instagram Ads (and My Cognitive Bias) Convinced Me to Buy $100 Leggings," Helen Lee Bouygues, December 16, 2022, Forbes.com.

15 "How Instagram Ads (and My Cognitive Bias) Convinced Me to Buy $100 Leggings," Helen Lee Bouygues, December 16, 2022, Forbes.com.

16 2022: The Year in Pictures—CNN.com.

17 Native American elder Nathan Phillips, teen Nick Sandmann give versions of encounter—YouTube.

18 "Everyone Has Invisible Bias. This Lesson Shows Students How to Recognize It," Jacquelyn Whiting, EdSurge, September 4, 2019, Everyone Has Invisible Bias. This Lesson Shows Students How to RecogniIt. | EdSurge News.

19 "Poor Schools Need to Encompass More Than Instruction to Succeed," Prudence L. Carter, September 14, 2016, Poor Schools Need to Encompass More Than Instruction to Succeed—NYTimes.com.

20 Smedley BD, Stith AY, Colburn L, et al. Institute of Medicine (US). The Right Thing to Do, the Smart Thing to Do: Enhancing Diversity in the Health Professions: Summary of the Symposium on Diversity in Health Professions in Honor of Herbert W Nickens, MD. Washington (DC): National Academies Press (US); 2001. Inequality in Teaching and Schooling: How Opportunity Is Rationed to Students of Color in America. Available from: https://www.ncbi.nlm.nih.gov/books/NBK223640/.

21 Smedley BD, Stith AY, Colburn L, et al. Institute of Medicine (US). The Right Thing to Do, the Smart Thing to Do: Enhancing Diversity in the Health Professions: Summary of the Symposium on Diversity in Health Professions in Honor of Herbert W Nickens, MD. Washington (DC): National Academies Press (US); 2001. Inequality in Teaching and Schooling: How Opportunity Is Rationed to Students of Color in America. Available from: https://www.ncbi.nlm.nih.gov/books/NBK223640/.

22 Smedley BD, Stith AY, Colburn L, et al.; Institute of Medicine (US). The Right Thing to Do, the Smart Thing to Do: Enhancing Diversity in the Health Professions: Summary of the Symposium on Diversity in Health Professions in Honor of Herbert W Nickens, MD. Washington (DC): National Academies Press (US); 2001. Inequality in Teaching and Schooling: How Opportunity Is Rationed to Students of Color in America. Available from: https://www.ncbi.nlm.nih.gov/books/NBK223640/.

23 Smedley BD, Stith AY, Colburn L, et al. Institute of Medicine (US). The Right Thing to Do, the Smart Thing to Do: Enhancing Diversity in the Health Professions: Summary of the Symposium on Diversity in Health Professions in Honor of Herbert W Nickens, MD. Washington (DC): National Academies Press (US); 2001. Inequality in Teaching and Schooling: How Opportunity Is Rationed to Students of Color in America. Available from: https://www.ncbi.nlm.nih.gov/books/NBK223640/.

24 "Everyone Has Invisible Bias. This Lesson Shows Students How to Recognize It," Jacquelyn Whiting, EdSurge, September 4, 2019, Everyone Has Invisible Bias. This Lesson Shows Students How to Recognize It. | EdSurge News.

25 "Everyone Has Invisible Bias. This Lesson Shows Students How to Recognize It," Jacquelyn Whiting, EdSurge, September 4, 2019, Everyone Has Invisible Bias. This Lesson Shows Students How to Recognize It. | EdSurge News.

The Information and Social Media Ecosystems

Walter Cronkite, longtime CBS Evening News anchorman, was not quite right when he signed off each night saying, "And that's the way it is." He should have said something like, "And that's the way *we want you to see it*." As I have said, all media have a **point of view** they want their audience to adopt. Given that we are living at a time in which many cultural and social issues have been politicized and reduced to "us" versus "them," Wilhelm and colleagues suggest[1] that understanding point of view is more critical than ever.

Media express their point of view through explicit messages—messages that are clear and complete, without vagueness, implication, or ambiguity—or implicit messages—messages that are understood, although not clearly or directly expressed or conveyed.[2] Media employ these messages using information along a spectrum of news, infotainment, and entertainment—what I call the **information ecosystem**. Each of these parts includes verifiable facts, opinions, or a combination. Students swimming in this ecosystem may wonder what these information categories mean and how they differ.

DOI: 10.4324/9781003471301-5

Here are definitions for each part of the ecosystem:

Data
Individual facts, statistics, or items of information used to analyze something or make decisions,[3] the smallest units of factual information that can be used as a basis for calculation, reasoning, or discussion.[4] Example: *These data represent the results of our analyses.*

Information
Information is often thought of as data that are thematically connected, organized, or structured by a human or artificial intelligence (see Chapter 13) and presented in a relevant context so that a reasonably intelligent person can derive meaning from the data.[5] Data that are unorganized or unstructured do not provide meaning and are not information.

News
Information about recent events or of something unknown.[6,7] News is sometimes called "hard news"—what preteens and teens call "the news." This differs from "soft news" or infotainment—what preteens and teens call "news" (see Chapter 1).[8]

Infotainment
Sometimes called "soft news," information that provides a combination of information and entertainment or is personally useful.[9,10] It is usually provided via television or online.

Entertainment
Amusement or diversion[11] provided via photos, videos, memes, games, music, or other media or activities.[12,13] *Example: The TikTok videos provided a diversion for the teen during the eight-hour flight.*

I illustrate these relationships in the chart in Figure 3.1:

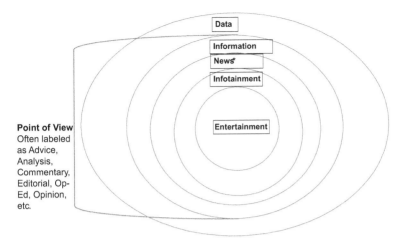

*Tweens and teens view 'news' to include topics like sports, entertainment, celebrity gossip, culture, and science. They see 'the news' as the narrow, traditional agenda of politics and current affairs, according to a 2022 study by the Reuters Institute for the Study of Journalism.

Figure 3.1 The information ecosystem.

Here are more definitions:

The news: Preteens and teens consider "the news" as the narrow, traditional agenda of politics and current affairs, according to a study from 2022 by the Reuters Institute for the Study of Journalism. This type of news should use fair and accurate reporting and "open-minded inquiry" to inform consumers, according to Tom Rosenstiel, professor at the University of Maryland Philip Merrill College of Journalism, in a podcast produced by the News Literacy Project.[14] Rosenstiel describes "inquiry" as attempting to learn information about something and "open-minded" as not forming conclusions about that something before you start.

News: Preteens and teens consider "news" to include reporting on topics like sports, entertainment, celebrity gossip, culture, and science, according to the Reuters study. This type of news should also use fair and accurate reporting and "open-minded inquiry" to inform consumers, according to Rosenstiel.[15]

Point of view: A position or perspective that the author or media outlet wants the viewer to adopt. It comes in lots of flavors; many credible media outlets label it as advice, analysis, commentary, editorial, op-ed, opinion, etc.

Opinion:[16] Often described by credible news outlets as commentary, editorials, or op-eds. It offers a particular perspective on an issue. While opinion may use emotional appeals to persuade readers, viewers, or listeners to consider the position it's arguing for or against, it includes confirmable facts or evidence that are clear and supported with reasoning. Some reputable news outlets may include other perspectives for balance and contrast. The most persuasive opinion pieces use strong arguments backed by facts and reasoning (see Chapters 15–16) to explain why we should agree with the position.

Students may hear the terms "persuasion" and propaganda" and wonder what they mean and how they differ. Let's explore them.

▶ PERSUASION

Renee Hobbs, a leading authority on media literacy education, indicates that many scholars have defined **persuasion** as an intent to change or strengthen beliefs, attitudes, or behaviors of one or a few people using classical Greek rhetoric to appeal to the audience's **ethos** (audience respect for the speaker), **logos** (the strength of the ideas presented using the audience's logical reasoning), and **pathos** (audience's emotions).[17] For example, a teen might persuade their group of friends to go to a rap concert, attend a climate change rally, or try a new challenge on TikTok.

▶ PROPAGANDA

According to Hobbs, many scholars have defined **propaganda** as mass communication, a type of persuasion that seeks to influence the beliefs, attitudes, and behaviors of a "large" audience, not a single person or small group.[18] For example, TV public service announcements from the US Centers for Disease Control during the COVID-19 pandemic that urged everyone to get vaccinated were **informational propaganda**.

Encyclopedia Britannica defines **propaganda** as the dissemination of information—facts, arguments, rumors, half-truths, or lies—to influence public opinion. Deliberateness and a relatively heavy emphasis on manipulation distinguish propaganda from casual conversation or the free and easy exchange of ideas.[19]

However we define it, Hobbs reminds us that contemporary propaganda is everywhere—in information, traditional news, advertising, infotainment, and entertainment. It is impossible to avoid.[20]

Whatever differences there are between **persuasion** and **propaganda**, they have something in common, according to Hobbs:[21] both seek to change or strengthen people's beliefs, attitudes, and behaviors through communication and symbolic expression.

Yet distinctions between persuasion and propaganda are eroding as social media allows us to communicate at once with a family member, a group of friends, or the world on the same platforms. For example, that photo you intended to share with your best friend can create misunderstanding and confusion when a mass audience sees it. Content shared on social media has the potential to go viral and reach a wide audience.[22]

Hobbs illustrates one way to think of the relationship between persuasion, propaganda, information, and entertainment (Figure 3.2):[23]

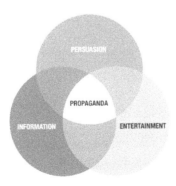

Figure 3.2 Propaganda at the intersection of persuasion, information, and entertainment.

For the purposes of this book, I view the relationship this way (Figure 3.3):

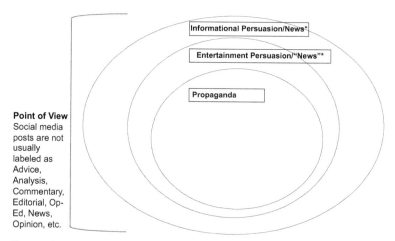

Point of View
Social media posts are not usually labeled as Advice, Analysis, Commentary, Editorial, Op-Ed, News, Opinion, etc.

Tweens and teens view 'news' to include topics like sports, entertainment, celebrity gossip, culture, and science. They see 'the news' as the narrow, traditional agenda of politics and current affairs, according to Reuters Institute for the Study of Journalism.

Figure 3.3 The social media ecosystem.

Of course, in the real world, distinguishing between information, entertainment, news, persuasion, and propaganda involves considerable nuance.[24]

The bottom line is this: It is less important for students to understand precise distinctions between these categories than to know that all media have a point of view they want students to adopt.

Let's look at some examples of propaganda and persuasion from social media.

Information Propaganda

The following post was part of a campaign by the US government's Department of Health and Human Services to promote vaccine awareness during the COVID-19 pandemic (Figure 3.4).

Figure 3.4 Getting vaccinated against #COVID-19 is your best protection from severe illness. Find vaccines near you at vaccines.gov. You may need parental consent to get vaccinated if you're under 18. #WeCanDoThis.[25]

"Social Media Graphic Posts for High School Students," hhs.gov, Social Media Graphic Posts for High School Students I WECANDOTHIS.HHS.GOV.

Wishes – A Public Service Announcement

The following PSA—made for the good of the public[26]—aired in early 2017 and encourages future generations to learn math and science and pursue a STEM career.

Video (https://www.youtube.com/watch?v=ON6hAudgqMg) QR Code 3.1

Entertainment Propaganda

Leaders from government, business, entertainment, and other sectors have also used entertainment propaganda to achieve their objectives. For example, Hollywood routinely uses it to persuade us to buy a product or watch a movie. A good example of entertainment propaganda is the promotion for the movie *Top Gun: Maverick*:

 Photo (https://www.adweek.com/convergent-tv/paramounts-cross-portfolio-campaign-helped-top-gun-maverick-reach-new-box-office-heights/) QR Code 3.2

This is a still image from a skit on the May 23, 2022, episode of the Late Late Show, in which Tom Cruise teaches James Corden how to fly a Top Gun fighter jet. The skit had racked up more than 25 million views on YouTube as of July 2022.[27]

The movie, released in late May 2022, gave the US military an opportunity to portray itself offering patriotic, adventurous, and cool jobs and careers as it grappled with some of its biggest recruitment challenges in decades. The US Army faced a "war for talent" amid shrinking battalion numbers, the Air Force had seen the number of qualified candidates fall by half since the beginning of COVID-19, and the Navy was short 5,000 to 6,000 sailors. The skit helped the movie gross more than $639 million at the US box office, surpassing the movie Titanic's first-run release as the highest-grossing domestic film in Paramount's history.[28,29] The effect on recruitment is hard to measure, but the skit will at least bring increased awareness of what the military does and no doubt persuade young men and women who may not have considered joining the military to take another look.

The study of **persuasion** and **propaganda** has virtually disappeared in the study of English since the rise of the Common Core Standards in ELA,[30] even though ELA has long recognized the need to highlight the power of misleading language (NCTE, 2019a).[31,32] Instead, the standards encourage English teachers to focus on narrative and expository forms of expression, including argumentation, rather than on persuasion, propaganda, and advertising, according to Hobbs. One reason given is that analysis of persuasion, propaganda, and advertising that targets middle and high school students is unlikely to have sufficiently advanced vocabulary and complex sentence structure to meet Common Core guidelines about the required intricacy of written text.[33]

A participant in the Northeast Media Literacy Conference in 2023 echoed this view in a discussion of the role of persuasion and propaganda, commenting that some educators have created an artificial hierarchy where evaluating facts is more important than evaluating opinions as a form of persuasion. The participant said that it is usually the curriculum that mandates this hierarchy.

Indeed, outside the classroom, students are immersed in digital media from across the social media ecosystem, much of it using persuasion and propaganda to convey their points of view. Students' engagement with it continues to increase (Eales et al., 2021).[34] As a result, ELA classrooms that rely on the study of literature and academic writing but do not also examine media use of persuasion and propaganda are becoming more and more disconnected and remote from students' lived experiences.[35]

An English teacher might respond that analyzing and producing argumentative writing activates logic and reasoning to prove a point. But from this perspective, persuasion merely appeals to the reader's emotions, and propaganda is thought to be exaggeration or even a lie (Taithe & Thornton, 1999).[36] Students can get the message that propaganda is always negative. Yet propaganda's ethical dimensions, social value, and utility can only be evaluated in context. In fact, propaganda can be at least partly true and can help us make informed choices.[37]

Teachers should help students critically examine contemporary propaganda and other persuasive genres, including advertising, politics, business, pop culture, and other spheres of public life. [38,39] When teachers expand literacy to include the analysis and production of video, infographics, podcasts, graphic novels, fanfiction, and other diverse modes that usually contain persuasion and propaganda, they are often pleasantly surprised that their students are willing to invest time and effort in their work.[40] Hobbs elaborates on the need for and value of critically examining propaganda and other persuasive genres in her book, *Mind Over Media: Propaganda Education for a Digital Age*,[41] and website, www.mindovermedia.us.[42]

Fortunately, there is a new movement to include the study of propaganda and persuasion in ELA. After the US presidential election in 2016, several professional organizations responsible for teaching writing, composition, and speech reaffirmed their goal to teach the responsible use of language as a form of social power.[43] In 2019, the National Council of Teachers of English called for educators to instruct students in analyzing and evaluating persuasive techniques in all types of media and subject matter.[44] If states don't reinstate teaching techniques of persuasion and propaganda in their standards, students will continue to have trouble evaluating good and bad examples in social media news.

Propaganda can be used in positive and negative ways. We have already examined a PSA about COVID-19 that people consider positive or negative, depending on their point of view, and another about the movie *Top Gun*: Maverick, which most people would consider neutral.

Here are two more examples that most people would consider positive and negative, respectively:

Positive Propaganda

Video   (https://www.youtube.com/watch?v=S4Z2UxGaPas) QR code 3.3

Negative Propaganda

Figure 3.5 This poster, an example of negative propaganda, helped create the cult of personality around Adolf Hitler.

Source: "WWII German Nazi Propaganda Poster." Design/illustration by K.Stauber circa 1933–1935. URL: https://commons.wikimedia.org/wiki/File:WWII_German_Nazi_Propaganda_Poster.jpg. Licensed under the Creative Commons Attribution-Share Alike 4.0 International license: https://creativecommons.org/licenses/by-sa/4.0/.

This was one of the most common posters that helped create the cult of personality around Adolf Hitler (Figure 3.5). Notice the appearance of light around Hitler, giving a halo-like effect. The winged bird lends angelic characteristics to the poster, enhanced by the presence of wreath-like flowers in the poster's border. These are designed to trigger responses in the viewer, especially the **halo effect**, a cognitive bias where people generalize from one highlighted trait of a person to form a favorable view of the person's entire personality. In addition, the commanding stance and shepherd-like portrayal of someone leading the people seek to trigger **authority bias**, where people respond favorably to a person's authority.[45]

Here are some photos that help illustrate the propaganda that Hitler and the Nazis used during World War II (Figures 3.6 and 3.7).

Figure 3.6 Nazi Party rally at Zeppelin Field, Nuremberg, Germany. At the top of the photo in the distance is the Grandstand, with the "Fuhrer's Rostrum," where Hitler addressed the masses, at its center.

Bundesarchiv—Bilddatenbank.

Figure 3.7 In this photo by the author, the remains of the Grandstand and "Fuhrer's Rostrum" (background) and spectators' stands (foreground) can be seen at Zeppelin Field, Nuremberg, Germany, in May 2018. Try to imagine the Nazis holding rallies here, with Hitler speaking from the Rostrum, to spread National Socialist propaganda.

 And finally, below is a more contemporary piece of negative propaganda.

Image (https://imgur.com/gallery/H2e7Ijc/) QR Code 3.4

According to the Simon Wiesenthal Center,[46] this image featuring green, blue, and red paint being mixed to form brown was posted to Facebook by the Canadian Nationalist Front (CNF). The image is no longer available on social media; Facebook shut down the CNF account in 2019. CNF is a Toronto-area white supremacist group that believes that those who promote multiculturalism—cultural pluralism or diversity within a society, organization, or educational institution[47]—seek to breed the white race out of existence.

▶ LESSON PLAN

Divide students into groups of three to four. Share a mix of examples of data, information, news, infotainment, and entertainment; I recommend using examples from trending pop culture to pique students' interest early in the school year.

This lesson requires all students to identify the functions of the parts of the information and social media ecosystems and what slice of the ecosystems each example represents.

It requires higher achieving students to also determine whether the example is persuasion or propaganda and how persuasion and propaganda interact with these ecosystems and appeal to their biases when they evaluate social media.

Teachers may want to omit the examples of negative propaganda around Hitler if they have not yet taught their students about the Nazis.

▶ NOTES

1 "Fighting Fake News: Teaching Students to Identify and Interrogate Information Pollution, Copyright 2023, Corwin Press.

2 "An Explication on the Use of 'Explicit' and 'Implicit,'" Explicit vs Implicit: Usage Guide | Merriam—Webster.

3 Data—Definition, Meaning & Synonyms | Vocabulary.com.

4 Data—Wikipedia.

5 Data—Wikipedia.

6 NEWS | English meaning—Cambridge Dictionary.

7 News Definition & Meaning—Merriam—Webster.

8 Sex, Lies, and War: How Soft News Brings Foreign Policy to the Inattentive Public, American Political Science Review, 2002.

9 John Zaller (2003) A new standard of news quality: Burglar alarms for the monitorial citizen, *Political Communication*, 20:2, 109–130, DOI: 10.1080/10584600390211136.

10 Dictionary of mass communication & media research: a guide for students, scholars and professionals, David Demer, 2005.

11 Entertainment Definition & Meaning—Merriam—Webster.

12 Cambridge Dictionary, ENTERTAINMENT | English meaning—Cambridge Dictionary.

13 IGI Global, What Is E—Entertainment | IGI Global (igi—global.com).

14 "Opinion Creep: How facts lost ground in the battle for our attention," NLP podcast, "Is That a fact?," June 1, 2023.

15 "Opinion Creep: How facts lost ground in the battle for our attention," NLP podcast, "Is That a fact?," June 1, 2023.

16 "Distinguishing among news, opinion and propaganda," John Silva, News Literacy Project, June 20, 2018, NLP Blog: Distinguishing among News, Opinion And Propaganda (newslit.org).

17 "Mind Over Media: Propaganda Education for a Digital Age," Renee Hobbs, Norton (2020).

18 "Mind Over Media: Propaganda Education for a Digital Age," Renee Hobbs, Norton (2020).

19 Smith, Bruce Lannes. "Propaganda." Encyclopedia Britannica, 28 Nov. 2023, https://www.britannica.com/topic/propaganda. Accessed 31 December 2023.

20 "What Is Propaganda?," MoM contemporary curriculum (mediaeducationlab.com).

21 "Mind Over Media: Propaganda Education for a Digital Age," Renee Hobbs, Norton (2020).

22 "Mind Over Media: Propaganda Education for a Digital Age," Renee Hobbs, Norton (2020).

23 "Mind Over Media: Propaganda Education for a Digital Age," Renee Hobbs, Norton (2020).

24 Mind Over Media: Propaganda Education for a Digital Age, Renee Hobbs and Douglas Rushkoff, Norton, 2020.

25 "Social Media Graphic Posts for High School Students," hhs.gov, Social Media Graphic Posts for High School Students | WECANDOTHIS.HHS.GOV.

26 Public service announcement Definition & Meaning—Merriam—Webster.

27 "Paramount's Cross—Portfolio Campaign Helped Top Gun: Maverick Reach New Box Office Heights," Paramount's Cross—Company Campaign Let Top Gun: Maverick Fly (adweek.com).

28 "Propaganda with your popcorn: How cinema became the military's key promotional tool," Top Gun Maverick: How cinema became the military's key promotional tool | The Independent, Joe Ellison, May 26, 2022.

29 "Propaganda with your popcorn: How cinema became the military's key promotional tool," Top Gun Maverick: How cinema became the military's key promotional tool | The Independent, Joe Ellison, May 26, 2022.

30 Mind Over Media: Propaganda Education for a Digital Age, Renee Hobbs and Douglas Rushkoff, Norton, 2020.

31 Position Statements: Media Education in English Language Arts, April 9, 2022, Media Education in English Language Arts—National Council of Teachers of English (ncte.org).

32 Position Statements: Media Education in English Language Arts, April 9, 2022, Media Education in English Language Arts—National Council of Teachers of English (ncte.org).

33 Mind Over Media: Propaganda Education for a Digital Age, Renee Hobbs and Douglas Rushkoff, Norton, 2020.

34 Position Statements: Media Education in English Language Arts, April 9, 2022, Media Education in English Language Arts—National Council of Teachers of English (ncte.org).

35 Position Statements: Media Education in English Language Arts, April 9, 2022, Media Education in English Language Arts—National Council of Teachers of English (ncte.org).

36 Mind Over Media: Propaganda Education for a Digital Age, Renee Hobbs and Douglas Rushkoff, Norton, 2020.

37 Mind Over Media: Propaganda Education for a Digital Age, Renee Hobbs and Douglas Rushkoff, Norton, 2020.

38 Mind Over Media: Propaganda Education for a Digital Age, Renee Hobbs and Douglas Rushkoff, Norton, 2020.

39 Position Statements: Media Education in English Language Arts, April 9, 2022, Media Education in English Language Arts—National Council of Teachers of English (ncte.org).

40 Position Statements: Media Education in English Language Arts, April 9, 2022, Media Education in English Language Arts—National Council of Teachers of English (ncte.org).

41 Mind Over Media: Propaganda Education for a Digital Age, Renee Hobbs and Douglas Rushkoff, Norton, 2020.

42 Mind Over Media: The Book.

43 Mind Over Media: Propaganda Education for a Digital Age, Renee Hobbs and Douglas Rushkoff, Norton, 2020.

44 Mind Over Media: Propaganda Education for a Digital Age, Renee Hobbs and Douglas Rushkoff, Norton, 2020.

45 "Analysis of Nazi Propaganda A Behavioral Study," Karthik Narayanaswami, Harvard University.

46 Digital Terrorism and Hate Project (digitalhate.net).

47 Multiculturalism Definition and Meaning—Merriam-Webster.

The Persuasive Power of Visuals

4

I learned over and over as a CIA imagery analyst that visuals play on our emotions and biases. For part of my career, I was assigned to determine the political, economic, and security situation on the ground after gut-wrenching humanitarian crises, some caused by nature, some by humans, some by a mix of the two. In nearly every case, the most effective tool I had to communicate foreign intelligence to busy US diplomats, military personnel, the United Nations, etc., was photographic intelligence. Whether I was writing about ethnic cleansing in Bosnia in 1992 or in Rwanda in 1994; conflict, drought, and starvation in Sudan's Darfur region; or political instability in the wake of the devastating tsunami in Asia in late 2004, visuals grabbed their attention. When I briefed US officials in person, I often used visuals to help them understand the issue more fully.

Entertainment media in our social media feeds do this particularly well for the general reader. They use visuals to try to activate our feelings and emotions to persuade us to think or do something. They try to grab our attention before we can read accompanying text that might dampen their effects. They are everywhere on social media and include all imaginable formats, including advertisements, cartoons, charts, comic books, graphic novels, maps, memes, photos, signs, storyboards, symbols, time lines, and videos, to name a few.[1]

DOI: 10.4324/9781003471301-6

Romain Vaktilibar indicates that we are more likely to be persuaded, for good or bad, when we consume visuals for entertainment.[2] Entertainment TV, for example, holds our attention because we develop bonds with favorite characters. The bond can cause us to abandon our critical thinking tools. On the other hand, the appeal of entertainment media to a politically diverse audience can help us set aside our biases and consider alternative viewpoints that help unite us.[3]

If we don't teach students how to "read" visuals effectively, we leave students open to misreading them. To that end, students should understand how visuals try to communicate with them via explicit and implicit messages.

An explicit message is usually text that comes right out and tells the audience what the messenger wants them to believe or do.

An implicit message implies what the messenger wants the audience to believe or do; it does not come right out and say it. Most visuals use implicit messages and appear in a context to help us understand them.

The skill of "reading" a visual is called "visual literacy," defined in part as the ability to identify, understand, and get meaning from the messages that visuals send.[4] That "meaning making" is influenced by our prior knowledge, beliefs, and experiences.

Teaching students to examine visuals critically does not seem common in US education.[5] Although many of us have heard the saying, "A picture is worth a thousand words," how many teachers ask students to deeply reflect on what that means and why people say it? This reflection is more and more important because of the spread of manipulated visuals, including shallow fakes and deepfakes (see Chapters 5 and 13).[6]

Driven by their emotions and biases, many students form first impressions of visuals out of context and before reading the explanatory caption. To counter this, we should teach students to interrogate visuals as dispassionately as possible by considering visuals' implicit and explicit messages and in their proper context.

This chapter introduces basic techniques to interrogate any visual for explicit and implicit messages. Subsequent chapters provide a variety of other techniques to evaluate specific types of visuals that students will encounter in social media, including photos, videos, memes, and ads.

▶ LESSON PLAN

This lesson requires all students to identify implicit and explicit messages in social media. Higher achieving students should also examine how the message makes them feel and how it interacts with their biases and mindset.

Remove the caption from each of the following visuals and have students determine if each has explicit and/or implicit messages trying to persuade them, and what those messages are. You might also use examples of trending pop culture to pique students' interest early in the school year.

▶ PHOTOS

 Photo[7] (https://www.gettyimages.com/detail/news-photo/trump-supporter-known-as-t-shows-off-his-outfit-during-the-news-photo/1245500535?adppopup=true) QR Code 4.1

Answer: Explicit

Tie to social studies-civics-ELA: Freedom of expression, First Amendment, US politics, US government

 Photo[8] (https://www.gettyimages.co.uk/detail/news-photo/scene-from-new-york-citys-pride-parade-by-carolyn-van-news-photo/1245500073) QR Code 4.2

Answer: Implicit

Tie to social studies-civics-ELA: Social justice, civil rights, freedom of expression, First Amendment

 Photo[9] (https://www.gettyimages.co.uk/detail/news-photo/previously-submerged-boat-on-lake-mead-on-june-14-2022-in-news-photo/1242008369?adppopup=true) QR Code 4.3

Answer: Implicit

Tie to science-social studies-civics-ELA: Environmental issues

Photo[10] (https://imagn.com/setImages/523047/preview/21661 966) QR Code 4.4

Answer: Implicit

Tie to social studies-civics-ELA: Racial equality, civil rights, freedom of expression, First Amendment

Photo[11] (https://www.gettyimages.com/detail/news-photo/ french-president-emmanuel-macron-meets-with-russian- news-photo/1238272145) QR Code 4.5

Answer: Implicit

Tie to social studies-civics-ELA: US foreign policy, politics

Video[12] (https://www.youtube.com/watch?v=9PodDl4DTNI) QR Code 4.6

Answer: Explicit

Tie to social studies-civics-ELA: Health education

▶ MEMES

Many memes carry implicit messages; they are usually directed at an "in group" who will pick up the implied message more quickly than the "out group," on which the meme also relies in order to spread rapidly. Some, but not all, memes are animated GIFs (Graphics Interchange Format).

Here are examples of memes with explicit or implicit messages (Figures 4.1 to 4.4):

Figure 4.1 A meme of Queen Elizabeth and Peppa Pig.

Tweet from Peppa Pig Official Twitter account @peppapig, https://twitter.com/peppapig/status/1567958357302022146?s=20.

Answer: Explicit

Tie to social studies-civics-ELA: Civics

When you finally graduate
from high school in the USA

Figure 4.2 Meme about gun violence in high schools in the USA showing graduating
        high school students throwing bulletproof vests in the air instead of grad-
        uation caps.

Meme about gun violence in high schools in the USA. (20+) Facebook.

Original image behind meme: Cheerful Students Throwing Graduation Caps in the
Air Stock Photo 188674772 I Shutterstock.

Answer: Implicit
Tie to social studies-civics-ELA: Civics

▶ **ADS**

Figure 4.3 Example of a pizza ad.

Pizza Emblem Stock Vector (Royalty Free) 455886493 | Shutterstock.

Answer: Explicit

Tie to social studies-civics-ELA: Civics

An **implicit message** in advertising sells an idea to the consumer rather than telling them specific details about a company, product, or service.[13]

Example of an ad that uses implicit messaging.

Figure 4.4 Example of a pizza ad.

Hungry Little Girl Enjoys Italian Pizza Stock Photo 2381544101 | Shutterstock.

Answer: Implicit
Tie to social studies-civics-ELA: Civics

▶ CHARTS

Charts are easy to misunderstand if we do not pay close attention.[14] All charts say things their makers intend, but many say things their makers did not anticipate. In other words, all charts have explicit messages, and many have implicit messages.

There are key differences between what charts say explicitly and implicitly. Explicit messages come from data in their axes, labels, and annotations and in the text in their figure descriptions. The explicit channel is active and purposeful. Annotations, figure descriptions, and axis labels relay data points with text in a more obvious manner than color and other graphical designs.[15]

Their implicit messages come from what their data say as a whole, which can be up to the viewer's interpretation. The implicit channel is passive and affects the reader subconsciously. For example, it includes the color choices and fonts used in the chart.[16]

An academic study from 2018 indicated that titles of charts and other visualizations have explicit and implicit messages comparable to the importance of news article headlines in how well the reader understands and remembers the information. Like news article headlines, visualization titles may be biased.[17]

Look at the chart in the link below. Orienting it upward, changing its title, and using blue instead of dark red dramatically reinforce the explicit and implicit messages about the death rate in Iraq in Figure 4.5.

Chart[18,19]   (https://www.scmp.com/infographics/article/128 4683/iraqs-bloody-toll) QR Code 4.7

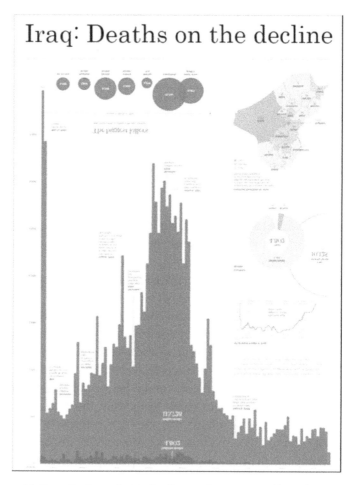

Figure 4.5 "Iraq: Deaths on the Decline," a visualization created by Andy Cotgreave in 2016.

Teachers whose students are not familiar in a broad sense with US involvement in Iraq may want to provide general background before giving them the charts on Iraq.

▶ NOTES

1 Visual Literacy: Definition & Examples. (2021, November 9). Retrieved from https://study.com/learn/lesson/visual-literacy-skills-overview-examples-what-is-visual-literacy.html.

2 Romain Vaktilibar, Northeast Media Literacy Conference, January 13, 2023.

3 Romain Vaktilibar, Northeast Media Literacy Conference, January 13, 2023.

4 Visual Literacy: Definition & Examples. (2021, November 9). Retrieved from https://study.com/learn/lesson/visual-literacy-skills-overview-examples-what-is-visual-literacy.html.

5 "Teach Kids to 'Read' the Images They See," Frank Baker, Middleweb.com, March 17, 2021, Teaching Students How to Analyze Images and Detect Fakery (middleweb.com).

6 "Teach Kids to 'Read' the Images They See," Frank Baker, Middleweb.com, March 17, 2021, Teaching Students How to Analyze Images and Detect Fakery (middleweb.com).

7 Trump supporter known as T shows off his outfit during the Save… News Photo—Getty Images.

8 Scene from New York Citys Pride Parade by Carolyn Van Houten Veronica…News Photo—Getty Images.

9 A previously submerged boat on Lake Mead on June 14, 2022 in Boulder…News Photo—Getty Images.

10 Imagn: Syndication: Rockford Register Star.

11 TOPSHOT—French President Emmanuel Macron meets with Russian…News Photo—Getty Images.

12 Mental Health Matters PSA students to student message (60 sec.)—YouTube.

13 Media Literacy: Implicit vs Explicit Ads—YouTube.

14 Graphics That Seem Clear Can Easily Be Misread: Misreading data visualizations can reinforce biased perceptions, Albert Cairo, Graphics That Seem Clear Can Easily Be Misread—Scientific American, September 1, 2019.

15 https://medium.com/nightingale/what-charts-say-6e31cbba2047, What Charts Say, Elijah Meeks, May 7, 2018.

16 https://medium.com/nightingale/what-charts-say-6e31cbba2047, What Charts Say, Elijah Meeks, May 7, 2018.

17 Kong, Ha—Kyung & Liu, Zhicheng & Karahalios, Karrie. (2018). Frames and Slants in Titles of Visualizations on Controversial Topics. 1—12.

18 Iraq's bloody toll | South China Morning Post (scmp.com).

19 Living With Data: Lies, damn lies, and statistics: How to take something positive from the UK's EU referendum campaign | InfoWorld, Andy Cotgreave, InfoWorld, June 28, 2016.

Evaluate Photos

5

We often give more credibility to photos than words because we think the camera never lies. We think photos capture a moment of reality.

But a photo can actually be a "**shallow fake**," edited with minimal effort by a human; it does not rely on an algorithm or deep-learning systems. It could be a real photo with edits out of context.[1] Or it may be a **deepfake**, manipulated by an algorithm, in which a depicted face or body has been digitally modified to appear as someone or something else to make a person look like they said or did something they did not do.[2]

I will discuss deepfake photos in more detail in Chapter 13 on artificial intelligence. As I write this, shallow fake photos are more worrisome on social media than deepfakes because they are more common. They have been manipulated using cheaper, simpler editing software and are lower quality than deepfakes.

Shallow fake photos can also omit important context or appear out of order to deceive you and shape your opinion.[3] They do not need to be realistic to succeed; their strength lies in their ability to confirm your preexisting biases.[4]

▶ **LESSON PLAN**

Have groups of two to three students answer the following questions as they study the photo in Figure 5.1 with the caption removed.

DOI: 10.4324/9781003471301-7

Figure 5.1 Original caption left off and revealed in text: "Dr. Martin Luther King, Jr. is arrested for loitering outside a courtroom where his friend and associate Ralph Abernathy is appearing for a trial in Montgomery, Alabama."

Source: Martin Luther King, Jr. Montgomery arrest 1958.jpg—Wikimedia Commons.

All students should examine the photo closely and make inferences based on their observations. They should identify what they see, whether they are looking at the original version, and where and when it was first published. They should also ask how the photo makes them feel and how their biases and mindset influence their reaction.

Higher achieving students should also critique the photo more deeply. They should ask questions like the following. I include my responses and possible answers students might come up with.

- *What do you think the message might be behind the photo? What was the photographer trying to capture?* The arrest of a Black man by police.
- *What is the possible setting? What are the clues about the setting?* A public facility. The specific function is not obvious.
- *What and who may be just out of the frame?* Possibly more people, including police, photographers and reporters, and onlookers.
- *Is the message implicit or explicit?* Implicit.
- *Examine the people's faces. What might their expressions communicate?* The man under arrest looks calm and somewhat stoic, suggesting he has been through this before. The onlookers also look stoic.
- *Is this an example of propaganda?* Without a caption, it is hard to determine.
- *How does the propaganda appeal to my biases?* Not applicable.

Note: This may be a good time to introduce **reverse image search**, a skill that students can use in this lesson. A student can validate the origin of an image or video by taking a screen capture of the image or individual frames of a video and running them through a reverse image search platform. Please see the "Tools" section for popular reverse image search tools.

Have a discussion with the students about their observations.

Next, show the photo with the caption included (Figure 5.2). The caption reads: *"Enroute To Jail—Police officers taking the Rev. Martin Luther King Jr. to a cell at Police Headquarters in Montgomery, Ala., yesterday, stop at the desk sergeant's counter for the keys to the cell. King was arrested on a city street on a charge of loitering."* [5]

Figure 5.2 "Enroute To Jail—Police officers taking the Rev. Martin Luther King Jr. to a cell at Police Headquarters in Montgomery, Ala., yesterday, stop at the desk sergeant's counter for the keys to the cell. King was arrested on a city street on a charge of loitering." A subscription database indicates the Standard Sentinel newspaper used a cropped version of the photo on its front page the day after the event.

"Teach Kids to 'Read' the Images They See," Frank Baker, Middleweb.com, March 17, 2021, Teaching Students How to Analyze Images and Detect Fakery (middleweb.com). Newspapers.com, September 4, 1958, 1—Standard-Speaker at Standard-Speaker (newspapers.com)

All students should identify what they see. They should determine again whether they are looking at the original version of the image and where and when it was first published. They should also ask how the image makes them feel and how their biases and mindset influence their reaction.

Higher achieving students should also critique the photo more deeply. They should ask questions like the following. I include possible answers students might come up with.

- *What's the actual message behind the photo? What was the photographer trying to capture?* The arrest of MLK at police headquarters in Montgomery, Alabama, on September 3, 1958. Moore was documenting struggles during the civil rights era.
- *What is the actual setting? What are the clues about the setting?* Police station, Montgomery, Alabama. The caption tells us so.
- *What may be just out of the frame?* We know from the uncropped photo that MLK's wife, Coretta, is out of the frame to the right, along with two other people.
- *Is the message implicit or explicit?* The caption makes it explicit.
- *Examine the people's faces again. What might their expressions communicate?* MLK looks calm and somewhat stoic, suggesting he has been through this before.
- *Is this an example of propaganda?* No.
- *How does the propaganda appeal to my biases?* Not applicable.
- *How have your initial thoughts about the photo changed given this new information?* I have a much greater appreciation for the photo now that I know what it depicts and the historic significance of the event.

Although students will find the photo all over the Internet, Wikimedia indicates photographer Charles Moore took the photo for the *Montgomery Advertiser* newspaper on September 3, 1958, to capture the arrest of MLK at police headquarters in Montgomery, Alabama, where he was charged and jailed for loitering.[6,7,8] Moore, who was covering a case involving Ralph

Abernathy at the Montgomery, Alabama, courthouse for the newspaper, saw two policemen arrest MLK there. Moore followed the police to the station.

Homework: Ask students to bring in a news photo from a social media platform they use to get their news. Have them present a photo analysis to the class based on their research and investigation.

▶ NOTES

1 Cheap fakes vs. deepfakes—Poynter.
2 Cheap fakes vs. deepfakes—Poynter.
3 "Cheap fakes vs. deepfakes," Poynter, Cheap fakes vs. deepfakes—Poynter.
4 Todd C. Helmus, Artificial Intelligence, Deepfakes, and Disinformation: A Primer, July 2022, Rand Corporation.
5 "Teach Kids to 'Read' the Images They See," Frank Baker, Middleweb.com, March 17, 2021, Teaching Students How to Analyze Images and Detect Fakery (middleweb.com).
6 "Teach Kids to 'Read' the Images They See," Frank Baker, Middleweb.com, March 17, 2021, Teaching Students How to Analyze Images and Detect Fakery (middleweb.com).
7 Newspapers.com, September 4, 1958, 1—Standard-Speaker at Standard-Speaker (newspapers.com).
8 File: Martin Luther King, Jr. Montgomery arrest 1958.jpg—Wikimedia Commons.

Evaluate Videos

6

As with photos, we often give more credibility to videos than words because we think the camera never lies. We think videos capture a moment of reality.

As with a photo, a video can actually be a shallow fake, edited with minimal effort by a human.[1] Or it may be an artificial intelligence (AI)–generated deepfake, in which a depicted face or body has been digitally modified to appear as someone or something else to make a person look like they said or did something they did not do.[2]

I will discuss deepfake videos in Chapter 13 on AI. As I write this, shallow fakes are more worrisome on social media than deepfakes because, like shallow fake photos, they are more common.[3] They are lower quality and have been manipulated using cheaper, simpler, more widely available editing software.[4] Shallow fake videos can omit important context or have clips that are out of order to deceive you and shape your opinion.[5]

As with shallow fake photos, shallow fake videos do not need to be realistic to succeed; their strength lies in their ability to confirm preexisting prejudices. For example, a video of then–Speaker of the US House of Representatives Nancy Pelosi was edited to slow down her speech and make her appear to slur her words during an interview so that she seemed intoxicated.[6] The video

DOI: 10.4324/9781003471301-8

went viral and was widely popular among politically conservative audiences who were inclined to cheer the video's contents.[7]

▶ LESSON PLAN

Remove the captions and mute the dialogue in the following video from pop culture. Have groups of two to three students answer the following questions as they study the video.

Will Smith slaps comedian Chris Rock at the 2022 Academy Awards:
Video[8]   (https://www.youtube.com/watch?v=h-UeElTIh5c)
      QR Code 6.1

All students should examine the video closely and identify what they see, whether they are looking at the original version of the video, and where and when it was first published. They should also ask how the video makes them feel and how their biases and mindset influence their reaction.

Higher achieving students should also critique the video more deeply. They should ask questions like the following. I include possible answers students might come up with.

- *What do you think the message might be behind the video? What was the videographer trying to capture?* The videographer was trying to capture a Black man walking toward another Black man.
- *What is the possible setting? What are the clues about the setting?* A formal awards ceremony. Clues include the tuxedo worn by the Black man on a stage, who holds a red envelope.
- *What and who may be just out of the frame?* Audience members at an awards ceremony.
- *Is the message implicit or explicit?* Implicit.
- *Examine the people's faces. What might their expressions communicate?* One Black man looks expressionless as he walks up to the other, who looks surprised and stunned.

- *Is this an example of propaganda?* No.
- *How does the propaganda appeal to my biases?* Not applicable.

Have a discussion with the students about their observations.

Next, play the video with the captions and dialogue included, and have all students identify what they see. They should also ask how the video makes them feel and how their biases and mindset influence their reaction.

Higher achieving students should also critique the video more deeply. They should ask questions like the following. I include my responses and possible answers students might come up with.

- *What's the actual message behind the video? What was the videographer trying to capture?* Comedian Chris Rock made a joke about Will Smith's wife, which caused Will Smith to become angry and slap Mr. Rock on the face.
- *What is the actual setting? What are the clues about the setting?* The Oscars on March 27, 2022. References to the "Oscars" at the 1:20 minute mark and being "nominated."
- *What may be just out of the frame?* Audience members at the awards ceremony.
- *Is the message implicit or explicit?* Explicit.
- *Examine the people's faces again. What might their expressions communicate?* Will Smith looks expression-less as he walks back to his seat after slapping Rock, who looks surprised and stunned.
- *Is this an example of propaganda?* No.
- *How does the propaganda appeal to my biases?* Not applicable.
- *How have your initial thoughts about the video changed given this new information?* The video is even more dramatic and impactful now that I know it depicts the actions of these two well-known actors on live TV at the Oscars.

Homework: Ask students to bring in a news video from a social media platform they use to get their news. Have them present a video analysis to the class based on their research and investigation.

▶ NOTES

1 Cheap Fakes vs. Deepfakes—Poynter.
2 Cheap Fakes vs. Deepfakes—Poynter.
3 Todd C. Helmus, *Artificial Intelligence, Deepfakes, and Disinformation: A Primer*, July 2022, Rand Corporation.
4 Cheap Fakes vs. Deepfakes—Poynter.
5 Cheap Fakes vs. Deepfakes—Poynter.
6 Donie O'Sullivan, "Doctored Videos Shared to Make Pelosi Sound Drunk Viewed Millions of Times on Social Media," CNN, May 24, 2019.
7 Todd C. Helmus, July 2022. *Artificial Intelligence, Deepfakes, and Disinformation: A Primer*, Rand Corporation.
8 Watch Dramatic Oscars Moment as Will Smith Slaps Chris Rock Over Jada Joke—YouTube.

Figure 7.1 I don't think this memes what you think it memes.

Author-created meme, Home—Canva.

Chapter 7

Evaluate Memes

DOI: 10.4324/9781003471301-9

Memes are usually funny images and text used to make social or political statements. In his book, *The Selfish Gene*, published in 1976, British scientist Richard Dawkins describes a meme as a unit of information, culture, or conduct that passes from one person to another. The term has evolved to describe the Internet memes we know today (Figure 7.1). [1,2]

The *Merriam-Webster Dictionary* defines a meme as "an amusing or interesting item (such as a captioned picture or video) or genre of items that is spread widely online especially through social media."[3] Readers who recognize the core component of the meme, such as an image of an actor or an idiosyncratic expression in the meme's text, will often be quick to reinterpret it as it spreads.

We are often lured by memes because they are funny or arouse our emotions with their unique combination of short text and an image or GIF. They can appear credible, but they rarely provide links to sources. They have no nuance or context, often contain fake or manipulated images, and often misquote celebrities, politicians, and historical figures. It is difficult to trace a meme to its creator and even harder to determine why the creator made it.[4]

A key aspect of memes is their culture, in which jokes like the one in the caption for the meme introducing this chapter appeal to an "in group." The "in group" gets smaller as memes become more obscure to many viewers, often because they require recognizing references to previous memes.[5]

In today's connected world, the number of people who "get" a meme is large enough to form a community, like support groups for sharing and debating issues on whether Bigfoot is real.[6] The ability to create inside and outside groups while uniting those groups makes memes uniquely persuasive in today's world of connected but often tribal political and social groups, according to Jonathan Haber, an educational researcher and consultant specializing in critical thinking education.[7]

Let's examine a few memes.

▶ LESSON PLAN

First, present the photo behind the meme and the photo's caption (Figure 7.2). All students should examine the photo closely and identify what they see, whether they are looking at the original version of the photo, and where and when it was first published. They should ask how the photo makes them feel and how their biases and mindset influence their reaction.

Higher achieving students should also critique the photo more deeply. They should ask questions like the following. I include possible answers students might come up with.

- *What message do you think is behind the photo? What was the photographer or uploader trying to capture?* The photographer or uploader was probably trying to capture how cute the dog is.
- *Is the message implicit or explicit?* Implicit.
- *What is the possible setting? What are the clues about the setting?* Unknown. There are no clues as to the setting.
- *What and who may be just out of the frame?* Unknown.
- *Examine the dog's face. What might its expression communicate?* The dog looks disturbed or worried, which detracts from the photographer's or uploader's probable desire to show a cute dog.
- *Is this an example of propaganda?* It is unlikely the photographer or uploader was trying to use propaganda.
- *How does the propaganda appeal to my biases?* Not applicable.

Figure 7.2 Photo of a dog wearing a denim collar.

Photo by charlesdeluvio on Unsplash.

Have a discussion with the students about their observations.

Now students should look at the meme derived from the photo (Figure 7.3). They should compare their initial thoughts with the actual information.

Figure 7.3 Meme of a dog.

Selected Media from My Book – *Media Literacy Sleuth*

All students should identify what they see. They should determine whether they are looking at the original version of the meme and where and when it was first published. They should ask how the meme makes them feel and how their biases and mindset influence their reaction.

Higher achieving students should also critique the meme more deeply. They should ask questions like the following. I include possible answers students might come up with.

Are you looking at the original version? Find out.
This is the original version.
Where was the original version published? The photo behind the meme was first posted to Unsplash.com. I posted the meme to my website, https://medialiteracysleuth.com/figure-7-3/. QR Code 7.1

When was it first published? The photo behind the meme was first posted on February 7, 2018. I uploaded the meme to my website on January 19, 2024.

Who first made/posted the meme? Students should discover that Charles Deluvio, a graphic designer in Montreal, Canada, posted the photo behind the meme. They should find through a reverse image search that the photo has appeared on several social media platforms, including Facebook, X, and Instagram. The author first posted the meme.

How does the meme make me feel, and how do my biases and mindset influence my reaction?
I grew up with dogs in my family. I love dogs, especially short-nosed ones like this one. I find the dog cute, but I wonder if the dog is worried or stressed, given its expression. I also was a middle and high school student, and I often felt worried and stressed when doing my homework. I would have felt especially worried if I had possibly violated a homework policy.

What's the actual message behind the meme? What was the meme maker or uploader trying to capture?
The author was trying to reinforce the need for students to use AI carefully and responsibly when doing homework.

Does this meme use explicit or implicit messaging? Implicit.

What is the actual setting? What are the clues about the setting? The setting of the photo behind the meme is unknown.

What may be just out of the frame? Unknown.

Examine the dog's face again. What might its expression communicate? Worry, stress.

Is this an example of propaganda? No.

How does the propaganda appeal to my biases? Not applicable.

How have your initial thoughts about the meme changed given this new information? I realize now that the meme seeks to encourage students to use AI responsibly, not just spur positive feelings about a cute dog.

Have a discussion with the students about their observations.

▶ LET'S LOOK AT ANOTHER MEME

Tweet (no title or caption)[8] (https://www.capitalfm.com/artists/harry-styles/covid-19-t-shirt-donate-stay-safe-stay-home/) QR Code 7.2

First, have students look at the meme without the tweet's title and caption and answer the following questions. All students should examine the meme closely and identify what they see, whether they are looking at the original version of the meme, and where and when it was first published. They should ask how the meme makes them feel and how their biases and mindset influence their reaction.

Higher achieving students should also critique the meme more deeply. They should ask questions like the following. I include possible answers students might come up with.

- *What message do you think is behind the meme? What was the meme maker or uploader trying to capture?* The meme maker or uploader was trying to connect the message about COVID on the T-shirt with the young man in the photo, who appears to be an entertainer.
- *Is the message implicit or explicit?* The message on the T-shirt makes the message explicit, though the identity of the young man gives it an implicit component.
- *What is the possible setting? What are the clues about the setting?* The microphones and the probable keyboard player behind the young man suggest the setting is a concert.
- *What and who may be just out of the frame?* Musicians, other entertainers, and concert attendees.
- *Examine the person's face. What might their expression communicate?* The possible entertainer looks as though he is emphasizing something, perhaps the message on the T-shirt.
- *Is this an example of propaganda?* This might be an example of positive propaganda in the form of a de facto public service announcement.
- *How does the propaganda appeal to my biases?* I vividly remember the COVID-19 pandemic, and I have a bias toward protecting oneself from the virus. I tend to have positive feelings toward the meme.

Have a discussion with the students about their observations.

Now, have students look at the meme with the tweet's title and caption included. In addition to asking what they see, whether they are looking at the original version, and where and when it was first published, they should ask how the meme makes them feel and how their biases and mindset influence their reaction. Higher achieving students should also answer the additional questions. I include possible answers students might come up with.

 Tweet (with title and caption)[9] (https://knowyourmeme. com/memes/events/harry-styles-coronavirus-merch-controversy/ photos) QR Code 7.3

- *Are you looking at the original version?*
  The entire meme that uses both images seems to be the original. However, a reverse image search turned up the image on the left of the T-shirt, dated February 18, 2020. Numerous reputable news outlets, however, report that Styles released the shirt on his website on April 7, 2020, for World Health Day. The shirt has since been removed from the website. The image on the right appeared on www.glamourmagazine.com and was taken in February 2020, when Styles performed on NBC's *Today* show at Rockefeller Plaza in New York City.
- *Where was the original version published?* The original version of the meme was published on X to the account @ CapitalOfficial.
- *When was it first published?* April 7, 2020.
- *Who first made/posted the meme?* X account @Capital-Official posted the meme. Since the tweet includes two images from different sources, @CapitalOfficial probably made the tweet.
- *What's the actual message behind the meme? What was the producer/poster trying to capture?* X account @ CapitalOfficial is probably trying to portray Harry Styles as a kind person by highlighting his humanitarian action to fight COVID-19 through the sale of his T-shirt. According to several news outlets[10,11,12] Styles donated 100

percent of profits from his shirt sales to the World Health Organization's Solidarity Response Fund, which is powered by the UN Foundation. Earlier in 2020, Styles launched the Treat People With Kindness (TPWK) movement and created a range of merchandise, with profits distributed to local charities around the world. A portion of the money made from his ticket sales on tour was also donated to various charitable organizations.

- *Does this meme use explicit or implicit messaging?* Implicit. The tweet's headline says, "Treat People With Kindness," implying that Styles is a kind person.
- *What is the actual setting? What are the clues about the setting?* The setting for the photo of Styles is NBC's *Today* show at Rockefeller Plaza in New York City. The setting of the T-shirt photo is probably a website associated with Styles.
- *What may be just out of the frame?* Musicians, other entertainers, and concert attendees.
- *Examine the person's face again. What might their expression communicate?* Styles looks as though he is emphasizing something, but he could just be gesturing as he performs rather than emphasizing the message on the T-shirt.
- *Is this an example of propaganda?* Yes, this is part positive propaganda but also part advertising. The propaganda message is to promote health and safety during COVID. The advertising message is to promote Harry Styles's concert ticket and merchandise sales.
- *How does the propaganda appeal to my biases?* Since I have a bias toward protecting oneself from the virus, I have positive feelings toward the meme's message of protecting people. These outweigh my neutral or slightly cynical feelings about the advertising for Styles's concert and merchandise.

How have your initial thoughts about the meme changed given this new information? I have a slightly more cynical view of the meme now that I know a famous entertainer is promoting it and selling his merchandise in the process. Some students are likely to say they have a deeper appreciation for Styles and see him as compassionate, despite a controversy over whether he should have contributed more money to COVID-19, delays in T-shirt orders, etc.

Have a discussion with the students about their observations.

Let's look at another meme. Teachers in school districts that do not teach about climate change may want to use these examples to teach some basic science concepts.

 Tweet[13,14] (https://medialiteracysleuth.com/qr-code-7-4/) QR Code 7.4

First, have students look at the meme without the title and caption and answer the following questions. All students should examine the meme closely and identify what they see, whether they are looking at the original version of the meme, and where and when it was first published. They should ask how the meme makes them feel and how their biases and mindset influence their reaction.

Higher achieving students should also critique the meme more deeply. They should ask questions like the following. I include possible answers students might come up with.

- *What do you think the message might be behind the meme? What was the meme maker or uploader trying to capture?* The meme maker or uploader was trying to say that melting icebergs do not cause sea levels to rise. This suggests they are trying to debunk the adverse effects of climate change.
- *Is the message implicit or explicit?* Implicit.
- *What is the possible setting? What are the clues about the setting?* The use of water and measuring cups suggests the setting is a kitchen in the person's home.
- *What and who may be just out of the frame?* Unknown.
- *Is this an example of propaganda?* If one thinks climate change causes sea level rise, this would probably be an example of negative propaganda. If one thinks climate change does not cause sea level rise, this would probably be an example of positive propaganda.
- *How does the propaganda appeal to my biases?* As a believer in the adverse effects of climate change, I have a dismissive attitude toward the meme.

Have a discussion with the students about their observations.

Now have them look at the meme with the title, caption, and a social media site where the meme appeared. All students should consider what they see, how the meme makes them feel, and how their biases and mindset influence their reaction. Higher achieving students should answer the additional following questions. I include possible answers students might come up with.

Are you looking at the original version? Find out.

No. The meme was shared to X by the now-suspended Project TABS account on June 4, 2022, according to Snopes.[15] A reverse image search indicates the earlier version of the meme, with just the two side-by-side photos and five text labels, appeared on Facebook on June 9, 2019[16] or earlier.

Where was the original version of the meme published?

Facebook

When was it first published?

June 9, 2019, or earlier.

Who first made/posted the meme?

The Facebook account Konspirasi Dunia posted the earlier version of the meme, but the meme no longer appears on that account. The @ProjectTabs account posted the later version. @ProjectTabs probably created the later meme using this or an earlier one.

What's the actual message behind the meme? What was the producer/poster trying to capture?

@ProjectTabs was trying to debunk climate change by showing that melting sea ice (represented by ice cubes) placed in a measuring cup does not contribute to sea level rise (represented by the unchanging water level of the cup).[17] The meme is a simplification of complex processes that make our planet's climate.[18]

Carly Shabo of California Sea Grant told Snopes that although sea ice melt is not a big contributor to sea level rise, ice in other forms, such as that found in glaciers or on land, is.[19] She indicated that sea ice forms from the seawater it floats on, and it acts similar to an ice cube in a glass of water. The ice cube does not change the water level of the glass when it melts, and melting sea ice in the

Arctic also does not markedly change sea level.[20] Shabo explained that melting land ice, such as that from the Greenland or Antarctic ice sheets, does cause sea level to rise, releasing water that had been frozen on land and adding it to the oceans.[21]

According to Heather Goldstone of the Woodwell Climate Research Center, the meme is misleading. It uses one finely scoped, factually true statement but distorts it to suggest that all climate science should be questioned.[22]

In short, the measuring cup metaphor used by the meme is an inaccurate and oversimplified explanation that does not debunk sea level rise or climate change.[23] It is malinformation.

Does this meme use explicit or implicit messaging?
Implicit.

What is the setting? What are the clues about the setting?
The water and measuring cups suggest the setting is a kitchen. This implies that the meme was created by an amateur in their home.

What may be just out of the frame? Unknown.

Is this an example of propaganda? Yes, if one thinks climate change causes sea level rise, this would be an example of negative propaganda, using malinformation, that sought to get users on Facebook and X to believe a misleading experiment. If one thinks climate change does not cause sea level rise, this would be an example of positive propaganda that sought to get users on Facebook and X to believe allegedly demonstrable facts.

How does the propaganda appeal to my biases? I consider this to be negative propaganda and have a dismissive attitude toward the meme.

How have your initial thoughts about the meme changed given this new information? Now that I have found credible evidence that the experiment depicted in the meme is misleading, I dismiss the meme even more strongly.

Some students who were persuaded by the meme initially will say the new information caused them to debunk the meme. Some will remain persuaded.

Have a discussion with the students about their observations.

Homework: Ask students to bring in a news-related meme from a social media platform they use to get their news. Have them present a meme analysis to the class based on their research and investigation.

▶ **NOTES**

1 Memes, Memes (logiccheck.net), December 1, 2021.
2 "The 20 Best Memes of 2022 You Couldn't Help but Laugh At," Kelly Kuehn, Reader's Digest, rd.com, January 24, 2023, 20 Best Memes of 2023: Relatable and Funny Memes from the Past Year (rd.com).
3 Meme Definition & Meaning - Merriam-Webster.
4 "True or False: A CIA Analyst's Guide to Spotting Fake News," Cindy Otis, Chapter 20.
5 Memes, Memes (logiccheck.net), December 1, 2021.
6 Memes, Memes (logiccheck.net), December 1, 2021.
7 Memes, Memes (logiccheck.net), December 1, 2021.
8 Harry Styles Drops 'Protect Each Other' T—Shirts & Is Donating 100% Of Profits To...—Capital (capitalfm.com).
9 Who's making it? | Harry Styles' Coronavirus Merch Controversy | Know Your Meme (archive.org).
10 "Harry Styles Supports COVID—19 Solidarity Response Fund With New Shirt," Brittany Spanos, Rolling Stone, April 7, 2020, Harry Styles Supports COVID—19 Solidarity Response Fund With New Shirt – Rolling Stone.
11 "Harry Styles Has Released A T—Shirt to Raise Funds for COVID—19 Efforts," Icon, Harry Styles Has Released A T—Shirt To Raise Funds For COVID—19 (icon.ink).
12 "Coronavirus: Harry Styles Is Selling 'Stay Home' T-Shirts for £21," Sarah Young, Independent, April 8, 2020, Coronavirus: Harry Styles is selling 'stay home' T-shirts for £21 | The Independent | The Independent.
13 "No, This Meme Doesn't 'Debunk' Sea Level Rise, Climate Change," Madison Dapcevich, Snopes, July 8, 2022, No, This Meme Doesn't 'Debunk' Sea Level Rise, Climate Change | Snopes.com.
14 elsonwarcraft. "CLIMATE CHANGE DEBUNK, PROOF." R/Insanepeoplefacebook, June 12, 2022, CLIMATE CHANGE DEBUNK, PROOF: r/insanepeoplefacebook (reddit.com).
15 "No, This Meme Doesn't 'Debunk' Sea Level Rise, Climate Change," Madison Dapcevich, Snopes, July 8, 2022, No, This Meme Doesn't 'Debunk' Sea Level Rise, Climate Change | Snopes.com.

16 (20+) Konspirasi Konspirasi Dunia | Facebook.

17 "No, This Meme Doesn't 'Debunk' Sea Level Rise, Climate Change," Madison Dapcevich, Snopes, July 8, 2022, No, This Meme Doesn't 'Debunk' Sea Level Rise, Climate Change | Snopes.com.

18 "No, This Meme Doesn't 'Debunk' Sea Level Rise, Climate Change," Madison Dapcevich, Snopes, July 8, 2022, No, This Meme Doesn't 'Debunk' Sea Level Rise, Climate Change | Snopes.com.

19 "No, This Meme Doesn't 'Debunk' Sea Level Rise, Climate Change," Madison Dapcevich, Snopes, July 8, 2022, No, This Meme Doesn't 'Debunk' Sea Level Rise, Climate Change | Snopes.com.

20 "No, This Meme Doesn't 'Debunk' Sea Level Rise, Climate Change," Madison Dapcevich, Snopes, July 8, 2022, No, This Meme Doesn't 'Debunk' Sea Level Rise, Climate Change | Snopes.com.

21 "No, This Meme Doesn't 'Debunk' Sea Level Rise, Climate Change," Madison Dapcevich, Snopes, July 8, 2022, No, This Meme Doesn't 'Debunk' Sea Level Rise, Climate Change | Snopes.com.

22 "No, This Meme Doesn't 'Debunk' Sea Level Rise, Climate Change," Madison Dapcevich, Snopes, July 8, 2022, No, This Meme Doesn't 'Debunk' Sea Level Rise, Climate Change | Snopes.com.

23 "No, This Meme Doesn't 'Debunk' Sea Level Rise, Climate Change," Madison Dapcevich, Snopes, July 8, 2022, No, This Meme Doesn't 'Debunk' Sea Level Rise, Climate Change | Snopes.com.

Evaluate Ads

These days, students can be particularly influenced by endorsements from social media 'influencers'—individuals who are celebrities or, more often, those who have generated a following through flashy marketing and engaging content. More traditional ads posted by companies can also influence if they use catchy imagery and language.

Social media has influenced half of the purchases of Generation Z—those born between 1998 and 2006, according to Consumers' Checkbook, citing a survey from 2021 by Statista.com.[1] The best way to persuade Gen Z is often with a subtle mention or testimonial by an online influencer that does not come across as a sales pitch and seems authentic and trustworthy. The influencer could be an actor, musician, sports figure, or someone who has a large social media following and can persuade their audience to act based on their recommendations.

A survey from 2016 of X users indicated that influencers rival friends in building consumer trust. When looking for product recommendations, 56% of respondents said they relied on tweets from friends, barely edging out the 49% who said they looked to influencers.[2] The findings should also generally hold true for preteens and teens on X.

Some advertisers use virtual influencers—computer-generated characters that often look lifelike—to pose with products and

DOI: 10.4324/9781003471301-10

promote brands, just like human influencers.[3] The US Federal Trade Commission (FTC) stresses that advertisers and endorsers should reveal any relationships, such as compensation, and those relationships should be authentic.[4]

In May 2022, the FTC proposed changes to its Endorsement Guides, which require "clear and conspicuous" disclosure if there is a "material connection" between an endorser and marketer that consumers would not otherwise realize and that would affect how they evaluate the endorsement.[5] The disclosure should stand out from other text or visual elements so viewers can easily notice, read, and understand it.[6] Disclosure in the credits would no longer be adequate. The changes would target fake reviews and other misleading marketing, including by 'influencers.' They would expand the definition of 'endorser' to include virtual influencers, such as computer-generated avatars and fictional characters, that show up more and more on social media.[7]

If a celebrity has a material connection to an advertiser and talks about its products or services in an interview, the celebrity must disclose the relationship at that time. If product review bloggers include affiliate links that earn them a commission when their readers make a purchase, their compensation needs to be disclosed, even if they independently produce their reviews.[8]

Students do not need to worry about finding the original version of an ad because they are not concerned with subsequent manipulation of the original. An ad is an ad. However, they should be interested in determining how the ad seeks to persuade them. As we learned earlier, ads do that with explicit and implicit messages.

▶ LESSON PLAN

In-class activity: Have groups of two to three students examine the following ads from Instagram (Figure 8.1) and TikTok (video), answer the following questions, and present their findings to the class. Students should use the same techniques to evaluate ads that they use to evaluate other media.

This lesson requires all students to identify what they see, what is the ad's main message, whether they are looking at the original version, and where and when it was first published. It requires higher achieving students to also critique the ad more deeply, including by reflecting on how the ad affects them. They should ask questions like the following:

What do you see?
How does the ad make you feel?
How do your biases and mindset influence your reaction?

▶ DEFINITION

Hashtag: a metadata tag that is prefaced by the hash symbol, #. On social media, hashtags are used as a form of user-generated tagging that enables cross-referencing of content by topic or theme.

▶ INSTAGRAM AD

Figure 8.1 Instagram "ad" for Drift Net Securities.

Ad for International Women's Day 2023: Drift Net Securities: Free Download, Borrow, and Streaming: Internet Archive.

Who paid for the ad? A company called Drift Net Securities (now Drift Net) paid for the ad, which ran on March 8, 2023, for International Women's Day. It no longer appears on Instagram. According to its website, the company aims to provide a "culture of safety" for school communities.

Are you viewing an "influencer"? If so, what is the influencer trying to influence? Why? This is an ad for a company, not an individual influencer.

What is the advertiser behind the influencer trying to influence? Why? The ad targets diverse mothers of children in elementary, middle, and high school. It uses International Women's Day to appeal to moms of these kids. The company hopes that the moms will click on the link to its website to find out more about the company's services to make schools safer.

Is there a "clear and conspicuous" disclosure of a "material connection" between the influencer and the advertiser that is hard to miss—i.e., does it stand out from other text or visual elements so students can easily notice, read, and understand it? Not applicable.

Notice the people's faces. What might their expressions communicate? The sketches of the four presumed moms show they are diverse. Their expressions are a mix of happiness and concern, presumably for school safety.

Does the ad use explicit or implicit messaging? What is the message? The ad uses implicit messaging. It does not come right out and say that the company can provide school safety for the mothers' kids; it does so implicitly by providing the hashtags #schoolsafety and #driftnetsecurities in the ad.

Have a discussion with the students about their observations.

▶ **TIKTOK AD**

Video[9] (https://www.tiktok.com/@grammarlyofficial/video/7138844045094161706) QR Code 8.1

What do you see? The thumbnail on the TikTok app shows a smiling high school or college-age student with her phone on a bed, with the label, "Back to School." This will catch the eye of high school students and some middle schoolers. On the video posted on the app the company and product name, "Grammarly," appears in the lower left, but there is no "sponsored" label anywhere on the screen during the video to suggest that this is an ad.

How does the ad make you feel? At least some students will say they have a positive feeling about the product. Some may say they think the product would be easy and quick to use because the young lady smiles when she downloads and uses it in a matter of seconds. She says things like "start off the year strong" and "impress my professors," "instantly proofread," "mistake free," and "get better grades," for example.

How do your biases and mindset influence your reaction? Students who care a lot about grammar and have a relatively fixed mindset that amplifies their bias toward detail and perfection would be vulnerable to being persuaded that Grammarly will help them perfect their writing.

Who paid for the ad? A company called Grammarly paid for the ad. According to its website,[10] the company's mission is to "improve lives by improving communication."

Are you viewing an "influencer"? If so, what is the influencer trying to influence? Why? The ad does feature an influencer, Olivia Dunn (https://www.tiktok.com/@livvy), with 7.9 million followers as of this writing. She is trying to persuade viewers to buy the product.

What is the advertiser behind the influencer trying to influence? Why? The company hopes that the influencer will persuade high school students (and perhaps middle school students) to click on the link to its website, find out more about the company's service, and buy the product.

Is there a "clear and conspicuous" disclosure of a "material connection" between the influencer and the advertiser that is hard to miss—i.e., does it stand out from other text or visual elements so students can easily notice, read, and understand it? No.

Notice the people's faces. What might their expressions communicate? The influencer generally has a determined or smiling expression on her face as she goes about her routines with Grammarly. She smiles and gives a "thumbs up" as she looks at her cell phone at the end of the video, suggesting she has been using the product and that the product has made her happy. This suggests the app will make teens and preteens who use the app happy too!

Does the ad use explicit or implicit messaging? What is the message? The ad uses a mix of explicit and implicit messaging. The narrator explicitly describes how to fix grammar errors by quickly downloading the Grammarly app, but the ad implicitly suggests that the teens, preteens, and young adults it is targeting will be happy because the app will help them spell better.

Have a discussion with the students about their observations.

Homework: Ask students to bring in ads from a social media platform they use to get their news. Have them present an ad analysis to the class.

▶ NOTES

1 "FTC Proposes New Advertising Guidelines Against Misleading Endorsements," Consumers' Checkbook, FTC Proposes New Advertising Guidelines Against Misleading Endorsements—Washington Consumers' Checkbook.

2 "FTC Proposes New Advertising Guidelines Against Misleading Endorsements," Consumers' Checkbook, FTC Proposes New Advertising Guidelines Against Misleading Endorsements—Washington Consumers' Checkbook.

3 "FTC Proposes New Advertising Guidelines Against Misleading Endorsements," Consumers' Checkbook, FTC Proposes New Advertising Guidelines Against Misleading Endorsements—Washington Consumers' Checkbook.

4 "FTC Proposes New Advertising Guidelines Against Misleading Endorsements," Consumers' Checkbook, FTC Proposes New Advertising Guidelines Against Misleading Endorsements—Washington Consumers' Checkbook.

5 "FTC Proposes New Advertising Guidelines Against Misleading Endorsements," Consumers' Checkbook, FTC Proposes New Advertising Guidelines Against Misleading Endorsements—Washington Consumers' Checkbook.

6 "FTC Proposes New Advertising Guidelines Against Misleading Endorsements," Consumers' Checkbook, FTC Proposes New Advertising Guidelines Against Misleading Endorsements—Washington Consumers' Checkbook.

7 "FTC Proposes New Advertising Guidelines Against Misleading Endorsements," Consumers' Checkbook, FTC Proposes New Advertising Guidelines Against Misleading Endorsements—Washington Consumers' Checkbook.

8 "FTC Proposes New Advertising Guidelines Against Misleading Endorsements," Consumers' Checkbook, FTC Proposes New Advertising Guidelines Against Misleading Endorsements—Washington Consumers' Checkbook.

9 TikTok Ad Grammarly: Grammarly: Free Download, Borrow, and Streaming: Internet Archive.

10 About Us | Grammarly.

Evaluate Charts

9

A survey of 2,000 pizza-loving adults in the United States in early 2022 found that 72% said they love pizza so much they could eat it for breakfast, lunch, and dinner without growing sick of it.[1]

How would middle and high school students, many of whom eat their share of pizza, feel about that? Poll results like this usually elicit three kinds of responses:

1. "That can't be true. Who could eat that much pizza in one day?"
2. "Sure, that sounds right."
3. "Well now that I think about it, pizza has a perfect blend of salty and sweet, so maybe I could eat it for breakfast, lunch, and dinner too."

If we ourselves like pizza, our response is more likely to be number two—if we could eat it that often, everyone else should be able to also. If we don't like pizza that much, our response is probably number one. The poll likely did not change the preexisting habits of respondents who like pizza or don't like it that much.

But the poll probably did change the habits of at least a few people who responded with number three—these on-the-fencers are likely to find numbers and stats like these persuasive. They are also the most likely to fall for fake or misleading

DOI: 10.4324/9781003471301-11

use of numbers and statistics. Actually, the best response to the pizza poll should be, "That poll is questionable. I need to find out more."

We often give more credibility to numbers and statistics—especially when they are displayed as charts, maps, graphs, diagrams, and tables than as words. They seem more complex, precise, and sophisticated, so we often think they are more accurate. Media producers know this and use them to make their information seem more credible. These days, they are all over social media, which has made it easier than ever to share them widely.

Our tendency to trust numbers and statistics more than other information is called **precision bias**. The bias can get us into trouble though. It is possible to be very precise but not very accurate, and it is also possible to be accurate without being precise. Indeed, Mark Twain said as much when he reportedly popularized the quote most, though not definitively, attributed to the prime minister of Great Britain, Benjamin Disraeli: "There are three kinds of lies: lies, damn lies and statistics."[2]

In this book, I refer to charts, maps, graphs, diagrams, tables, etc., as simply charts to keep the writing concise. Data visualization expert Alberto Cairo writes that good charts can make us smarter by revealing patterns and trends hidden behind the numbers—if we know how to read them.[3]

There are five common ways chart makers misrepresent and distort statistics to support their explicit or implicit message, according to Ryan McCready, managing editor at Reforge, a company providing growth-focused programs for experienced professionals in marketing, product, data, and engineering.[4]

▶ OMITTING THE BASELINE

Omitting or manipulating one or more baselines, or axes, is one of the most common ways data are used deceptively in charts. Some chart makers omit or manipulate the baseline because they think it distracts from the data. That can actually make the data harder to read. Some do it deceptively to make one thing look better than another, causing something insignificant to look like a huge difference.[5]

There are no baselines in the chart in Figure 9.1, which appeared on Instagram. The chart makes it appear that the number of people viewing Drake's song lyrics on the Genius.com website in 2018 was almost double that of XXXTentacion and Kanye West and more than double that of Post Malone and Eminem.

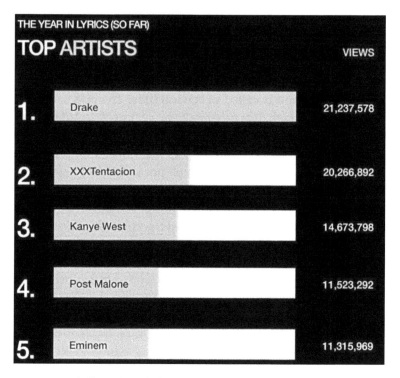

Figure 9.1 It's halfway through the year, so we crunched some numbers—here are the most popular artists on Genius in 2018 so far.

Genius on Instagram: "It's halfway through the year, so we crunched some numbers—here are the most popular artists on Genius in 2018 so far 👀."

BlF56u0htTK (1385×1966) (archive.org).

You can see the real story when the chart is adjusted and the axes are added. Drake generated a lot of views, but not as much as the first chart made it seem (Figure 9.2).[6,7]

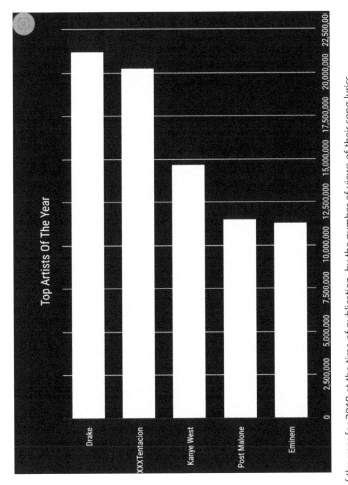

Figure 9.2 Top artists of the year for 2018 at the time of publication, by the number of views of their song lyrics.

5 Ways Writers Use Misleading Graphs to Manipulate You [INFOGRAPHIC], Vennage.com, Ryan McCready, April 17, 2020.

▶ MANIPULATING THE Y-AXIS

Chart manipulators will often distort the scale of a chart to minimize or maximize a change. They will include the axis and baselines but change them so much that they lose meaning. These manipulated charts are often used to push false or misleading stories on social media.[8]

Take a look at these two charts that illustrate this manipulation (Figures 9.3 and 9.4):

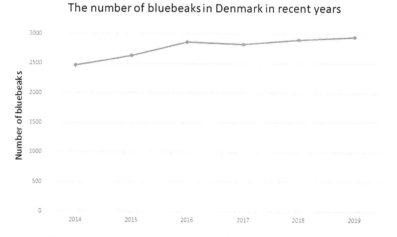

Figure 9.3 The number of bluebeaks in Denmark in recent years.

Driessen Jep, Vos Dac, I. Smeets, C. J. Albers (2022) Misleading graphs in context: Less misleading than expected, *PLoS ONE*, 17(6), e0265823, DOI: 10.1371/journal. pone.0265823

The chart was published on June 15, 2022, in the peer-reviewed Public Library of Science Journal. The chart depicts the proportional increase of the number of the 'bluebeak', a fictional, non-native bird in Denmark from 2014 to 2019. The chart maker uses a y-axis that starts at zero to make the line as flat as possible, so it appears at first glance that the increase in bluebeaks is relatively small.

To show a more dramatic change, we need to restrict the y-axis to a narrower range:

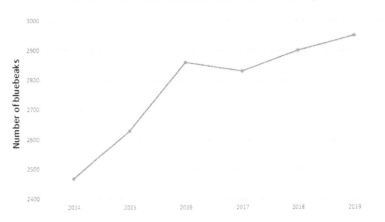

Figure 9.4 The number of bluebeaks in Denmark in recent years.

Driessen Jep, Vos Dac, I. Smeets, CJ Albers (2022) Misleading graphs in context: Less misleading than expected, *PLoS ONE*, 17(6), e0265823, DOI: 10.1371/journal. pone.0265823.

When the y-axis is truncated to a narrower range, the increase in bluebeaks appears much greater. A chart maker who wants to downplay the increase in bluebeaks might use the nontruncated y-axis; a chart maker who wants to emphasize the increase might use the truncated y-axis.

▶ CHERRY-PICKING DATA

Another way to create a misleading chart is to cherry-pick—pick and choose—only part of the data, usually the part that makes the chart appear to support the chart maker's viewpoint or undermine their opponent's.[9]

For example, it is relatively easy to mislead readers with a stock price. Look at this chart, which appears to show that then Twitter, as of May 2017, had been on a large upward swing for about a month.[10]

Chart (Cherry-Picking)[11] (https://venngage.com/blog/ misleading-graphs/) QR Code 9.1

There are thousands of data points that stock analysts examine before they trade or recommend a purchase. There are a lot of things they can omit to make it appear a company's stock looks better or worse overall.[12]

From this chart alone, Twitter's stock price appeared to have been soaring! This was not the case, as we see in this corrected chart:

Chart[13]   (https://venngage.com/blog/misleading-graphs/) QR code 9.2

Twitter's stock price had actually been on an unprecedented decline for roughly the prior year, and the increase that the earlier chart focused on was just a blip on this longer-term chart. A dishonest stock trader could have tried to sell a lot of X stock by using the first graph![14]

Cherry-picking data is a useful tool for manipulators, who can make any chart appear to support their view or undermine their opponent's.

▶ USING THE WRONG TYPE OF CHART

So far, we've talked about deceptive tactics chart makers use to support their agendas. But charts can mislead us simply through unintentional mistakes, often from sheer incompetence. This usually means picking the wrong type of chart to present the data.

The pie chart is often the biggest offender.[15] Here is one about calories from fast-food consumption of children and teens (Figure 9.5). It is similar to one that I recently saw on social media.

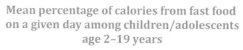

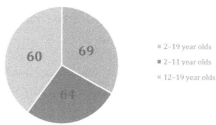

Figure 9.5 Pie chart incorrectly using data from the National Center for Health Statistics on calories from fast-food consumption among children and teens.

Author, using data incorrectly from the National Center for Health Statistics, National Health and Nutrition Examination Survey, 2015–2018.

It's not clear what the chart maker (the author) was trying to say with this pie chart. First, 60% is not more than 69%, as the chart appears to show. Second, a bar chart would be more appropriate for this data because the totals do not need to add up to 100%.[16,17]

If you saw a chart like this on social media, you would understandably think all age groups consumed about the same number of calories from fast food during the time period 2015—2018. But if the author wanted to convey the story more accurately and clearly, he could have created a bar chart like the one in Figure 9.6.

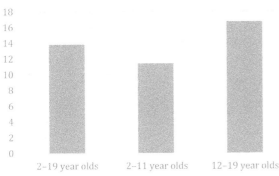

Figure 9.6 Bar chart correctly rendering data from the National Center for Health Statistics on calories from fast-food consumption among children and teens.

National Center for Health Statistics, National Health and Nutrition Examination Survey, 2015–2018.

Source: National Center for Health Statistics, National Health and Nutrition Examination Survey, 2015–2018.

▶ GOING AGAINST CONVENTIONS

Finally, let's look at misleading charts that break long-held customs or relationships. For example, in politics, think about a chart where red represents Democrats and blue represents Republicans. Or, in economics, using green for losses and red for profits. These attributes would rile a competent chart maker but would be a powerful tool to manipulate an audience.[18]

Here's a chart (Figure 9.7) that the creator flipped upside down to push an agenda. This made it appear that global temperatures were declining from 1980 to 2016 when in fact they were increasing.[19,20]

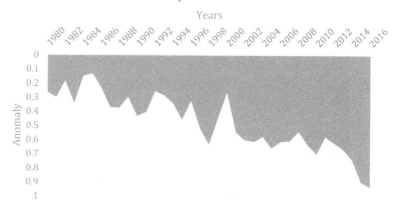

Figure 9.7 Misleading (inverted) chart showing global temperature change.

5 Ways Writers Use Misleading Graphs to Manipulate You [INFOGRAPHIC], Vennage.com, Ryan McCready, April 17, 2020.

The chart uses data from NASA in a misleading way to depict global temperatures trending downward during 1980–2016. Chart makers often "invert" the y-axis to push a misleading or false narrative. Similar misleading charts often appear on social media. Data source: NASA's Goddard Institute for Space Studies (GISS). Credit: NASA/GISS.

A simple rotation and mirroring of the chart shows what it should have looked like (Figure 9.8).

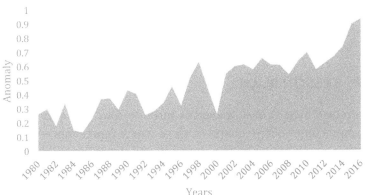

Figure 9.8 Accurate chart showing global temperature change.

5 Ways Writers Use Misleading Graphs to Manipulate You [INFOGRAPHIC], Vennage.com, Ryan McCready, April 17, 2020.

This chart correctly depicts global temperature trending upward during the time period.

How can we avoid being deceived by charts? As with any type of news story, first, check where the chart came from and then examine the data by checking other sources. For example, if a company that sells ice cream shares a chart on social media showing the benefits of eating ice cream, the chart may be inaccurate. Another red flag is if just one person or group shares the chart. As Alberto Cairo says, chart makers can make a chart say whatever they want—up to a point—by deciding how it is constructed, how detailed it is, and what patterns it displays.[21] This is a key reason we need to learn to evaluate charts accurately.

Cairo shares some tips for evaluating charts:[22]

- Don't trust charts made or shared by a source unfamiliar to you until you evaluate the chart and/or its source.
- Don't trust chart makers or publishers who don't name their sources or link directly to them.

- Don't automatically dismiss a chart just because you dislike the ideology or other aspects of its designers or publishers.
- A chart shows only what it shows. Don't read too much into it by letting your biases and mindset take over.

▶ LESSON PLAN

In class: Direct each group of three to four students to electronic copies of five charts, each of which represents one of the five ways charts often misrepresent and distort data. Have each group identify which one of the five ways each chart shows.

This lesson requires all students to identify what type of chart they see, what its main message is, what way or ways it misrepresents and distorts data, whether they are looking at the original version, where it was first published, and when it was first published. It requires higher achieving students to also critique the chart more deeply, including by reflecting on how the chart affects them. They should ask questions like the following:

- *How have your biases and mindset influenced your reaction?*
- *What was the creator of the chart trying to do? Why?*
- *Is the message implicit or explicit?*
- *What story do you think is behind the chart?*

Homework: Ask each student to bring in charts from a social media platform they use to get their news. Have them present a chart analysis to the class based on their research and investigation.

Note: Math teachers should consider including these techniques in modules on fractions and percentages.

▶ NOTES

1 "How Do You Eat Your Pizza? A New Survey Reveals 1 in 12 Americans Use a Fork and Knife," Madeline Buiano, Yahoo Finance, January 28, 2022, How Do You Eat Your Pizza? A New Survey Reveals 1 in 12 Americans Use a Fork and Knife (yahoo.com).

2 "There Are Three Kinds of Lies: Lies, Damned Lies, and Statistics: Mark Twain? Benjamin Disraeli? St. Swithin? Eliza Gutch? Charles Dilke? Charles Stewart Parnell? Robert Giffen? Arthur James Balfour? Francis Bacon? Anonymous?," There Are Three Kinds of Lies: Lies, Damned Lies, and Statistics – Quote Investigator®, June 22, 2022.

3 Front flap in "How Charts Lie: Getting Smarter about Visual Information," Alberto Cairo, 2019, W. W. Norton & Company.

4 5 Ways Writers Use Misleading Graphs to Manipulate You [INFOGRAPHIC], Vennage.com, Ryan McCready, April 17, 2020.

5 5 Ways Writers Use Misleading Graphs to Manipulate You [INFOGRAPHIC], Vennage.com, Ryan McCready, April 17, 2020.

6 5 Ways Writers Use Misleading Graphs to Manipulate You [INFOGRAPHIC], Vennage.com, Ryan McCready, April 17, 2020.

7 5 Ways Writers Use Misleading Graphs to Manipulate You [INFOGRAPHIC], Vennage.com, Ryan McCready, April 17, 2020.

8 5 Ways Writers Use Misleading Graphs to Manipulate You [INFOGRAPHIC], Vennage.com, Ryan McCready, April 17, 2020.

9 5 Ways Writers Use Misleading Graphs to Manipulate You [INFOGRAPHIC], Vennage.com, Ryan McCready, April 17, 2020.

10 5 Ways Writers Use Misleading Graphs to Manipulate You [INFOGRAPHIC], Vennage.com, Ryan McCready, April 17, 2020.

11 5 Ways Writers Use Misleading Graphs to Manipulate You [INFOGRAPHIC], Vennage.com, Ryan McCready, April 17, 2020.

12 5 Ways Writers Use Misleading Graphs to Manipulate You [INFOGRAPHIC], Vennage.com, Ryan McCready, April 17, 2020.

13 5 Ways Writers Use Misleading Graphs to Manipulate You [INFOGRAPHIC], Vennage.com, Ryan McCready, April 17, 2020.

14 5 Ways Writers Use Misleading Graphs to Manipulate You [INFOGRAPHIC], Vennage.com, Ryan McCready, April 17, 2020.

15 5 Ways Writers Use Misleading Graphs to Manipulate You [INFOGRAPHIC], Vennage.com, Ryan McCready, April 17, 2020.

16 National Center for Health Statistics, National Health and Nutrition Examination Survey, 2015–2018.

17 5 Ways Writers Use Misleading Graphs to Manipulate You [INFOGRAPHIC], Vennage.com, Ryan McCready, April 17, 2020.

18 5 Ways Writers Use Misleading Graphs to Manipulate You [INFOGRAPHIC], Vennage.com, Ryan McCready, April 17, 2020.

19 Author's misleading rendering of data from NASA's Goddard Institute for Space Studies (GISS).

20 5 Ways Writers Use Misleading Graphs to Manipulate You [INFOGRAPHIC], Vennage.com, Ryan McCready, April 17, 2020.

21 "How Charts Lie: Getting Smarter about Visual Information," pp. 104—106, Alberto Cairo, 2019, W. W. Norton & Company.

22 "How Charts Lie: Getting Smarter about Visual Information," pp. 104—106 and p. 188, Alberto Cairo, 2019, W. W. Norton & Company.

Chapter 10

Can You Fact-Check It?

As a CIA analyst, I routinely evaluated intelligence reports to determine whether to use them as evidence in my analysis. Some reports had a line that said, "Source comment...," which described the source's opinion or observation about the topic. I could decide whether to accept the source's comment as credible based on whether it was consistent with other reports and the CIA's prior assessment of the issue. But sometimes I found myself treating the source's opinion as fact, even when it was not consistent with other evidence or could not be cross-checked.

Some of the analysts I trained would fail to distinguish opinions unsupported by facts from fact-based opinions and even straight factual reporting, even though many of them had experience evaluating information before we hired them. I realized that if CIA analysts were vulnerable, middle and high school students scrolling their social media feeds would definitely be.

Here's another story. In early 2022, when COVID-19 was still common and a debate continued about the effectiveness of face masks to slow its spread, I found myself agreeing with a tweet. The tweet's author said they would not be surprised if masks were used for a month during a COVID-19 outbreak to reduce spread. Masks would be worn as surges start and would be

DOI: 10.4324/9781003471301-12

optional during periods when COVID-19 was under better control. The author pointed out that many other countries use that approach.

I wanted to verify the tweet before sharing it. I quickly realized that most of this tweet is uncheckable. It is mostly opinion and conjecture about what might happen in the future and is not backed with evidence. What part is checkable? The part about many other countries doing it that way. But even that statement hinges on how one defines "many." Sharing this tweet with my friends as fact could mislead them.

My most recent experience with fact versus opinion goes like this: back when the game Wordle was popular, I ran across a tweet that said that the day's Wordle was especially challenging and was the hardest that the person posting the tweet had ever tried. I braced myself, gave it a go, and discovered that, well, it was not as hard as others. I asked myself, "How could this person think that?" My first thought was to look for data comparing various Wordle challenges with one another. But then I realized that the tweet was not checkable. The remark that it was the toughest yet was an opinion. It had no supporting evidence.

Social media are full of opinions that are not supported by facts. Reputable news outlets usually label their social media posts as opinion, op-ed, analysis, advice, perspective, etc., but many other social media posts do not. Moreover, many readers, including middle and high schoolers, may not see these labels in their social media feeds if they are in a small font or are not at the top center of the post. They may have an even harder time knowing the difference between these labels.[1]

There are often no harmful consequences to believing that social media posts on relatively innocuous topics are facts—e.g., the Wordle example. But assuming uncheckable opinions are "fact" can spread disinformation and potentially harm people.

▶ LESSON PLAN

First, ask the class why they think it is important to distinguish between facts and opinions in news on social media.

Activity: Distinguish Fact-Based from Opinion-Based Statements

You could use statements trending in pop culture to pique students' interest. You could also use the following example to support the social studies curriculum.

a) Martin Luther King Jr. died by an assassin's bullet.
b) Martin Luther King Jr. was a great orator.
c) Martin Luther King Jr. died in Memphis, Tennessee.

Divide students into groups of three to four and have them discuss the three statements. All students should identify the similarities and differences among the statements. They should also determine how their biases and mindset influence their reaction.

Higher achieving students should also create a list of characteristics for fact-based and opinion-based statements using the example as a guide. They should critique the statements more deeply by asking questions like the following:

- *What was the creator of the statement trying to do?*
- *Is the message implicit or explicit?*
- *What story is behind the statement?*

Bring the class back together. Ask each group to share their thoughts.

Hand out this decision chart (Figure 10.1) and discussion worksheet (Figure 10.2) on fact- versus opinion-based statements:

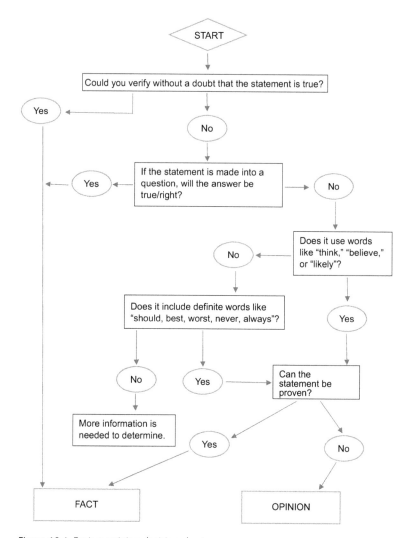

Figure 10.1 Fact or opinion decision chart.

Roy Whitehurst.

Fact vs Opinion Discussion Worksheet
Use the decision chart provided (Figure 10.1) to assist with this exercise.

FACT Something that can be proven or is verifiable	OPINION A person's thoughts, feelings, beliefs
Point to evaluate:	Point to evaluate:
Provide information to determine:	Provide information to determine:
Point to evaluate:	Point to evaluate:
Provide information to determine:	Provide information to determine:
Point to evaluate:	Point to evaluate:
Provide information to determine:	Provide information to determine:
Point to evaluate:	Point to evaluate:
Provide information to determine:	Provide information to determine:

Figure 10.2 Fact versus opinion discussion worksheet.

Roy Whitehurst.

Use the decision chart in Figure 10.1 to assist with this exercise.

Discuss how the students' ideas compare with how the chart would evaluate the three statements.

- Highlight that "a" and "c" are the fact-based statements and "b" is the opinion-based statement.
- Discuss how fact-based statements are "checkable." Your students can use web searches to see whether such statements are true or false.

Activity: More Practice Determining Fact Versus Opinion

- Divide students into groups of three to four.
- Direct each group to a different electronic packet of fact- and opinion-based pop culture or social studies-related news, along with the decision chart and the discussion worksheet.
- Have each group identify the fact- and opinion-based statements in their packets, using web searches to look for evidence. Have each group enter its findings in their discussion worksheet.
- For opinion-based statements, have students try to identify evidence that supports each opinion and say whether the author offers reasons for the opinion. Are any of those reasons fact-based?

▶ NEXT STEPS

- To pique your students' interest in the first semester, have them practice spotting fact- and opinion-based pop culture news using these techniques. Go to my website for some examples.

- In the second semester, have students use their skills to spot fact- and opinion-based news supporting your social studies, civics, and ELA curriculum and the learning standards. Go to my website for some examples.

▶ NOTE

1 "Opinion Creep: How Facts Lost Ground in the Battle for Our Attention," NLP podcast, "Is That A Fact?," June 1, 2023.

Fact-Check It!

11

I was a CIA officer analyzing satellite imagery in the wake of 9/11 and the run-up to the US war in Iraq in early 2003. Among other duties, I was tangentially involved in helping determine if Iraq was operating mobile biological weapons facilities on its soil.

As most readers of this book know, the United States and its allies did not find evidence of the facilities in Iraq. *The Report of the Commission on the Intelligence Capabilities of the United States Regarding Weapons of Mass Destruction* (*WMD Report*) concluded after the war that[1] just one source provided nearly all of the information the Intelligence Community (IC) had on Iraq's alleged mobile biological weapons facilities. The report said that CIA analysts gave too much weight to the source's reporting because the source's stories were consistent with what they already thought. In other words, the failure resulted in part from **confirmation bias** and analysts' poor evaluation of the reporting. The *WMD Report* prompted major changes in how the IC, including the CIA, collected and analyzed intelligence.

Students' failure to properly fact-check news reports on social media can have as far-reaching implications for US democracy as the IC's failure to properly fact-check intelligence

DOI: 10.4324/9781003471301-13

reporting on Iraq. It can contribute to the spread of false and misleading information across social media that can lead to events like the protests at the Capitol on January 6, 2021.

▶ WHY FACT-CHECKING NEWS IS CRITICAL

Evaluating the credibility of news with fact-checking is incredibly important for students as they research for class and take on civic responsibilities outside the classroom. It helps them minimize their biases, which makes them less vulnerable to being persuaded by social media.

▶ LESSON PLAN: FACT-CHECKING NEWS WITH SIFT

This lesson requires all students to apply the four steps of SIFT (Figure 11.1), developed by Mike Caulfield, a research scientist at the University of Washington's Center for an Informed Public.[2] SIFT will help students evaluate the credibility of news on social media. The lesson requires higher achieving students to also critique the news more deeply, including by determining how the news affects them. They should ask questions like the following:

- How have my biases and mindset influenced my reaction?
- What was the creator of the media trying to achieve? What might their biases be?
- Is the message implicit or explicit?
- If people's faces are visible, what might their expressions communicate?
- What story do you think is behind the media?

Provide students with a hardcopy or electronic copy of the SIFT steps:

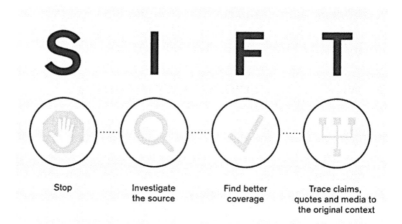

Figure 11.1[3] The four steps of SIFT.

1. Stop!
2. Investigate the source that posted the media.
3. Find trusted coverage.
4. Trace claims, quotes, and media to their original context.

▶ STOP! PLAYING ON OUR EMOTIONS, BIASES, AND MINDSET: WORD CHOICE

When you encounter a piece of media and read the headline, **Stop!** Ask yourself: "What emotions, biases, and mindset does the media reveal in me?" Let your emotions subside before you evaluate the media. Do not dismiss the media as fake, wrong, or misleading just because you don't agree with its message. As we know from Chapter 1, our mindset and biases can kick in, causing us to close our minds to the media. Instead, ask, "Can I evaluate the media?" to determine if the media has facts you can evaluate or is opinion unsupported by evidence, which you cannot (see Chapter 2 for a review).

Word choice can influence how students feel about a news story. News producers choose which words they use to describe a product, service, event, or situation, but news consumers interpret the meaning of words differently, largely due to their unique biases and mindsets. Students need to be aware of this to think rationally.

Divide students into groups of three to four. Have each group examine the following two tweets about the events at the Capitol on January 6, 2021. Each group should identify key words that influence how they feel about the tweets and think of other words that would change how they would feel about the tweets. Have them report their thoughts to the class.

This lesson requires all students to identify key words that affect how they feel about the tweets and explain how the words make them feel. It requires higher achieving students to also evaluate the tweets more deeply, generating new words that would change how they feel. They should ask questions like the following:

- How have my biases and mindset influenced my reaction?
- What is the author or poster of the tweet trying to achieve? What might their biases be?
- What implicit and explicit messages do the word choices in the tweet convey?

Tweet[4] (https://twitter.com/mayorlightfoot/status/1611384967 266959361) QR Code 11.1, dated January 6, 2023.

Tweet (https://medialiteracysleuth.com/qr-code-11-1-5/) QR Code 11.1.5, dated February 20, 2023.[5]

After the students provide their thoughts, provide the following observations:

- The first tweet refers to the people as "domestic terrorists." This word choice suggests the poster is less sympathetic to the motives of the people who approached and entered the Capitol.
- The second tweet, from an account that no longer exists, refers to the same people as "crowds" versus "insurrectionists" or "terrorists." This word choice suggests the poster is more sympathetic to the people's motives.

Ask the students what final thoughts they have.

▶ S̲TOP! CAN YOU BELIEVE THE HEADLINE?

In 2014, National Public Radio (NPR) posted a news article on Facebook with the headline, "Why Doesn't America Read Anymore?" and the caption, "What Has Become of Our Brains?"[6] According to Snopes, many users replied with their opinions about the two questions in the post. They had apparently not clicked to read the article. If they had, they would have discovered that it was an April Fools' Day message. NPR was trying to remind readers of a key point: There is value in the stories beyond a headline and a picture in social media posts.[7]

In 2018, NPR posted the story a second time with the same headline, this time on X.[8] The tweet's caption read, "Americans just don't read like they used to." People fell for it again, responding with their opinions about the headline. They apparently had not clicked to see that it was an April Fools' trick.[9]

Why did the posts fool so many people? Because they played on our emotions, mindset, and biases.

Headlines of news articles on social media are supposed to give readers an accurate preview of the article's content. Headline writers (who are often not the author of the article) can cram key words and phrases into a headline, but not context. That is why it is important to read beyond the headline to get the full scope of the topic.[10]

I taught new CIA analysts to write as objectively as possible. This included using a title that accurately reflected the content of the article or visual to which it was attached, yet "hooked" the busy policymaker so they would read or view the article. This was hard because the title had to fit on two lines yet capture the key points of what were usually complex, nuanced stories. To do otherwise would have misled readers who often only read the titles, and worse, contributed to their making poor decisions affecting US national security.

I was not in a profit-making industry. A person looking to get "likes," sell something, or otherwise will sometimes use eye-catching titles that may not reflect the content of the media.

Unfortunately, many students often do not read beyond the headlines. Headlines serve as a kind of menu, allowing us to judge from brief descriptions which articles we want to read. In the process, we get snippets of information about many different things, but nobody has time to read every article in detail. As Maggie from the United States, aged 21–24, said, "If I'm somewhere where I don't really have time to read a news story, I do rely on headlines."[11]

How do students avoid falling prey to false or inaccurate headlines? First, they need to pause and ask themselves these questions:

- Does the headline make sense, according to what I know about the topic?
- Is the headline too good to be true?
- Could it be a joke or satire? **Satire** is a literary device such as ridicule and irony that is used to criticize elements of society.

Satire can also use photos for this purpose. It can become misinformation if audiences misinterpret it as fact.

A misleading or incorrect headline can be particularly damaging when the social media post includes the views of an expert or public figure whose opinion is a persuasive piece of evidence for many readers.[12]

In November 2020, for example, the *Guardian* published an article[13] about Professor David Spiegelhalter of the UK Statistics Authority with a headline that the COVID-19 lockdown was essential but that graphs showing COVID-19 data were messy. The article did not quote Professor Spiegelhalter saying that a lockdown was needed, and he had not said this. Yet it did not keep another prominent scientist from sharing it on X and paraphrasing the headline in the following tweet (Figure 11.2).[14,15]

Figure 11.2 Tweet with a misleading headline and a reply with a correction request. (a) Top half[16]; (b) Bottom half[17]

The *Guardian* fixed the headline after the professor's request.[18]

Ask the students: How does the headline influence your interpretation of the tweet? Would your interpretation change if you saw a different headline?

▶ LESSON PLAN

Divide students into groups of three to four. Have each group examine headlines of several news posts from social media and determine if the headline accurately reflects the content of its associated media. Ask them to think of an alternative headline that would change how they would feel. Ask the groups to report their thoughts to the class.

Higher achieving students should also evaluate the headline more deeply, generating new words that would change how they feel. They should ask questions like the following:

• How have my biases and mindset influenced my reaction to the headline?

- What is the author or poster of the headline trying to achieve? What might their biases be?
- What implicit and explicit messages do the word choices in the headline convey?

Ok, let's continue to the second step of SIFT.

▶ INVESTIGATE THE SOURCE THAT POSTED THE MEDIA

If you can evaluate the media, immediately leave the page. **Investigate** the source that posted it.

- Do you know and trust the source? Do you know the author and their previous work? What is their expertise? What is their agenda? Do they have a financial or ideological stake in the issue they are posting about? What is their record of fairness or accuracy?
- If the source is well-known to you as credible—e.g., it is a standards-based media outlet you recognize and trust—this may be the only step you need to take if you just want to repost, read an interesting story, or get a high-level explanation of a concept.
- If the source is not well-known to you, go to the next step.

▶ FIND TRUSTED COVERAGE

After a quick scan of the post, open a new browser tab and search for reports from trusted sources in order to judge the credibility of the original post.[19] This is called **reading laterally**—leaving a website after a quick scan and opening up new browser tabs in order to judge the credibility of the original site.[20] It is especially important if you need to cite a more reliable source, say, for use in a school report.

- Consult at least one reputable fact-checking site—i.e., one that is a member of the International Fact-Checking Network (IFCN). The URL https://cse.google.com/cse?cx= 009843066196008418578:5c4h08rfa8q#gsc.tab=0 allows searches of several fact-checking sites at once.

If the search yields no results, open another tab and do a "smart" search (see "**How to search the Internet more effectively**") and scan the results to see if there is consensus or disagreement about the social media post's key points. Use **click restraint**—resist the urge to immediately click on the first search result and instead scan the results to make an informed choice about where to go first.[21] The best result may not be the one at the top of the list.

HOW TO SEARCH THE INTERNET MORE EFFECTIVELY:

- **Be specific**: Use clear, specific words in your search query to get more relevant results. For example, instead of searching for "supermarket," search for "Safeway."
- **Use quotation marks**: Use quotation marks to get results that include exact phrases. See the example above.
- **Use the minus sign to exclude certain terms**: Use the minus sign (—) to exclude certain words from your search results. For example, if you are looking for beaches in the Caribbean without black sand, you would search like this: "Caribbean beaches"—"black sand."
- **Limit your search to a specific website or section of a website**: If you know the information you need is included in a specific website, or you are interested only in the website's information, you can limit your search to that website. Add this to the search: "site:WEBSITENAME" followed by ".com," ".org," ".gov," etc. To get results from a section of the website, add a subdirectory to the search, such as: "site:WEBSITENAME.org/mediterranean diet."
- **Limit your search to news or other specific sources**: If you are looking for news articles, narrow your search by clicking the "News" button in the row of buttons below the search bar. You can also narrow your search to videos, images, etc., by clicking on the appropriate button.
- **Use 'AND' and 'OR'**: Do this when you need results that contain more than one search term or you need information containing only one of your terms. Make sure you use upper case 'AND' and 'OR.' For example: "Maryland Malls" OR "Maryland Shopping Centers".
- **Use parentheses to group items**: This will give you more relevant and specific results. For example: ("Maryland Malls" OR "Maryland Shopping Centers") AND "shoe stores."
- **No need to use common words and punctuation**: There is usually no need to add words such as 'The' or 'A,' periods, or commas to your search terms. They are usually ignored by search engines.

- **Customize your searches**: Most search engines provide options that allow you to customize your search. For example, you can search by date, time frame, language, or file type.
- **Take advantage of autocomplete**: Use the autocomplete feature of your search engine to get suggestions for your search query. As you start typing, let the autocomplete provide suggestions. This can save you time and effort.
- **Drop the suffixes**: Drop the suffixes from words in your search to get more results. For example, instead of searching for "swimming," search for "swim."
- **No need for capitalization**: You can use all lowercase letters without affecting search results.

▶ TRACE CLAIMS, QUOTES, AND MEDIA TO THEIR ORIGINAL CONTEXT

Even if you find trusted media that verifies the post you are looking at, a lot of posts on the Internet have been stripped of context. Maybe there is a video of a fight between two people that you have verified. But what happened before the video was taken? Who started the fight? What was clipped out of the video, and what stayed in? Maybe there is a picture that you have verified, but the caption is dubious. In these cases, you should trace the claim, quote, or media back to its original context and determine if the version you saw was accurately presented.

- **Origin**: Search for the media in the form in which it originally appeared online. Understanding its origin unlocks the context and motivation for its creation. To evaluate photos and videos, right-click on the image (or a video frame) and use a reverse image search tool (see "Tools" section), or search on a phrase that describes the image. Scan the results to see if the same image is present in a trusted media outlet.

- **Source**: Determine who created or captured the original form of the media. Be careful to distinguish between who posted it—which you would do in step two (**investigate**)—and the primary source who created or captured it. Do you know the author and their previous work? A well-respected journalist has a track record.

- **Motivation**: Try to determine why the original version was created or captured. This is hard and may not always be possible, but here are some things to consider.
  - ➤ Did the person attend an event to capture it from a particular perspective?
  - ➤ Is the person affiliated with a government, corporation, or research organization that has a specific financial, ideological, or other agenda?
  - ➤ Is the person a member of online communities that support or promote a specific cause?

▶ THE CHALLENGE OF BREAKING NEWS

When I followed fast-developing humanitarian crises around the world as a CIA analyst, I often had to provide my analysis to US policymakers within just a few hours. This was particularly challenging because I had to determine if the information I was receiving in the hours after the event was accurate or whether it was incomplete, misleading, or downright wrong.

For example, just after Christmas in 2004, I was called off my holiday leave to come into the office. A major earthquake had occurred off the coast of Indonesia, resulting in a tsunami that swept across the Indian Ocean. I had to take the lead in writing a preliminary, quick-turnaround piece on the humanitarian needs in the wake of the disaster that killed hundreds of thousands of people and displaced almost two million in countries around the Indian Ocean. The piece was to be published the next morning, which meant I had to get it to my editors that evening, in a few hours.

I cobbled together as credible a story as I could. All of the information I had received by then was incomplete, which is unavoidable hours after a large natural disaster. My US policy-maker customers and I were used to that. What was harder was figuring out what information was credible. I focused on reporting from respected local and international nongovernmental organizations—nonprofit entities that operate independently of any government—that already had relief workers on the ground in the disaster areas. They were the ones most likely to have the most credible information. Although I normally trusted reporting from the US Embassy, in this case, the US Embassies in the affected countries generally did not have personnel on site yet.

I wrote the piece as best I could and sent it on its way. Of course, I updated the piece in the coming days and weeks as more information came in, but I continued to closely evaluate each report for credibility.

When students scroll through their social media feeds, they can often feel like everything is breaking news. In a vacuum of information and a quest for certainty, people take to social media, claiming to know what is happening because they are on the ground or have special sources. Even credible media outlets are reporting on the event. These sources may repeatedly update readers as they scramble to get new information.

In this uncertainty, some individual social media users and less credible news outlets will label something "breaking news" to generate clicks. Sometimes they recycle old stories or make up new ones just to have something to say.

What can students do to sort fact from fiction, or at least from exaggeration, during an actual breaking news event?

In a fast-breaking situation where the temptation to share is high, I recommend that students consider these things:

- **Stop and take a breath**.
  - ➢ Students' emotions can run high during fast-breaking news events, especially those that interest them. Students should not share a post that they feel emotional about but have not verified to avoid spreading disinformation.
- **Make sure it's really breaking news**.
  - ➢ Students should check news sources they trust to discover what they are saying and make sure the event actually happened. Chances are, if a news source you are not sure about reports a big event, reputable news outlets should be covering the story too. If none are, students should not share the story until one or more do.
- **Look for news outlets nearest to the event**.
  - ➢ For example, if students see a breaking news story claiming a mass shooting occurred at a school in San Francisco, California, reputable media outlets with journalists in the city are probably the best places for students to get accurate information. Reporters who cover that area are more likely to have well-placed

sources who have access to facts more quickly than other journalists.

- **Be skeptical of posts that don't link to sources**.
  - ➢ During fast-breaking news stories, unreliable news outlets and anyone with an opinion can post what they think is happening. They don't usually have access to reliable information, especially if they are not on the scene. People claiming to be experts churn up disinformation, and trolls and bots—sometimes run by foreign governments—jump into the vacuum to spread propaganda and confusion and create or exacerbate polarization among people about hot-button issues. In this environment, students should check that social media posts cite or include links to sources.
- **Be patient with your trusted news sources**.
  - ➢ The most trusted news outlets are often not the first to report on a story, especially if they do not have journalists and sources on the scene. It is tempting to share what random people and unfamiliar news outlets are saying on social media. When trusted outlets do make their first report, they usually do not have all the facts. Students should know that this does not mean they cannot trust the outlet; it means they should wait for the outlet to provide more information once they verify it.

▶ LESSON PLAN: CREDIBLE OR NOT? EVALUATE A REAL BREAKING NEWS STORY

The following are actual social media posts that appeared during a real breaking news event. This was the mass shooting at Robb Elementary School in Uvalde, Texas, on May 24, 2022, that killed 19 students and 2 teachers and injured 17 others.

Note: Some teachers may decide this topic is too disturbing for their students. If so, they can use the same lesson format for a different topic.

Divide students into groups of three to four. Direct each group to the posts. Each group should discuss each post and put a checkmark for those they think are credible; an asterisk for the ones worth investigating further, with a note of what they would want to check; and an 'X' for those they discount.[22]

All students should apply the four SIFT steps and consider the additional things I discussed earlier in the chapter.

Higher achieving students should also critique the posts more deeply, including by determining how the posts affect them. They should ask questions like the following:

- How have my biases and mindset influenced my reaction?
- What was the creator of the post trying to achieve? What might their biases be?
- Is the message implicit or explicit?
- If people's faces are visible, what might their expressions communicate?
- What story do you think is behind the post?

The Snopes fact-checking organization reported on May 25, 2022, that racial justice activist Shaun King tweeted on the day of the Uvalde mass shooting that one or more law enforcement officers rescued their own children 91 minutes before the shooter, Salvador Ramos, was stopped.[23] The tweet has been deleted, but another person responded with a tweet that contained a video.[24,25]

Video in tweet (https://twitter.com/_Sir_Perfluous/status/1 529585786848411651?cxt=HHwWhoCw6eiKl7oqAAAA)

QR Code 11.2

Snopes rated the tweet as generally true,[26] and students should determine that it looks credible. Clues include a link to the video from a local news station, taken hours after the shooting, featuring an interview at the scene. The local station, KENS 5, posted the following longer clip,[27] which gives more context, to its YouTube channel. This increases the probability the post is credible.

Video (https://www.youtube.com/watch?v=59w8uu87OrM)

QR Code 11.3

Snopes reported that Jacob Albarado, an off-duty US Border Patrol officer, helped evacuate his daughter and several other children with the assistance of other officers and that the evacuation occurred prior to the officers confronting the shooter. However,

Snopes said the shooter was in the school for about 77 minutes, making the "91 minutes" part of King's tweet incorrect.[28]

Facebook post[29] (https://www.facebook.com/bravenewfilms/ posts/pfbid0xbbjTTw1uSduaWVZFYjFL1njENWYLBJrucdo buLrg34yTHC14g6iXnwvoRJ7bg8el) QR Code 11.4

This post was shared more than 300 times in less than a day. It lists the number of school shootings by country, including 288 in the United States; two each in France and Canada; one each in Germany, China, and Russia; and none in the United Kingdom, Switzerland, Netherlands, Australia, Japan, Spain, and Italy.[30]

USA Today rates this post as "missing context"—the post does not explain how the data were collected, which would help readers understand the country rankings. The United States has many more school shootings than other countries, but the data included in the post actually understate the problem. Research shows the number of school shootings in the United States is nearly ten times higher. One database puts the tally for the United States at more than 2,000 school shootings.[31]

The post should have explained that the tallies reflect one calculation of shootings from 2009 to 2018, so they don't account for US shootings since 2018 or before 2009. The statistics in the post are consistent with a CNN article from May 2018 about school shootings since 2009.[32]

Before sharing the post, students should discover the context if they **investigate the source**, which would uncover the date range of the tally and other research that puts the number of US school shootings much higher. They might also find this information if they **trace the post to its original context**.

Tweet[33]   (https://web.archive.org/web/20220531191305/ https:/twitter.com/AirielHicks/status/1530499300194762752) QR Code 11.5

This tweet calls the Uvalde shooting a "Black Hat/Red Faction/ Deep State Operation." It claims that two "crisis actors" saying they are the father of one of the victims is evidence of this.

USA Today fact-checkers reported that this tweet is false,[34] and students should discount it and refrain from sharing. One sign that the tweet is false is the lack of a blue checkmark next to the account owner's name, indicating the account is verified, meaning the owner may not be who they say they are. Other clues include the words in all caps and the reuse of the common but debunked conspiracy theory terms, "Black Hat," "Red Faction," and "Deep State Operation."

USA Today reported[35] that after the shooting, some social media posts began spreading a conspiracy theory about the father of Amerie Jo Garza, a 10-year-old girl who died during the shooting.[36] A Facebook post from May 29, 2022, included a CNN video clip showing an interview of Angel Garza, identified as Garza's father. The post also included part of an NBC News interview of another man identifying himself as Garza's father. The post falsely claimed that the interviews with the two men tied to the same Uvalde victim showed they were crisis actors and that the shooting was a false flag operation.[37] In recent years, some social media users have used the term "crisis actors"—actors who play victims or their families in a made-up crisis.

USA Today found no evidence the men are crisis actors. CNN had interviewed Garza's stepfather, while Guthrie had interviewed her biological father. They were both outside the school at the time of the shooting.[38]

▶ BIAS OF POPULAR NEWS MEDIA OUTLETS

These two charts from AllSides.com indicate the bias of some popular news media outlets.

Chart[39]   (https://www.allsides.com/media-bias/media-bias-chart) QR Code 11.6

Chart[40]   (https://www.allsides.com/media-bias/fact-check-bias-chart) QR Code 11.7

▶ LESSON PLAN

In-class activity: Fact-checking media

- Divide students into groups of three to four.
- Direct each group to an electronic or hardcopy packet of trending pop culture social media posts: for example, a tweeted article, an out-of-context captioned photo from Instagram, a TikTok video, a tweeted meme, and a tweeted poll. Ideally, each packet would contain different media so that follow-up class discussions expose students to more media evaluations.

- Have the groups apply the four SIFT steps to evaluate each post.
- Have each group report their findings to the entire class.
- Prompt an entire class discussion about each group's findings.

You can also do this activity with social studies-, civics-, or ELA-related media.

Higher achieving students should also critique the posts more deeply. They should ask questions like the following:

- How have my biases and mindset influenced my reaction?
- What was the creator of the post trying to achieve? What might their biases be?
- Is the message implicit or explicit?
- If people's faces are visible, what might their expressions communicate?
- What story do you think is behind the post?

▶ NEXT STEPS

To pique students' interest in the first semester, I suggest you have them practice fact-checking pop culture media using these techniques. Go to my website, **medialiteracysleuth.com**, for examples.

In the second semester, I suggest you have students evaluate social media supporting your social studies, civics, and ELA curriculum and the learning standards. Go to my website for examples.

▶ NOTES

1 "The Commission on the Intelligence Capabilities of the United States Regarding Weapons of Mass Destruction: Report to the President of the United States March 31, 2005,".
2 IFT (The Four Moves) – Hapgood.
3 SIFT (The Four Moves) – Hapgood.

4 https://twitter.com/mayorlightfoot/status/1611384967266959361.

5 https://twitter.com/LJisRight/status/1627643138608140295?
   lang=en.

6 "Why Doesn't America Read Anymore?," (9) NPR—What Has
   Become of Our Brains? | Facebook.

7 "This Headline Doesn't Tell You Everything You Need to Know,"
   Jordan Liles, Snopes.com, March 23,2022.

8 "Americans just don't read like they used to," (20) NPR on X:
   "Americans just don't read like they used to. https://t.
   co/02NkyLF7M6"/X (twitter.com).

9 "This Headline Doesn't Tell You Everything You Need to Know,"
   Jordan Liles, Snopes.com, March 23,2022.

10 "This Headline Doesn't Tell You Everything You Need to Know,"
    Jordan Liles, Snopes.com, March 23,2022.

11 How Young People Consume News and the Implications for
    Mainstream Media, https://reutersinstitute.politics.ox.ac.uk/our-
    research/how-young-people-consume-news-and-implications-
    mainstream-media, Reuters Institute for the Study of Journalism,
    September 2, 2019.

12 "The Media Must Stop Using Misleading Headlines," Leo Benedic-
    tus, FullFact.org, May 28, 2021, The media must stop using mis-
    leading headlines—Full Fact.

13 "England Lockdown Was Needed but Graphs Were a Mess, Says
    Statistics Guru," Mattha Busby, Guardian, November 7, 2020,
    England lockdown was needed but graphs were a mess, says statis-
    tics guru | Coronavirus | The Guardian (archive.org).

14 (20) Professor Susan Michie on Twitter: "England lockdown was
    needed but graphs were a mess, says statistics expert Spiegelhalter
    https://t.co/HFHxKLFUkp"/Twitter.

15 "The Media Must Stop Using Misleading Headlines," Leo Benedic-
    tus, FullFact.org, May 28, 2021, The media must stop using mis-
    leading headlines—Full Fact.

16 (21) Professor Susan Michie on X: "England lockdown was needed
    but graphs were a mess, says statistics expert Spiegelhalter https://t.
    co/HFHxKLFUkp"/X (twitter.com).

17 (21) Professor Susan Michie on X: "England lockdown was needed
    but graphs were a mess, says statistics expert Spiegelhalter https://t.
    co/HFHxKLFUkp"/X (twitter.com).

18 "The Media Must Stop Using Misleading Headlines," Leo Benedic-
    tus, FullFact.org, May 28, 2021, The media must stop using mis-
    leading headlines—Full Fact.

19 Sam Wineburg & Sarah McGrew Working Paper No 2017.A1/Stanford History Education Group sheg.stanford.edu September 2017.

20 Sam Wineburg & Sarah McGrew Working Paper No 2017.A1/Stanford History Education Group sheg.stanford.edu September 2017.

21 Click Restraint | Civic Online Reasoning (stanford.edu).

22 "True or False: A CIA Analyst's Guide To Spotting Fake News," Cindy Otis, Chapter 21.

23 "Did Officers Rescue Own Children During Uvalde School Shooting?," Jordan Liles, Snopes, July 14, 2022, Did Officers Rescue Own Children During Uvalde School Shooting? | Snopes.com.

24 (20) SirPerfluous on X: "@misstessowen "1st acknowledge the brave men and women of law enforcement," not condolences to the family first. Also, the cops engaged the shooter before he entered the school, and they are still alive? Finally, cops went in and pulled their own kids out during the active shooter threat. WTF? https://t.co/4okN01jGjq"/X (twitter.com).

25 Gale Farce on Twitter: ""1st acknowledge the brave men and women of law enforcement," not condolences to the family first. Also, the cops engaged the shooter before he entered the school, and they are still alive? Finally, cops went in and pulled their own kids out during the active shooter threat. WTF?... https://t.co/6KSpLq2ghk" (archive.org).

26 "Did Officers Rescue Own Children During Uvalde School Shooting?," Jordan Liles, Snopes, July 14, 2022, Did Officers Rescue Own Children During Uvalde School Shooting? | Snopes.com.

27 https://youtu.be/59w8uu87OrM?feature=shared.

28 "Did Officers Rescue Own Children During Uvalde School Shooting?," Jordan Liles, Snopes, July 14, 2022, Did Officers Rescue Own Children During Uvalde School Shooting? | Snopes.com.

29 https://www.facebook.com/bravenewfilms/posts/pfbid0xbbjTTw1uSduaWVZFYjFL1njENWYLBJrucdobuLrg34yTHC14g6iXnwvoRJ7bg8el.

30 "Fact Check: Comparison of School Shootings in the US, Other Countries Uses Old Data," BriAnna J. Frank, *USA Today*, June 3, 2022, Fact check: Claim understates number of school shootings in the US (usatoday.com).

31 "Fact Check: Comparison of School Shootings in the US, Other Countries Uses Old Data," BriAnna J. Frank, *USA Today*, June 3, 2022, Fact check: Claim understates number of school shootings in the US (usatoday.com).

32 "Fact Check: Comparison of School Shootings in the US, Other Countries Uses Old Data," BriAnna J. Frank, *USA Today*, June 3, 2022, Fact check: Claim understates number of school shootings in the US (usatoday.com).

33 Airiel Hicks on Twitter: "Two Crisis Actors claiming to be the FATHER of the Same girl 🙄 Amerie Jo Garza Lol This SHIT GLOWS FALSE FLAG CONFIRMATION Uvalde, Texas shooting is a Black Hat/Red Faction/Deep State Operation https://t.co/LPBRYSvvlS https://t.co/RZW533zBY7 https://t.co/k5wVAtomN4"/Twitter (archive.org).

34 "Fact Check: Interviews with Uvalde Victim's Family Spur Baseless Crisis Actors Conspiracy Theory," Sudiksha Kochi, *USA Today*, June 10, 2022, Fact check: Baseless conspiracy theory about Uvalde victim's father (usatoday.com).

35 "Fact Check: Interviews with Uvalde Victim's Family Spur Baseless Crisis Actors Conspiracy Theory," Sudiksha Kochi, *USA Today*, June 10, 2022, Fact check: Baseless conspiracy theory about Uvalde victim's father (usatoday.com).

36 "Fact check: Interviews with Uvalde victim's family spur baseless crisis actors conspiracy theory," Sudiksha Kochi, USA Today, June 10, 2022, Fact check: Baseless conspiracy theory about Uvalde victim's father (usatoday.com).

37 "Fact check: Interviews with Uvalde victim's family spur baseless crisis actors conspiracy theory," Sudiksha Kochi, USA Today, June 10, 2022, Fact check: Baseless conspiracy theory about Uvalde victim's father (usatoday.com).

38 "Fact check: Interviews with Uvalde victim's family spur baseless crisis actors conspiracy theory," Sudiksha Kochi, USA Today, June 10, 2022, Fact check: Baseless conspiracy theory about Uvalde victim's father (usatoday.com).

39 "AllSides Media Bias Chart," Media Bias | AllSides.

40 "AllSides Fact check Bias Chart," Media Bias | AllSides.

Chapter 12

How to Spot a Bot

In early 1990, a fire had apparently damaged a suspected chemical weapons factory in a North African country. I analyzed the apparent damage when I was a CIA imagery analyst and judged that the damage had probably shut down the factory for an extended period. Country officials claimed that the damage had closed the facility and denied that it was producing chemical weapons. As a result, the United States canceled a military strike on the facility. Although the Intelligence Community soon determined that the leadership of the country had staged the fire, the deception and disinformation had succeeded by warding off the strike.[1] This was not the first or only time I encountered foreign disinformation, including deception, in my CIA career.

Disinformation is not just something I dealt with as a CIA analyst. It affects all of us in our daily lives. Last year, my wife and I received an email purportedly from our power company. It said we had a past-due balance and that the company would cut the power to our home unless we called the provided phone number and gave our credit card information.

Something did not seem right. Instead of calling the phone number and providing our credit card information, we closed the email and logged into our account. To our relief, our account had been paid in full. The company website even said the

DOI: 10.4324/9781003471301-14

company would never solicit payment information via email or phone. It was a good example of disinformation.

We examined the email for signs of disinformation. Although the logo on the email resembled the one our power company used in its emails, and there were no misspellings or awkward grammar, we did not recognize the sender's email address. This was a telltale sign of disinformation, possibly from a bot.

▶ DEFINITIONS

Avatar: A graphical representation of a human user or the user's character or persona.[2]

Bot: A computer program that executes commands, replies to messages, or performs automatic and repetitive tasks, often mimicking the actions of a real person.[3,4]

▶ WHY BOTS ARE A PROBLEM

Social media accounts created by automation and run by bots are another common path for disinformation. Many of the known bot accounts occur on X, but Instagram, TikTok, and other platforms also have them. Although they are normally intended to make life easier for users, peddlers of disinformation also use them. Bots can severely warp debate, especially when they do so in coordination with one another. For example, they can magnify or condemn a message or article, make a phrase or hashtag trend, or bully other users.

Bots can generate professional-looking posts mimicking standard-based media organizations. The posts can easily persuade us to believe something or take some action. Students are not immune. Many have not learned how to pause and evaluate media before sharing it. They often reflexively accept media as true, or they reject it out of hand instead of taking time to evaluate it.

Bot accounts often inadvertently reveal themselves through metadata or behavior. Key indicators include missing avatars, mismatched male/female names, names that look like computer code, or accounts created within seconds of each other. Bot accounts may post content at precise intervals and repost every few seconds—faster than a typical human.[5]

In early 2022, First Draft tweeted a list of common signs of possible bot-like activity (Figure 12.1).[6,7] Each of the indicators by itself is not a good indicator of such activity, but the more indicators a social media account has, the more likely it is a bot.[8,9] Students should not automatically dismiss an account as a bot, even if it has several bot-like indicators. Instead, they should take extra care to evaluate the credibility of the post before using the content or sharing it with others.

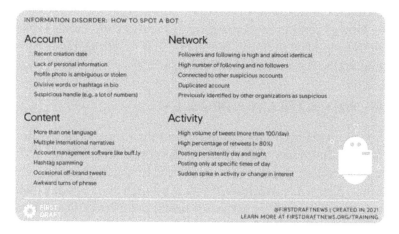

Figure 12.1 How to spot a bot.

First Draft on X: "Think before you share: How to spot a #bot (or not). Bot detection is no simple task. That's why we have put together a number of indicators that might suggest—but not prove—automated activity online. https://t.co/kTl8aBb20A"/ X (twitter.com).

Account Information

Creation Date

- Was the account or group of accounts created in the last year or few months? Does a dormant account with an earlier creation date suddenly show a spike in activity?

Bio Info
- Does the user profile have information about a real person or just hashtags, emojis, URLs, and politically divisive or highly partisan words? On the other hand, does it include bland claims that would be widely accepted by the target audience, such as "music lover" or "foodie"?

Suspicious Handle
- Does the account's handle or username include a generic name followed by numbers or a random sequence of numbers?

Profile and Background Picture
- Is the account missing a profile picture or avatar? Does the profile use stock photos or arbitrary images of cartoon characters, animals, landscapes, TV personalities, etc.? Is the account missing a background photo? If in doubt, use reverse image search to check the authenticity of the user's profile photo.

Pattern of Activity

High Volume of Activity
- Does the account generally produce a high rate of activity? There are no agreed criteria on what constitutes a high rate, but for accounts on X, First Draft has proposed a minimum of 100 tweets a day.[10]
- The rate of activity will vary depending on the organization operating the account. For example, journalists and news organizations typically post more frequently than other organizations, especially during breaking news events, so they may appear bot-like.

A High Percentage of Reposts
- Does the account primarily repost or "like" content from other users rather than post original content?

Pattern of Activity
- Does the account typically post only on certain days or at specific times, or does it have a sudden surge in activity and then stop posting altogether?

Content

International Narratives/Multiple Languages
- Does the account post in two or more languages? Does it post content about random, unrelated things, such as cat GIFs and hyperpartisan political statements?

Domains
- Does the account share URL shorteners, such as buff.ly, bit.ly, and ow.ly, to hide the actual names of malicious sites? Does it bury the URL of the malicious site within common domain names—e.g., google.com?[11]
- Does the account share URLs with odd hyphens and symbols that URLs of legitimate websites often do not have? Does it share URLs made entirely of numbers, such as IP addresses that mask the actual owner of the domain?[12]
- Does the account hide dangerous URLs inside credible-looking links, text, images, etc.? Hovering over the suspicious links will reveal the actual URL and allow you to compare it to the displayed URL. Avoid an actual URL that includes any warning signs I have just discussed or that differs significantly from the displayed URL.[13]

Stock Images and Memes
- Does the account use only images and memes from stock collections rather than the originals?[14]

Inflammatory Memes/GIFs
- Does the account share or post inflammatory, defamatory, or misleading memes and GIFs?

Hashtag Spamming
- Does the account post only hashtags or a few words followed by a long list of hashtags, especially ones that are hyperpartisan or concern controversial or inflammatory topics?

Links
- Does the account only use specific 'news' sources? For example, does it use several media sources of the same political leaning? Are these news sources questionable?

Low Engagement Quantity, Quality, and/or Diversity
- Are comments on the account random, contain only emojis, or all come from one person?[15]

Suspicious Turns of Phrase
- Does the account use awkward language or phrases in posts or bio descriptions?

Network Characteristics

Follow-for-follower strategy or high number of following and no followers
- Is the ratio of users who follow the account to users the account follows close to one? For example, does the account have 2,000 followers and 2,002 following? It is particularly suspicious if the numbers of following and followers are in the thousands. On the other hand, bots could have a large number of following but no followers.

Suspicious Mix of Followed Sources
- Is the account only following accounts in other countries? Bot accounts, especially when operated by state-controlled agencies, sometimes seek to influence users in several countries.

Duplicate Accounts
- Is the account connected to one or more accounts that are similar in appearance? Are other accounts posting the exact same content? Are the usernames or bio information the same or similar? Are the accounts referencing or interacting with each other?

Previously Identified by Other Organizations
- Has the account been flagged as a bot or bot-like by organizations that investigate disinformation, such as DFR Lab, EUvsDisinfo, or the Oxford Internet Institute? Does

the account appear in the Information Operation Archive? Researchers around the world are investigating bots and automation and may be able to give more information about a suspicious account.

The contest between bot creators and bot detectors will continue. Students who look for several or all of these indicators should have a good chance of detecting bot activity online.

▶ LESSON PLAN: IDENTIFYING POSSIBLE BOT-GENERATED CONTENT ON SOCIAL MEDIA

All students should recall indicators of a bot-run or bot-influenced social media account, identify possible accounts that contain one or more indicators, and explain why they think the account might be a bot. Students should use the "How to Spot a Bot" criteria in Figure 12.1. Higher achieving students should also critique the accounts more deeply by asking questions like the following:

- How have my biases and mindset influenced my reaction?
- What are the main themes of the content it posts or reposts?
- Do these themes contain implicit or explicit messages? What are they?
- What is the human creator and operator of the account trying to achieve? What might their biases be?

The following examples are from X, but the criteria also apply to accounts on Instagram, TikTok, and other social media platforms.

Account on X[16]   (https://twitter.com/sunneversets100) QR Code 12.1

School solution: This account showed clear bot-like behavior but is no longer active. The account displays little identifying information. Its avatar is an image of the cathedral in Florence, which is widely available online. Some bot makers are more careful and try to mask their anonymity by using images that are harder to determine are stolen. A good test of an account's veracity is therefore to reverse search its avatar on other sites to see if it has been pilfered.

The account also has an anonymous handle and screen name, a common sign of a bot. The only unique feature is a link to a US-based political action committee. None of these features are sufficient to identify a human user.

A key purpose of bots is to amplify the influence of other specific accounts by retweeting, liking, or quoting them. A typical bot will repeatedly repost content from those accounts and word-for-word quotes of news headlines liked by them, with few or no original posts.

Though this account posted almost no tweets of its own it, it showed a very high rate of amplification by reposting content, according to the DFR Lab.[17] It had an average of more than 1,000 reposts per day for 165 days—a feat no human could achieve.

A quick way to determine an account's activity and amplification is to click on 'posts' and 'replies.' As of August 28, 2017, for example, 195 of @Sunneversets100's last 200 tweets were reposts, according to the DFR Lab.[18] For context, there is no universal agreement on the threshold for suspicious activity. The Oxford Internet Institute's Computational Propaganda team considers an average of more than 50 posts a day to be suspicious; this is a commonly used benchmark, but it may be too low.[19] The DFR Lab considers 72 tweets per day (one every 10 minutes for 12 hours straight) as suspicious.[20]

Account on X[21] (https://twitter.com/pamela85758345?s=11& t=zlhb4-8sfHMY27CILJgpAg) QR Code 12.2

School solution: This example from X could be a bot because it does not have any followers, has no identifying profile imagery, and has a username that is followed by a random string of numbers.[22] During its short period of activity (November 11—December 11, 2019), it mostly reposted content (about 23 of its 31 posts), which focused mostly on politics in Bolivia.

Account on X (https://medialiteracysleuth.com/qr-code-12-3/) QR Code 12.3

School solution: This account from X, currently suspended, is probably not a bot because it has sufficient bio information and a level of activity typical of a human. Regarding the bio, it has a unique profile picture, a relevant background image, a handle without seemingly random numbers, and a specific location (Wisconsin). Regarding its activity, it has a following and followers count realistic for a human, and it posts and reposts on relevant topics (e.g., puppies) at a reasonable rate, with no apparent hashtag spamming on unrelated, provocative topics that would be indicators of possible bot amplification.

Account on X[23] (https://twitter.com/andreah83940354?s= 21&t=zlhb4-8sfHMY27CILJgpAg) QR Code 12.4

School solution: This account from X existed from November 11 to 20, 2019. It showed several bot-like indicators, including a handle with random numbers, a lack of bio information, and no background image. It appeared to engage in hashtag spamming during its short lifespan, tweeting and retweeting #EvoDictador, #EvoAsesino, #EvoTerrorista, and #NoHayGolpeEnBolivia, sometimes more than once a day.[24] Its two followers also had handles with random numbers and were unverified on X (meaning they could also have been bots because they did not meet certain criteria that X then had in place). One of the followers was an account with a similar short lifespan. The account also appeared to engage in similar hashtag spamming.

▶ NOTES

1 "Damage in Libyan Fire Reassessed as US See Possible Hoax," R. Jeffrey Smith, *The Washington Post*, March 31, 1990, Damage in Libyan Fire Reassessed as Us Sees Possible Hoax—The Washington Post.

2 Avatar (computing)—Wikipedia.

3 Bot Definition & Meaning—Merriam-Webster.

4 Bot Definition & Meaning | Dictionary.com.

5 Donara Barojan (on behalf of DFRLab), "#TrollTracker: Bots, Botnets, and Trolls," Medium, October 8, 2018, https://medium.com/ dfrlab/trolltracker-botsbotnets-and-trolls-31d2bdbf4c13.

6 First Draft on X: Think before you share: How to spot a #bot (or not) Bot detection is no simple task. That's why we have put together a number of indicators that might suggest—but not prove—automated activity online. https://t.co/kTl8aBb20A/ X (twitter.com).

7 "How to Spot a Bot (or Not): The Main Indicators of Online Auto-mation, Co-ordination and Inauthentic Activity," Carlotta Dotto and Seb Cubbon, First Draft, September 28, 2019, How to spot a bot (or not): The main indicators of online automation, co-ordination and inauthentic activity (firstdraftnews.org).

8 First Draft on X: Think before you share: How to spot a #bot (or not) Bot detection is no simple task. That's why we have put together a number of indicators that might suggest—but not prove—automated activity online. https://t.co/kTl8aBb20A/ X (twitter.com).

9 "How to Spot a Bot (or Not): The Main Indicators of Online Auto-mation, Co-ordination and Inauthentic Activity," Carlotta Dotto and Seb Cubbon, First Draft, September 28, 2019, How to spot a bot (or not): The main indicators of online automation, co—ordi-nation and inauthentic activity (firstdraftnews.org).

10 Donara Barojan (on behalf of DFRLab), "#TrollTracker: Bots, Bot-nets, and Trolls," Medium, October 8, 2018, https://medium.com/dfrlab/trolltracker-botsbotnets-and-trolls-31d2bdbf4c13.

11 5 URL Warning Signs to Watch For | INFORMATION TECH-NOLOGY (du.edu).

12 5 URL Warning Signs to Watch For | INFORMATION TECH-NOLOGY (du.edu).

13 5 URL Warning Signs to Watch For | INFORMATION TECH-NOLOGY (du.edu).

14 Foreign Policy CAN on X: Online #disinformation is often spread using fake social media accounts. Here are some signs to spot the fakes and stop the spread of false information. For more tips on identifying fake accounts, visit https://t.co/IOYywEUVFk https://t.co/Wn2FCdFpHn/ X (twitter.com).

15 Foreign Policy CAN on X: Online #disinformation is often spread using fake social media accounts. Here are some signs to spot the fakes and stop the spread of false information. For more tips on identifying fake accounts, visit https://t.co/IOYywEUVFk https://t.co/Wn2FCdFpHn/ X (twitter.com).

16 sunneversets100 (@sunneversets100) / X (twitter.com).

17 #BotSpot: Twelve Ways to Spot a Bot | by @DFRLab | DFRLab | Medium.

18 #BotSpot: Twelve Ways to Spot a Bot | by @DFRLab | DFRLab | Medium.

19 #BotSpot: Twelve Ways to Spot a Bot | by @DFRLab | DFRLab | Medium.

20 #BotSpot: Twelve Ways to Spot a Bot | by @DFRLab | DFRLab | Medium.

21 Amid the Crisis in Bolivia, a Twitter Flood of Coup Denial, Bot Accusations, and Memes | by @DFRLab | DFRLab | Medium.

22 Amid the Crisis in Bolivia, a Twitter Flood of Coup Denial, Bot Accusations, and Memes | by @DFRLab | DFRLab | Medium.

23 "How to Spot a Bot (or Not): The Main Indicators of Online Automation, Co-ordination and Inauthentic Activity," Carlotta Dotto and Seb Cubbon, First Draft, September 28, 2019, How to spot a bot (or not): The main indicators of online automation, co-ordination and inauthentic activity (firstdraftnews.org).

24 "How to Spot a Bot (or Not): The Main Indicators of Online Automation, Co-ordination and Inauthentic Activity," Carlotta Dotto and Seb Cubbon, First Draft, September 28, 2019, How to spot a bot (or not): The main indicators of online automation, co-ordination and inauthentic activity (firstdraftnews.org).

Chapter 13

Artificial Intelligence

Embracing It Responsibly to Enhance Learning

Artificial intelligence (AI) gathers and synthesizes information, concepts, and languages more quickly and widely than nearly all humans, according to *Washington Post* AI columnist Josh Tyrangiel.[1] It can enhance and inhibit news literacy, and it presents unique opportunities and challenges for middle and high school students.

First let's get familiar with some key AI terms.

▶ DEFINITIONS

Deepfake image: Synthetically altered footage in which a depicted face, body, or object has been digitally modified to appear as someone or something else.[2] It is often a headshot. The images are easily accessible via certain websites, such as Generated Photos (https://generated.photos/), allowing users to create fake headshots quickly and easily.[3] It got the name "deepfake" because it uses a special kind of machine learning (ML) called "deep" learning.

Deepfake video: Like a deepfake image, it is synthetically altered footage (really a series of images) in which a depicted face, body, or object has been digitally modified to appear as someone or something else.[4] It got the name "deepfake" because it uses a special kind of machine learning called "deep" learning.

DOI: 10.4324/9781003471301-15

Disinformation campaign: An influence operation that involves covert efforts to intentionally spread false or misleading information.[5]

Generative Adversarial Network (GAN): A machine learning (ML) technology that uses two neural networks—a generator and a discriminator—to compete against one another. The generator tries to create data to fool the discriminator, and the discriminator tries to detect fake data from the generator. As the networks compete, they learn from each other, and the process produces an increasingly realistic output in image, video, and audio formats.[6] GANs are the ML capability behind deepfakes.

Large Language Model (LLM): A language model that utilizes "deep" methods on an extremely large data set as a basis for predicting and constructing natural-sounding text.[7]

Machine learning (ML): The ability of machines to learn from a large amount of complex data, identify patterns, and make inferences about decision rules.[8]

Natural language processing (NLP) and generation (NLG): ML technologies that allow ML systems to read, write, and interpret text.[9] They also allow ML systems to produce **generative text**—artificial yet lifelike text produced with natural language computer models.[10] AI-generated text is predictable, follows patterns, and contains "probable" content.

One of the most widely used NLGs is the Generative Pre-Trained Transformer 3 (GPT-3), built by OpenAI, an AI research and deployment company. OpenAI's most recent GPT as of this writing is GPT-4, a relatively powerful AI chatbot.[11]

Psychographics: An advanced form of demographics that includes profiling of values, interests, activities, and opinions of population segments for advertising and election targeting.[12]

Sentiment analysis: A research field within NLP that mines attitudes and emotions—such as sarcasm, confusion, and suspicion—from text and interprets the text as negative, positive, or neutral. Some models can determine the degree of polarization from user comments and posts with 94%–96% accuracy.[13]

Social network analysis: Visualizes social and knowledge networks to show how people and organizations are linked together, and the nature of their relationships.[14] For example, in a 2019 study on the popular Chinese social media site Renren, researchers used available data, such as a user's friends list, to infer unstated information, such as their age, hobbies, and university majors.[15]

Stance detection: Uses ML techniques to identify if the sentiment of a post is negative or positive and if it agrees with a broader idea—such as atheism or feminism. It enables more accurate targeting of individuals by providing a deeper understanding of a user's positions and the strength of their beliefs.[16]

Text-to-image generators: An ML model that takes a natural language description as an input and produces an image that attempts to match that description—e.g., DALL-E.[17]

Voice cloning: Digitally altering a voice to make it sound like someone else. Various online and phone apps, such as Celebrity Voice Cloning[18] and Voicer Famous AI Voice Changer,[19] allow users to mimic the voices of popular celebrities.[20]

Now let's discuss how AI can enable and interfere with learning.

▶ HOW AI CAN BENEFIT STUDENTS IN THEIR DAILY LIVES

AI helps power so many things that can make life easier. For example, AI can predict and recommend the best routes to Uber drivers; enable language translators to tell us how to say, "Where is the bathroom?" when we travel; and help health-care organizations use their health data more effectively, just to name a few.

AI also plays a key role in several things that middle and high school students use or are directly affected by, including powering algorithms that continually recommend types of news content they tend to view most on social media and types of videos they like to watch on streaming services, powering electronic games, etc.

▶ HOW AI CAN ENABLE STUDENT LEARNING

AI can help students gather basic facts for their class assignments. For example, with the appropriate prompt, AI can summarize key facts about a US president or even a Hollywood celebrity, allowing students to focus, for example, on analyzing their influence on society. With its ability, in some cases, to automatically detect fake or bot accounts that spread disinformation and texts, videos, images, and even audio that contain disinformation, AI can help students read and evaluate news on social media with more confidence.

With the appropriate prompt, AI tools such as DALL-E can create images using text prompts to help students visualize and better understand complex relationships, inspire creative thinking, and help students explore alternative perspectives.[21] AI tools like DALL-E can also provide personalized visual content that helps students who learn best through visual cues to receive image-based explanations and visual summaries; students who prefer written text can still benefit from the generated images as supplementary materials. This adaptability can cater to diverse learning styles, promote inclusivity, and make the learning process more immersive and engaging. Tools like DALL-E can be an excellent way to help students be creative without having the technical skills of a graphic artist to create interesting digital images.

Finally, AI's ability to tutor could especially benefit students who are having trouble grasping the content.

▶ HOW AI CAN INTERFERE WITH LEARNING

On the flip side, AI can enable effective disinformation campaigns that can make it harder for students to determine which news sources are credible. According to the *Post's* Tyrangiel, it's nearly impossible to determine whether information is AI-generated. With text, it is easy to copy and reformat output from an LLM for your own use.[22]

Forensic tools can often identify a synthetic or AI origin for some, but not all, images, audio, and video. Many companies are producing digital watermarks for their content, in part because governments and other regulators might soon require them to have such identifiers, according to Tyrangiel.[23]

The implications are huge. The potential deluge of sophisticated AI-powered disinformation may disrupt sound decision-making and, ultimately, the ability to reach a consensus that is critical for Western democracy.[24]

Several US adversaries have gotten into the disinformation game. Since the late 2000s, Russia has increasingly pursued AI-enabled disinformation campaigns, including against the 2020 US presidential election. China and Iran have developed AI disinformation operations against their internal opposition movements and are also using them to try to sway international opinion in support of their geopolitical aims.[25] For example, China, echoing Russia's tactics, set up a high-volume network of inauthentic accounts on numerous social media platforms and in various languages to promote disinformation and conspiracy theories about the COVID-19 virus.[26] As of 2021, some 81 countries were using social media to spread propaganda and disinformation, some of it presumably AI-enabled, to target foreign and domestic audiences.[27]

Key ML technologies for disinformation campaigns include NLGs and GANs. Developers are incorporating a common NLG model, ChatGPT (GPT-3 and GPT-4), into apps to improve chat, translation, and ads.[28] In the future, AI systems that chat flawlessly like humans and are tailored to the interests of individual social media users may become a potent way to spread AI-enabled disinformation.

Deepfakes are especially worrisome. As we might conclude from our earlier look at visual persuasion, deepfakes can make a persuasive impression on viewers.[29] Research on the impact of deepfakes is just starting, and current findings are not conclusive, but some studies indicate viewers are apt to rate deepfake videos as more memorable, believable, and credible than fake news articles.[30]

For example, researchers in a 2020 study found that participants were more likely to share disinformation on social media when it contained a deepfake video. A 2021 study of more than 7,000 participants, one of the largest to date, confirmed the finding. However, the 2021 study concluded that the persuasiveness of deepfake videos produced only "small effects" on attitudes and intentions.[31]

GANs facilitate the production of images of fake humans that are nearly impossible to detect with the human eye.[32] For example, Facebook discovered high-quality ML-generated avatars on some profiles that were part of a disinformation campaign.[33] The platform has banned the use of GAN-generated content and has relied on various methods to detect them. But GAN-generated photos remain difficult to detect in real time as detection and generation technologies continue to overtake one another.

Deepfakes may also have a longer-term, strategic impact—namely, a declining trust in all types of media. Some research seems to validate this. A study in 2020 showed that participants who viewed deepfakes were more likely to distrust social media–based news content in general.[34]

Still, some researchers question the deepfake hype and suggest that weaponization of the technology will depend on factors that are largely out of a bad actor's control. These include ease of access, decreased cost, and the waning effectiveness of current, non-ML-enabled techniques.[35]

In sum, bad actors can weaponize AI in four ways:[36]

- Manipulate elections
- Exacerbate social divisions
- Lower trust in institutions and authorities
- Undermine journalism and trustworthy sources of information

Students can reduce the chance of getting fooled by AI-enabled content in their social media feeds. First, let's discuss text content.

As I noted earlier, NLGs create text that increasingly looks like an actual human wrote it. Two NLGs that have exploded in popularity are ChatGPT (GPT-3 and GPT-4), built by OpenAI. In January 2023, Newsguard asked ChatGPT to respond to 100 disinformation narratives from Newsguard's database; the chatbot produced false yet authoritative-sounding narratives—including false news articles and TV scripts—for 80 of them. Newsguard reported that the chatbot has safeguards that prevent it from spreading some disinformation and that OpenAI's future versions will be even better at doing so.[37] Nonetheless, an

80% failure rate is concerning because bad actors could easily use the technology to spread disinformation.

There are two key steps students should take to evaluate text.

First, students should check whether there is a notice or label that the text is AI-generated. This may be on the text itself (probably at the beginning or end) or—if the text is part of a longer social media post or article—somewhere on it, usually at the beginning or end.

Second, if the text is formal and formulaic, is awkwardly worded, includes facts and no opinion, is bland, and/or lacks details one would expect from a human, it is more likely to be AI-generated.

▶ LESSON PLAN: HARNESSING AI FOR LEARNING

Activity 1: Human- or AI-Generated Text?

Here is an activity for students to practice spotting AI-generated text.

- Divide students into groups of three to four.
- Provide each group with the following text and have them evaluate each piece to determine if it was written by a human or was AI-generated using ChatGPT, Bard, or a similar AI program. How do they know?
- Have each group report their findings to the class.

This activity requires all students to recall indicators of AI-generated text and explain why they think the text is or is not generated completely or partly by AI (Figure 13.1). Students should take the two steps previously discussed in this chapter to find out. Higher achieving students should also critique the human- or AI-generated text more deeply by asking questions like the following:

- How have my biases and mindset influenced my reaction?
- Does the text contain implicit or explicit messages? What are they?

- Does the text contain biases or stereotypes? What are they?
- What is the human or the AI tool that produced the text trying to achieve? What might their biases be?

The existence of Bigfoot has been a subject of intense speculation and debate for decades. While there have been numerous reports of sightings and encounters with this elusive creature, the scientific community has largely remained skeptical about its existence due to the lack of concrete evidence. The Bigfoot phenomenon has been the subject of many investigations and expeditions, but the results have been inconclusive and often dismissed as hoaxes or misidentifications of other animals.

Despite the skepticism, the existence of Bigfoot continues to captivate the public imagination and remains a topic of interest for cryptozoologists, enthusiasts, and skeptics alike. The debate surrounding Bigfoot's existence raises important questions about the nature of scientific inquiry and the role of evidence in determining the veracity of claims. While some argue that the absence of definitive evidence is sufficient reason to doubt Bigfoot's existence, others point to the many eyewitness accounts and anecdotal evidence as reasons to consider the possibility. Ultimately, the question of Bigfoot's existence remains unresolved, and it is up to individual interpretation whether the lack of evidence is sufficient grounds for skepticism or whether the existence of Bigfoot should be considered a genuine possibility.

Figure 13.1 Human- or AI-generated text?

"How to Check for Writing Made With ChatGPT (AI Detection)," July 3, 2023, Gold Penguin, How to Check for Writing Made With ChatGPT (AI Detection) | Gold Penguin.

Provide the 'school solution.'

The text was generated by ChatGPT.[38] How do we know?

First, there is no notice or label on the text indicating it was entirely or partly AI-generated, and there is no associated social media post or article to check for the notice or label.

Second, the text lacks details, such as examples of investigations, expeditions, or anecdotal evidence one would expect a human writer to include.

The results of the second step suggest, but do not prove, that the text was at least partly AI-generated.

Discuss students' reactions and answer any questions.

Activity 2: Human- or AI-Generated Text?

Here is another activity teachers can use with their students to give them practice spotting AI-generated text.

- Divide students into groups of three to four.
- Provide each group with the following dating app text profiles and have them evaluate each to determine if one or both were written by a human or were AI-generated using ChatGPT, Bard, or a similar AI program. How do they know?
- Have each group report their findings to the class.

This activity requires all students to recall indicators of AI-generated text and explain why they think the text is or is not generated completely or partly by AI. Students should take the two steps previously discussed in this chapter to find out. Higher achieving students should also critique the text—whether human- or AI-generated—more deeply by asking questions like the following:

- How have my biases and mindset influenced my reaction?
- Does the text contain implicit or explicit messages? What are they?
- Does the text contain biases or stereotypes? What are they?
- What is the human or AI tool that produced the text trying to achieve? Why? What might their biases be?

You're browsing a dating app when two profiles pique your interest. The profiles seem sincere and appealing, and the interests expressed fit your own. Here are their blurbs:

Quote (dating profiles)[39] (https://hai.stanford.edu/news/was-written-human-or-ai-tsu) QR Code 13.1

All else being equal, how would you decide between the two profiles? Which one is not a real person, i.e., which one did AI write?

Provide the 'school solution' to each question using the two steps.

This is a tough one. AI generated the blurb for 'Person 1,' and a human wrote the blurb for 'Person 2.'[40]

There is no notice or label on either blurb, and there is no associated social media post or article to check.

However, the awkward wording, "I…want to get to know each other better," in the 'Person 1' blurb suggests the blurb is at least partly AI-generated.

Discuss students' reactions and answer any questions.

Images and videos are another type of content students see in their social media feeds. Text-to-image generators such as DALL-E are increasingly used to create realistic images from text prompts.

There are five steps students can use to help distinguish real images and videos from shallow fakes and AI-generated ones, including deepfakes. I introduce the first two here and the remaining three in Activity Three to follow.

First, if the image or video is part of a social media post, check whether there is a notice somewhere on the post, in the comments section—where the author might have mentioned it—or on a linked article indicating that the image or video is AI-generated. Reputable news sources inform readers when they use AI.

Second, look for a 'watermark.' As of this writing, the following watermarks are still being rolled out; other watermarks exist. **One of these is a small, encircled 'i.'** When clicked, the icon will reveal the original photo or video and identify edits made to it. The icon will also identify when and where the photo or video was taken and with what type of device. The technology is being developed first for still images and video but is expected to work for other forms of digital content in the future.[41]

Activity 3: Human- or AI-Generated Image?

Here is an activity teachers can use with their students to give them practice spotting an AI-generated image.

- Divide students into groups of three to four.
- Provide each group with the following image and have them evaluate it to determine if it was a photo taken by a human or was AI-generated. How do they know?
- Have each group report their findings to the class.

This lesson requires all students to recall indicators of an AI-generated image and explain why they think the image is or is not generated completely or partly by AI. Students should take the steps previously discussed in this chapter to find out. Higher achieving students should also critique the image—whether AI- or human-generated—more deeply by asking questions like the following:

- How have my biases and mindset influenced my reaction?
- Does the image contain implicit or explicit messages? What are they?
- Does the image contain biases or stereotypes? What are they?
- What is the human behind the AI or real image trying to achieve? Why? What might their biases be?

Photo[42] (https://www.starlinglab.org/reflections/) QR Code 13.2

Ask students
- Is this a human-produced or AI-generated image? How do you know?
- Who produced the image
- How did they find this information?

Provide the 'school solution' using the two steps.

This is a human-produced image (photo). Here is how we know:

- The image is not part of a social media post, so we cannot check it to see if the author might have indicated that the image is AI-generated. The article in which the image is embedded does not indicate whether the image is AI-generated.
- The image does have a 'watermark,' the small, encircled 'i' in the upper right corner, indicating the image was not AI-generated. When clicked, it reveals who produced the image (Hannah McKay), what it was produced with (Starling Store using Numbers Protocol), when it was produced (November 7, 2020), and who provided it (Reuters). It also indicates if any edits were made to it (no).

Discuss students' reactions and answer any questions.

Here is **another watermark** from the Coalition for Content Provenance and Authenticity (Figure 13.2). The C2PA is developing technical specifications for establishing the provenance and authenticity of digital content, including whether at least part of the content has been AI-generated.

Figure 13.2 Watermark from the Coalition for Content Provenance and Authenticity (C2PA).

Introducing Official Content Credentials Icon—C2PA.

C2PA User Experience Guidance for Implementers: C2PA Specifications.

When clicked, the watermark displays data about a piece of content, such as the publisher or creator's information, where and when it was created, what tools were used to make it—including whether or not generative AI was used—as well as any edits made to it.

Here is a symbol created by the Four Corners Project (Figure 13.3).[43] It identifies where the reader can click for more information in each corner. A photographer can add context to each of the four corners of their image online. When clicked, the symbol in the lower right corner, shown below, displays the image's provenance and authenticity.

Figure 13.3 Symbol from the Four Corners Project.

Four Corners Project—An initiative to increase authorship and credibility in visual media.

Watermarks and symbols like these are not always adequate to identify AI-generated images because they are often applied like a label or sticker on an image and can easily be removed with editing. In response, Google in August 2023 launched a beta version[44,45] of a watermarking tool, SynthID, that creators can use to implant a digital watermark directly into AI-generated images. The tool makes the watermark invisible to the human eye but detectable using the tool and therefore more difficult to edit out. Google released a version for audio in September 2023. Improvements to the tool, and tools similar to Google's, will roll out in the near future.

Third, if there is no watermark and no notice, **students should read laterally to see if the verified social media account or website of a reputable news, government organization, or celebrity is reporting on the event or development and includes the apparent same image or video**. If not, there is a greater likelihood that the image or video is AI-generated.

Fourth, if there is no watermark or notice and no verified source is reporting on the event or development, **students can run the image through an AI image detector**. Some free ones as of this writing include Illuminarty, Optic AI or Not, and Everypixel Aesthetics.[46]

Students can also use a tool (https://contentcredentials.org/verify) from the Content Authenticity Initiative (CAI) to help trace the provenance of an image that they think looks real but may be AI-generated. Behind synthetic media and AI are people and organizations using them. The CAI creates a system that enables creators to transparently share the details of how they created an image.

Fifth, if the AI image detector does not flag the image as AI-generated, **students should** examine **the image themselves for signs that it may be AI-generated**.

As of this writing, key signs of AI-generated images include the following:[47,48]

- Misshapen hands, stretchy wrists, spindly fingers, or too many finger digits.
- Blurred or overly bright teeth.
- Blurred or oddly shaped shoelaces.

- Textures that are excessively smooth and look too perfect; human skin can come out looking like plastic with a glossy sheen.
- Inconsistencies in the logic of the image itself—for example, clothing fabric that blends together across different subjects or background patterns that repeat perfectly.
- Shadows do not align with the light sources or match the shape of the objects casting them.
- Overly dramatic lighting. Lighting in portraits may exaggerate the edge of the subject's face and hair; they may be lit with an exaggerated cool bluish light to one side and a warm orange light to the other; landscapes often have too much atmosphere, as in excessively murky backdrops or orange glow from the setting sun.
- Backdrops in portraits are usually blurry and lack detail. In landscapes, features like foliage or rocks may blend together.
- Text on the image, such as on street signs and in logos on clothing, may look pixelated or stretched; sometimes the text does not make sense, is out of context, or contains odd phrases that a human would not write.

Here are things students should look for to specifically identify AI-generated **deepfake images**, based on information from Poynter[49] and the Media Lab at the Massachusetts Institute of Technology.[50] This is not a complete list, and new indicators will probably be identified.

- **Face expressions**: Do they look awkward or unnatural? Do they show the appropriate emotion consistent with what the person is saying?
- **Cheeks and forehead**: Does the skin appear too smooth or too wrinkly? Blotchy or uneven? Is the agedness of the skin similar to the agedness of the hair and eyes? Deepfakes may be incongruent on some dimensions.
- **Eyes and eyebrows**: Do shadows appear in places that you would expect?
- **Eyeglasses**: Is there glare? Is there too much glare? Deepfakes may fail to fully represent the natural physics of lighting.

- **Facial hair or lack thereof**: Does the facial hair look real? Deepfakes might add or remove a mustache, sideburns, or beard but may fail to make facial hair transformations fully natural.
- **Facial moles**: Does the mole look real?
- **Lips**: Do their size and color match the rest of the person's face?
- **Teeth**. Do they look blurry?
- **Hair**: Does it look too "perfect"—e.g., no frizz? Does it look unnatural for the face?
- **Unnatural body shape**: Does the person's body look distorted?
- **Misaligned body parts**: Is there misalignment between the person's face and neck, neck and torso, arms and torso, or legs and torso?
- **Background**: Is it blurry, static, or does it appear out of place?[51]

When trying to determine if a video is a **deepfake**, students should look for the same indicators they use for images and also those that follow, according to Poynter[52] and the Media Lab at the Massachusetts Institute of Technology:[53]

- **Eyes and eyebrows**: Do eye movements look unnatural? Is there a lack of eye movement or blinking? Too much blinking? Do shadows appear in places that you would expect? Deepfakes may fail to fully represent the natural physics of a scene.
- **Eyeglasses**: Is there glare? Is there too much glare? Does the angle of the glare change when the person moves? Once again, deepfakes may fail to fully represent the natural physics of lighting.
- **Lips**: Some deepfakes are based on lip-syncing. Do the lip movements look natural? Do their size and color match the rest of the person's face?
- **Voice/audio**: Does it sound "off"? Is there poor lip-syncing, robotic-sounding voices, odd word pronunciation, background noise, or no audio when there should be?

- **Unnatural body movement or body shape**: Does the person look distorted when they turn to the side or move their head? Are their movements jerky and disjointed from one frame to the next?

Students can also do a reverse image search using tools included in the "Tools" section of the book to see if the image or frames of a video have been used before, which would suggest the image or video is not AI-generated, since AI-generated images are unique. However, AI is getting so good that there is a high chance that this method would not single out the unique AI image or video.

Activity 4: Human- or AI-Generated Image or Video?

Here is an activity teachers can use with their students to give them practice spotting an AI-generated image and video.

- Divide students into groups of three to four.
- Provide each group with the following image and video and have them evaluate them to determine if one or both were taken by a human or were AI-generated. How do they know?
- Have each group report their findings to the class.

This lesson requires all students to recall indicators of an AI-generated image and video and explain why they think the image and video is or is not generated completely or partly by AI. Students should take the steps previously discussed in this chapter to find out. Higher achieving students should also critique the image or video—whether human- or AI-generated—more deeply by asking questions like the following:

- How have my biases and mindset influenced my reaction?
- Does the image or video contain implicit or explicit messages? What are they?
- Does the image or video contain biases or stereotypes? What are they?

- What is the human creator and poster of the image or video trying to achieve? What might their biases be?

Image[54] (https://pixabay.com/illustrations/ai-generated-dog-puppy-hoodie-7897496/) QR Code 13.3

Provide the 'school solution': The image is AI-generated.

First, the image is not part of a social media post, so we cannot check whether there is a notice somewhere on the post, in the comments section, or on a linked article indicating that the image is AI-generated.

Second, there is no 'watermark.'

Third, a reverse image search does surface the image. It appears on the Pixabay.com website and is labeled as AI-generated.

There is no need to take the fourth step to check the image with an AI image detector.

Ask the students to examine the image themselves for signs that it is AI-generated. Signs for this image include the following:

- The puppy's nose looks too smooth or too 'perfect.'
- The puppy's fur looks too smooth and perfectly combed.
- The edge of the puppy's clothing is lit with an exaggerated whitish light.
- The background is unnaturally blurry. The depth of field is very shallow.
- The flowers in the field behind the puppy have an unnaturally bright orange glow, and the edges of the supposed flower in the upper right of the image are too smooth.

Discuss students' reactions and answer any questions.

Video[55] (https://www.tiktok.com/@kindnessrulesalways/video/7199603719590333742) QR Code 13.4

- Is the video real, a shallow fake, or an AI-generated deepfake? How do you know?
- Have each group report their findings to the class.

Provide the school solution: The video is a shallow fake or poorly done deepfake. It appears to show actor Morgan

Freeman criticizing a Super Bowl halftime show, including a performance by Rihanna. But if you look closely, Freeman's likeness does not blink, the teeth look unnatural, and the lips do not sync with the voice. The account owner probably did not try to generate the voice of Morgan Freeman with voice cloning or another AI tool; the voice just does not sound that convincing.

The video displays the apparent handle of the TikTok account, @themanofmanyvoices. An Internet search uncovers a report from the fact-checking site VERIFY, which confirmed the video is from that account, a celebrity impressionist who posts manipulated content like this regularly. The video shows the same background as similar videos from this account of Sylvester Stallone and Muhammad Ali; it's unlikely all three men would make their remarks in the same room or use the same simulated background. Ali died in 2016, so obviously, he could not have made this video in 2022.

Discuss students' reactions and answer any questions.

Remember: We can't prove **beyond any doubt** that AI has generated the text, photo, video, or other media we're looking at.

▶ THE ETHICS OF AI USE

Now that students have practiced identifying several types of AI-generated content, they will be in a better position to think about some of the ethical dilemmas around the use of AI to produce news—in students' broader definition of the term—for social media, and implications for their news literacy. There are many definitions of ethics and opinions on the ethical implications of AI. This book does not claim to offer the definitive definition of the term or the final opinion. This section is intended as food for thought and to generate discussion among students and teachers, drawing on my experience teaching ethics to CIA analysts.

What is "ethics"? The English word 'ethics' derives from the Greek root word 'êthos,' referring to one's character or moral nature.[56] It is considered synonymous with morality, according to the Cambridge Dictionary of Philosophy.[57] Rushworth Kidder agrees, stating that the definition usually includes language such as "the science of moral duty" and describes whatever is "good or right or proper."[58] It no longer signals dour condemnation or self-righteousness.[59]

Right/Wrong Dilemmas

These are situations that are widely understood to be wrong, according to Kidder.[60] Examples include violating the law (e.g., passing a stopped school bus), intentionally distorting long-standing facts (e.g., asserting that two times two equals five), or dismissing fundamental, widely understood inner values (e.g., failing to pick up after your dog when walking them in a public space).

Right/Right (Ethical) Dilemmas

Unlike right-versus-wrong situations, Kidder uses the term "ethical dilemma" to refer to right-versus-right situations— when two "core moral values" conflict.[61] Examples: It is right for a country to go to war to defend itself and right to protect innocent lives in the process; It is right to support freedom of expression on social media and right to support widespread desire to prohibit the display of pornographic material.

One of my ethical dilemmas at the CIA was when I recruited intelligence analysts. A common topic of discussion among my colleagues was whether to recruit highly qualified candidates from "tried and tested" traditional schools or equally qualified candidates from a wider variety of "less tested" schools to create a more diverse workforce. This was arguably not a right/wrong issue because, to my knowledge, the CIA generally did not have an explicit requirement to recruit from specific schools. This was a choice between "right versus right"—an ethical dilemma.

Many middle and high school students apparently struggle distinguishing between right/wrong and ethical dilemmas. A survey[62] by the Josephson Institute of Ethics of nearly 7,000 people in five age groups (17 and under, 18–24, 25–40, 41–50, and over 50) in 2009 found that 60% of young people said they had cheated on a test within the past year. It found that teens 17 or under are five times as likely than those over 50 to think that lying and cheating are necessary to succeed. It also found that high school students who cheated on exams two or more times were significantly more likely to be dishonest later in life.

A 2008 survey[63] for Deloitte of 750 teens 12 to 17 years of age living in the United States found that 80% thought they were prepared to make ethical decisions after they graduated. Yet more than a third said they had to break the rules at school to succeed. Granted, the survey was relatively small and was conducted 15 years ago, but the results suggest a need for teachers to help students reflect on the ethical implications of their actions, including their use of AI.

Kidder writes that schools can help students make ethical decisions by establishing guidelines for ethical decision-making.[64] Teachers can also help students do so by appealing to the so-called golden rule of "doing to others what you would like them to do to you." This appeal, what Kidder calls "care-based" thinking,[65] is behind the two activities below.

▶ LESSON PLAN: THE ETHICS OF AI USE OUTSIDE THE CLASSROOM

Divide students into groups of three to four. Give them the following question:

What are some ethical issues for you as <u>consumers</u> and <u>creators</u> of news content on social media?

You might also ask them questions like the following:

- How many of you create your own TikTok videos?
- How many upload your own photos and videos to Instagram?
- How many of you tweet AI-generated answers to prompts, such as: "Does the US government have plans to deal with a zombie apocalypse?"

Students are likely to come up with some insightful answers.

After the discussion, cover any of the following examples of ethical issues they do not mention.

This lesson requires all students to recall what the term "ethics" means, demonstrate their understanding by evaluating the fictitious but realistic scenarios below, and determine if the scenario illustrates an ethical dilemma. Higher achieving students should also determine how their biases and mindset may influence their reactions and responses to the scenarios.

Transparency of Sources

Scenario: You are reading a report online from your high school newspaper about the big win your school had against its main rival. The report lacks the details you have seen in prior reports, and it contains awkward language and odd expressions. You asked the editor-in-chief of the paper about it, and they said the story was AI-generated and that the paper planned to include more AI-generated sports reports because AI could easily do so and because the paper did not have the human staff to do it. Is this an ethical dilemma?

 Possible answer: Yes, this is an ethical dilemma. As of this writing, this is not a right-versus-wrong issue/illegal issue, but disclosing the use of AI is desirable and expected of credible news outlets, which should include high school newspapers. In the absence of such language, readers have a reasonable expectation that what they are reading is human-generated.

Amplification of Biases and Prejudices, Leading to Stereotyping, Discrimination, Inequity, and Violation of Civil Rights

 Scenario: You ask DALL-E to generate an image of a CEO and include it in your Instagram post about the latest trends in CEO pay around the world. The image it generated is of a white, middle-aged male in a suit and tie. You think nothing of it and go ahead with your post. Similar scenarios have occurred. Should you be cautious while using AI to avoid training AI that reinforces stereotypes and biases? Is this an ethical dilemma?

 Possible answer: Yes, this is an ethical dilemma because it could reinforce the bias of DALL-E to produce all images of CEOs as white, middle-aged males in suits and ties and ultimately deepen the stereotype in society. The *Post's* Tyrangiel claims, however, that students do not really need to worry about training AI models that reinforce stereotypes and biases. An individual prompt does not do much to train the models because the models and user base are large. Some models are now training on synthetic data and prompts, rendering an individual's single input even less meaningful to its overall knowledge and training base.[66]

Concerns over Privacy and Security of Personal Data

Scenario: You work for an AI company's information security team. One day, you discover that several user prompts and generative responses from the company's AI tool appeared on social media. Your company has specific security measures in place to prevent this. It also has a statement on its website saying that trust and protection of users' privacy are at the core of its mission. What do you do? Is this an ethical dilemma?

Possible answer: No, this is an issue of right versus wrong. In this case, your company has specific language on its website saying that trust and protection of users' privacy are at the core of its mission. Although this particular example is fictitious, it is based in truth: OpenAI's ChatGPT suffered a data breach in March 2023 that partly exposed conversations and some users' personal details, including email addresses and the last four digits of their credit cards.[67] There have also been numerous cases of doctored images spread on social media in an attempt to discredit someone.

Scenario: You used AI to make a video showing how to use a just-released cell phone. You noticed that the AI tool used someone else's video and added your image and voice in place of theirs, but you uploaded it to YouTube anyway—without asking permission. Is this an ethical dilemma?

Possible answer: No, this is an issue of right versus wrong. YouTube has specific rules in place requiring users to seek permission from the copyright holder when using their content. Although this particular example is fictitious, it is based in truth: there have been many cases of copyright infringement like this. When a creator uploads their content to a social media platform, they have a reasonable expectation that their work will be protected. But that expectation is only as good as the platform's information security team—and the integrity of other creators.

When using AI tools, the user typically shares their input in return for the right to use the tool, according to Tyrangiel. They have a reasonable expectation that their information will be anonymized, but that depends on the AI company's information security. It is best to avoid sharing details that you would not want to see all over social media.[68]

Efficiency/Cost Savings Versus Elimination of Jobs Once Done by Humans

Scenario: You enjoyed writing for your high school newspaper, so you decided to use your news literacy skills to become a reporter for a highly respected news outlet. Today, your employer laid you off; your job was replaced by AI. Did your employer face an ethical dilemma?

Possible answer: Yes, this is an issue of right versus right. It is an ethical dilemma because your employer faced the choice of saving money versus saving a job done by you. This is a realistic scenario: newsrooms have been hit relatively hard by AI. AI was responsible for nearly 4,000, or roughly 5%, of all jobs lost at US-based employers between April and May 2023, according to a report from the outplacement firm Challenger, Gray & Christmas.[69] According to Pew Research, exactly which or how many jobs are at risk is uncertain because AI could be used to either replace or supplement what workers do.[70] A report from Goldman Sachs[71] suggests that generative AI could expose up to 300 million full-time jobs around the globe, especially in administrative and legal fields, to automation. Yet worker job loss from automation has historically been offset by the creation of new jobs.

You can ask the students to consider whether actual and potential AI impacts on jobs would lead to greater efficiency and cost savings and the ethical questions around the issue.

Students may also mention known errors and inaccuracies of information and plagiarism/copyright infringement as ethical issues around AI. The first is a right-versus-wrong issue if it violates the policy that reputable news outlets have to correct such errors. The second is an example of right versus wrong because it violates the law.

Finally, bring the entire class back together and have a class discussion around the following questions:

- How would you feel if someone used your social media content to generate new AI-generated content without your permission and did not give you credit? What would you do? **Possible answer**: Contact the uploader of the AI-generated content and ask them to credit you conspicuously. If that is not possible or is unsuccessful, ask the social media platform to remove the AI-generated content.
- How does that possibility make you feel about your responsibility as a **consumer** of the content? What would you do? **Possible answer**: Pause and consider whether I should share AI-generated disinformation.
- How does that possibility make you feel about your responsibility as a **creator**? What should you do? **Possible answer**: Make sure to get permission for any content you use to produce new AI-generated content.

THE ETHICS OF AI USE IN THE CLASSROOM

As of this writing, teachers are facing decisions about to what extent and how to incorporate AI into the classroom and whether and to what extent students should use it in their homework. Though the focus of this book is on how to detect and evaluate disinformation and manipulated content such as AI, I briefly address the issue of classroom and homework use of AI here.

After students practice identifying various types of AI-generated content they increasingly find on social media and consider their roles as consumers and creators of such content, they will be in a better position to think about and discuss some of the ethical dilemmas around using AI in the classroom and for homework. **Teachers should partner with them in the discussion**.

Lesson Plan: Student-teacher group discussions on if and how they should use AI in the classroom

First, have a whole-class discussion. Give the students some "fodder" to provoke discussion around a variety of policies that education scholars and classroom teachers have proposed to govern AI use specifically by teachers and students.

In absence of a preexisting school policy specifically on the use of AI, there is probably an ethical dilemma. Teachers and students could work together to add a "Code of Conduct" as a suggested activity. This could be a care-based code of conduct—i.e., do unto others as you would have them do unto you—which would appeal to students' desire as creators not to have others "steal" their work. If there is a preexisting policy, the students and teachers face a right versus wrong, not an ethical, dilemma.

Include examples of positions along the spectrum of potential AI use by teachers and students. Examples could range from the strictest position to the most lenient:

- No use of AI at all.
- AI use is subject to preexisting yet vague classroom norms that teachers are required to follow.
- No policy. (As fodder to generate discussion on this position, teachers could have students read the approach (https://www.washingtonpost.com/opinions/2023/08/29/ai-student-policy-chatgpt-college/) that a University of Pennsylvania professor was taking as of August 2023.)
- No restrictions.

Now divide students into groups of three to four. Have each group discuss AI use for the teachers and students, drawing on the prior class discussion. Depending on how much "control" the teacher wants over the outcome, the teacher could have each group create a list of classroom norms they think should govern their teachers' and students' use of AI in the classroom and for outside assignments. Each group could brief the class and the teacher on their recommendations. The teacher and each student could vote, with the winning recommendations adopted.

Alternatively, teachers and students could work together to create a Code of Conduct.

▶ HARNESSING AI'S POWER AND REDUCING ITS THREAT: POLICY

Now that students have considered the ethical issues around the use of AI on social media and their use of AI to consume and create content inside and outside the classroom, they are in a better position to discuss and evaluate current and proposed government standards and best practices governing AI.

A discussion of international, regional, national (country-level), and US state policies is beyond the scope of this book. However, the general standards and best practices that the White House is proposing in an executive order as of this writing are broadly applicable to students around the world. I recommend teachers use it to initiate a discussion with students on the implications of general AI standards and best practices on society, including how they could affect future careers and jobs available to students.

President Joe Biden issued the executive order[72] on October 30, 2023, that, among other things, seeks to create "standards and best practices for detecting AI-generated content and authenticating official content." The order also seeks to safeguard "Americans' privacy" and "advance equity and civil rights."

Lesson Plan: Implications for Students of Executive Order on AI

This lesson requires all students to read and reflect on the key proposed provisions of the White House Executive Order on AI and determine how they will affect their use of AI.

Have students read the order:

Today, President Biden is issuing a landmark Executive Order to ensure that America leads the way in seizing the promise and managing the risks of artificial intelligence (AI). The Executive Order establishes new standards for AI safety and security, protects Americans' privacy, advances equity and civil rights, stands up for consumers and workers, promotes innovation and competition, advances American leadership around the world, and more.

A part of the Biden—Harris Administration's comprehensive strategy for responsible innovation, the Executive Order builds on previous actions the President has taken, including work that led to voluntary commitments from 15 leading companies to drive safe, secure, and trustworthy development of AI.

The Executive Order directs the following actions:

New Standards for AI Safety and Security

As AI's capabilities grow, so do its implications for Americans' safety and security. With this Executive Order, the President directs the most sweeping actions ever taken to protect Americans from the potential risks of AI systems:

- *Require that developers of the most powerful AI systems share their safety test results and other critical information with the US government. In accordance with the Defense Production Act, the Order will require that companies developing any foundation model that poses a serious risk to national security, national economic security, or national public health and safety must notify the federal government when training the model, and must share the results of all red—team safety tests. These measures will ensure AI systems are safe, secure, and trustworthy before companies make them public.*
- *Develop standards, tools, and tests to help ensure that AI systems are safe, secure, and trustworthy. The National Institute of Standards and Technology will set the rigorous standards for extensive red—team testing to ensure safety before public release. The Department of Homeland Security will apply those standards to critical infrastructure sectors and establish the AI Safety and Security Board. The Departments of Energy and Homeland Security will also address AI systems' threats to critical infrastructure, as well as chemical, biological, radiological, nuclear, and cybersecurity risks. Together, these are the most significant actions ever taken by any government to advance the field of AI safety.*
- *Protect against the risks of using AI to engineer dangerous biological materials by developing strong new standards for biological synthesis screening. Agencies that fund life—science projects will establish these standards as a condition of federal funding, creating powerful incentives to ensure appropriate screening and manage risks potentially made worse by AI.*
- *Protect Americans from AI—enabled fraud and deception by establishing standards and best practices for detecting AI-generated content and authenticating official content. The Department of Commerce will develop guidance for content authentication and watermarking to clearly label*

AI-generated content. Federal agencies will use these tools to make it easy for Americans to know that the communications they receive from their government are authentic—and set an example for the private sector and governments around the world.

- *Establish an advanced cybersecurity program to develop AI tools to find and fix vulnerabilities in critical software, building on the Biden—Harris Administration's ongoing AI Cyber Challenge. Together, these efforts will harness AI's potentially game—changing cyber capabilities to make software and networks more secure.*
- *Order the development of a National Security Memorandum that directs further actions on AI and security, to be developed by the National Security Council and White House Chief of Staff. This document will ensure that the United States military and intelligence community use AI safely, ethically, and effectively in their missions, and will direct actions to counter adversaries' military use of AI.*

Protecting Americans' Privacy

Without safeguards, AI can put Americans' privacy further at risk. AI not only makes it easier to extract, identify, *and exploit personal data, but it also heightens incentives to do so because companies use data to train AI systems. To better protect Americans' privacy, including from the risks posed by AI, the President calls on Congress to pass bipartisan data privacy legislation to protect all Americans, especially kids, and directs the following actions:*

- *Protect Americans' privacy by prioritizing federal support for accelerating the development and use of privacy-preserving techniques—including ones that use cutting—edge AI and that let AI systems be trained while preserving the privacy of the training data.*
- *Strengthen privacy—preserving research and technologies, such as cryptographic tools that preserve individuals' privacy, by funding a Research Coordination Network to advance rapid breakthroughs and development. The*

National Science Foundation will also work with this network to promote the adoption of leading—edge privacy-preserving technologies by federal agencies.

- *Evaluate how agencies collect and use commercially available information—including information they procure from data brokers—and strengthen privacy guidance for federal agencies to account for AI risks. This work will focus in particular on commercially available information containing personally identifiable data.*
- *Develop guidelines for federal agencies to evaluate the effectiveness of privacy-preserving techniques, including those used in AI systems. These guidelines will advance agency efforts to protect Americans' data.*

Advancing Equity and Civil Rights

Irresponsible uses of AI can lead to and deepen discrimination, bias, and other abuses in justice, healthcare, and housing. The Biden-Harris Administration has already taken action by publishing the Blueprint for an AI Bill of Rights (https://www.whitehouse.gov/ostp/ai-bill-of-rights/) and issuing an Executive Order directing agencies to combat algorithmic discrimination (https://www.whitehouse.gov/briefing-room/statements-releases/2023/02/16/fact-sheet-president-biden-signs-executive-order-to-strengthen-racial-equity-and-support-for-underserved-communities-across-the-federal-government/), while enforcing existing authorities to protect people's rights and safety. To ensure that AI advances equity and civil rights, the President directs the following additional actions:

- *Provide clear guidance to landlords, Federal benefits programs, and federal contractors to keep AI algorithms from being used to exacerbate discrimination.*
- *Address algorithmic discrimination through training, technical assistance, and coordination between the Department of Justice and Federal civil rights offices on best practices for investigating and prosecuting civil rights violations related to AI.*

- *Ensure fairness throughout the criminal justice system by developing best practices on the use of AI in sentencing, parole and probation, pretrial release and detention, risk assessments, surveillance, crime forecasting and predictive policing, and forensic analysis.*

Standing Up for Consumers, Patients, and Students

AI can bring real benefits to consumers—for example, by making products better, cheaper, and more widely available. But AI also raises the risk of injuring, misleading, or otherwise harming Americans. To protect consumers while ensuring that AI can make Americans better off, the President directs the following actions:

- *Advance the responsible use of AI in healthcare and the development of affordable and life—saving drugs. The Department of Health and Human Services will also establish a safety program to receive reports of—and act to remedy – harms or unsafe healthcare practices involving AI.*
- *Shape AI's potential to transform education by creating resources to support educators deploying AI-enabled educational tools, such as personalized tutoring in schools.*

Supporting Workers

AI is changing America's jobs and workplaces, offering both the promise of improved productivity but also the dangers of increased workplace surveillance, bias, and job displacement. To mitigate these risks, support workers' ability to bargain collectively, and invest in workforce training and development that is accessible to all, the President directs the following actions:

- *Develop principles and best practices to mitigate the harms and maximize the benefits of AI for workers by addressing job displacement; labor standards; workplace equity, health, and safety; and data collection. These principles and best practices will benefit workers by providing guidance to prevent employers from undercompensating*

*workers, evaluating job applications unfairly, or impinging
on workers' ability to organize.*
- *Produce a report on AI's potential labor—market impacts,
  and study and* identify *options for strengthening federal
  support for workers facing labor disruptions, including
  from AI.*

Promoting Innovation and Competition

*America already leads in AI innovation—more AI startups
raised first—time capital in the United States last year than in
the next seven countries combined. The Executive Order ensures
that we continue to lead the way in innovation and competition
through the following actions*:

- *Catalyze AI research across the United States through a
  pilot of the National AI Research Resource—a tool that
  will provide AI researchers and students access to key AI
  resources and data—and expanded grants for AI research
  in vital areas like healthcare and climate change.*
- *Promote a fair, open, and competitive AI ecosystem by providing small developers and entrepreneurs access to technical assistance and resources, helping small businesses
  commercialize AI breakthroughs, and encouraging the
  Federal Trade Commission to exercise its authorities.*
- *Use existing authorities to expand the ability of highly
  skilled immigrants and nonimmigrants with expertise in
  critical areas to study, stay, and work in the United States
  by modernizing and streamlining visa criteria, interviews,
  and reviews.*

Advancing American Leadership Abroad

*AI's challenges and opportunities are global. The Biden—Harris
Administration will continue working with other nations to support safe, secure, and trustworthy deployment and use of AI
worldwide. To that end, the President directs the following
actions*:

- *Expand bilateral, multilateral, and multistakeholder engagements to collaborate on AI. The State Department, in collaboration with the Commerce Department will lead an effort to establish robust international frameworks for harnessing AI's benefits and managing its risks and ensuring safety. In addition, this week, Vice President Harris will speak at the UK Summit on AI Safety, hosted by Prime Minister Rishi Sunak.*
- *Accelerate development and implementation of vital AI standards with international partners and in standards organizations, ensuring that the technology is safe, secure, trustworthy, and interoperable.*
- *Promote the safe, responsible, and rights-affirming development and deployment of AI abroad to solve global challenges, such as advancing sustainable development and mitigating dangers to critical infrastructure.*

Ensuring Responsible and Effective Government Use of AI

AI can help government deliver better results for the American people. It can expand agencies' capacity to regulate, govern, and disburse benefits, and it can cut costs and enhance the security of government systems. However, use of AI can pose risks, such as discrimination and unsafe decisions. To ensure the responsible government deployment of AI and modernize federal AI infrastructure, the President directs the following actions:

- *Issue guidance for agencies' use of AI, including clear standards to protect rights and safety, improve AI procurement, and strengthen AI deployment.*
- *Help agencies acquire specified AI products and services faster, more cheaply, and more effectively through more rapid and efficient contracting.*
- *Accelerate the rapid hiring of AI professionals as part of a government-wide AI talent surge led by the Office of Personnel Management, US Digital Service, US Digital Corps, and Presidential Innovation Fellowship. Agencies will provide AI training for employees at all levels in relevant fields.*

*As we advance this agenda at home, the Administration will work with allies and partners abroad on a **strong international framework** to govern the development and use of AI. The Administration has already consulted widely on AI governance frameworks over the past several months—engaging with Australia, Brazil, Canada, Chile, the European Union, France, Germany, India, Israel, Italy, Japan, Kenya, Mexico, the Netherlands, New Zealand, Nigeria, the Philippines, Singapore, South Korea, the UAE, and the UK. The actions taken today support and complement Japan's leadership of the G-7 Hiroshima Process, the UK Summit on AI Safety, India's leadership as Chair of the Global Partnership on AI, and ongoing discussions at the United Nations. The actions that President Biden directed today are vital steps forward in the US's approach on safe, secure, and trustworthy AI. More action will be required, and the Administration will continue to work with Congress to pursue bipartisan legislation to help America lead the way in responsible innovation.*

Ask the students the following:

- How would these measures, if fully implemented, affect your use of AI outside the classroom? How would they change the types of careers available in the future? How would they affect the job market and skills you would need to get a job?
- How would they affect your use of AI inside the classroom?

▶ AI POLICIES BY SOCIAL MEDIA PLATFORM

Meta (Facebook and Instagram)

Beginning in 2024, advertisers have to disclose whenever an advertisement on a "social issue, electoral, or political issue" contains a photorealistic image or video or realistic-sounding audio that was digitally created or altered to

- depict a real person as saying or doing something they did not say or do,
- depict a realistic-looking person who does not exist or a realistic-looking event that did not happen,

- alter footage of a real event that happened, or
- depict a realistic event that allegedly occurred but is not a true image, video, or audio recording of the event.[73]

Advertisers running these ads do not need to disclose when content is digitally created or altered in ways that are "inconsequential or immaterial" to the claim, assertion, or issue raised in the ad. These ways may include adjusting image size, cropping an image, color correction, or image sharpening, unless such changes are "consequential or material" to the claim, assertion, or issue raised in the ad.

Meta will add information on the ad when an advertiser discloses in the advertising flow that the content is digitally created or altered.

TikTok

In late September 2023, TikTok began launching a new tool[74] to help creators label their AI-generated content. It also indicated that it was beginning to test ways to label AI-generated content automatically. It said the tool would make it easier to comply with its policy on synthetic and manipulated media[75] that requires creators to label AI-generated content that contains realistic images, audio, or video. The platform said it would also begin testing an "AI-generated" label that it would at some point apply automatically to content that it determined was edited or created with AI.

YouTube

In a blog post in November 2023,[76] YouTube indicated that it planned to require creators on its platform to disclose whether they used AI to alter their content. It also planned to give users the option to request the removal of videos that contain AI or other altered content that "simulates an identifiable individual, including their face or voice, using our privacy request process." It said that not all content would be removed and that it would consider a variety of factors when evaluating requests. This could include whether the content is parody or satire, whether the person making the request is uniquely identifiable, or whether it features a public official or well-known individual, in which case the threshold could be higher. YouTube is implementing similar protections for music artists.

YouTube indicates these steps are particularly important for content that discusses "sensitive topics," such as elections, ongoing conflicts, public health crises, or public officials. Creators who consistently choose not to disclose this information may be subject to content removal, suspension from the YouTube Partner Program, or other penalties.

YouTube also indicated that it will inform viewers of altered or synthetic content with a new label in the description panel indicating that some of the content was altered or synthetic. For certain types of content about sensitive topics, it will apply a more conspicuous label to the video player.

X

As of this writing, X had not announced specific measures governing the use of AI on the platform.[77]

▶ LESSON PLAN: IMPLICATIONS FOR STUDENTS OF SOCIAL MEDIA PLATFORMS' AI POLICIES

Ask the students the following:

- How would these measures, if fully implemented, affect your use of AI outside the classroom? How would you feel as a consumer? As a creator?
- How would they affect your use of AI inside the classroom? How would you feel as a consumer? As a creator?
- What should X do, if anything, to govern AI use on the platform?

This lesson requires all students to recall the various policies of popular social media platforms, distinguish them from one another, and determine how they will affect their use of AI.

▶ NOTES

1 Opinion | 5 Questions about Artificial Intelligence, Answered— *The Washington Post*, December 18, 2023.

2 Todd C. Helmus, Artificial Intelligence, Deepfakes, and Disinformation: A Primer, July 2022, Rand Corporation.

3 Todd C. Helmus, Artificial Intelligence, Deepfakes, and Disinformation: A Primer, July 2022, Rand Corporation.

4 Todd C. Helmus, Artificial Intelligence, Deepfakes, and Disinformation: A Primer, July 2022, Rand Corporation.

5 Select Committee on Intelligence, Russian Active Measures Campaigns and Interference in the 2016 US Election, United States Senate, Volume 2, November 10, 2020, https://www.intelligence.senate.gov/sites/default/files/documents/Report_Volume2.pdf.

6 Katerina Sedova, Christine McNeill, Aurora Johnson, Aditi Joshi, and Ido Wulkan, "AI and the Future of Disinformation Campaigns" (Center for Security and Emerging Technology, December 2021). https://doi.org/10.51593/2021CA011.

7 Large Language Model Definition & Meaning – Merriam-Webster.

8 Glossary," CSET.

9 IBM Cloud Education, "What Is Natural Language Processing?," IBM, July 2, 2020, https://www.ibm.com/cloud/learn/natural-language-processing.

10 Todd C. Helmus, Artificial Intelligence, Deepfakes, and Disinformation: A Primer, July 2022, Rand Corporation.

11 About OpenAI, www.openai.com/about.

12 "Psychographics," Dictionary of Psychology, American Psychological Association, https://dictionary.apa.org/psychographics; "What Is Psychographics? Understanding the Tech That Threatens Elections" (CBInsights, 2020), https://www.cbinsights.com/research/what-is-psychographics/.

13 Sebastian Ruder, "NLP—Progress: Sentiment Analysis," GitHub, https://github.com/sebastianruder/NLPprogress/blob/master/english/sentiment_analysis.md; Zhilin Yang et al., "XLNet: Generalized Autoregressive Pretraining for Language Understanding," arXiv preprint arXiv:1906.08237 (2020), https://arxiv.org/pdf/1906.08237.pdf.

14 "*ORA—LITE Project," Center for Computational Analysis of Social and Organizational Systems, Carnegie Mellon University, http://www.casos.cs.cmu.edu/projects/ora/; Kathleen M. Carley, "NetMapper for Extracting Networks from Texts Has Been Released," Netanomics, January 4, 2017, https://netanomics.com/

netmapper-for-extracting-networks-from-texts-has-been-released/.

15 Yuxin Ding et al., "Predicting the Attributes of Social Network Users Using a Graph—Based Machine Learning Method," Computer Communications 73 (2016): Part A, https://doi.org/10.1016/j.comcom.2015.07.007.

16 Dilek Küçük and Fazli Can, "Stance Detection: A Survey," ACM Computing Surveys 53, no. 1 (May 2020): Article 12, https://doi.org/10.1145/3369026.

17 Text-to-Image Model—Wikipedia.

18 Hobantay Inc., Celebrity Voice Cloning, mobile app, undated. As of April 12, 2022: https://apps.apple.com/us/app/celebrity-voice-cloning/id1483201633.

19 Voloshchuk, Alexander, Voicer Famous AI Voice Changer, mobile app, Version 1.17.5, Apple App Store, undated. As of November 10, 2021: https://apps.apple.com/us/app/voicer-famous-ai-voice-changer/id1484480839.

20 Todd C. Helmus, Artificial Intelligence, Deepfakes, and Disinformation: A Primer, July 2022, Rand Corporation.

21 The Digital Engine: DALL-E Can Help Students Express Their Creativity.

22 Opinion | 5 Questions about Artificial Intelligence, Answered—*The Washington Post*, December 18, 2023.

23 Opinion | 5 Questions about Artificial Intelligence, Answered—*The Washington Post*, December 18, 2023.

24 Katerina Sedova, Christine McNeill, Aurora Johnson, Aditi Joshi, and Ido Wulkan, "AI and the Future of Disinformation Campaigns" (Center for Security and Emerging Technology, December 2021). https://doi.org/10.51593/2021CA011.

25 Carly Miller et al., "Sockpuppets Spin COVID Yarns: An Analysis of PRC—Attributed June 2020 Twitter Takedown," Stanford Internet Observatory, June 17, 2020, https://stanford.app.box.com/v/sio-twitter-prc-june-2020. For Iran's evolution: Ben Nimmo et al., "Iran's Broadcaster: Inauthentic Behavior" (Graphika, May 2020), https://publicassets.graphika.com/reports/graphika_report_irib_takedown.pdf.

26 Miriam Matthews, Katya Migacheva, and Ryan Andrew Brown, "Superspreaders of Malign and Subversive Information on COVID—19: Russian and Chinese Efforts Targeting the United States" (RAND Corporation, 2021), https://www.rand.org/content/dam/rand/pubs/research_reports/RRA100/RRA112-11/RAND_RRA112-11.pdf.

27 Samantha Bradshaw, Hannah Bailey, and Philip N. Howard, "Industrialized Disinformation: 2020 Global Inventory of Organized Social Media Manipulation" (Computational Propaganda Project, Oxford Internet Institute, University of Oxford, January 2021), https://demtech.oii.ox.ac.uk/wp-content/uploads/sites/12/2021/02/CyberTroop-Report20-Draft9.pdf.

28 OpenAI Beta, "OpenAI Technology, Just an HTTPS Call Away," OpenAI, https://beta.openai.com/; Sid Bharath (@Siddharth87), "I'm now playing around with writing ads on Google. I've fed the AI the top ad copy for 'sales engagement software'" and it generated two really useful outputs below the dotted line that I could run without any edits," Twitter, July 13, 2020, https://twitter.com/Siddharth87/status/1282823360825581568.

29 Todd C. Helmus, Artificial Intelligence, Deepfakes, and Disinformation: A Primer, July 2022, Rand Corporation.

30 Todd C. Helmus, Artificial Intelligence, Deepfakes, and Disinformation: A Primer, July 2022, Rand Corporation.

31 Todd C. Helmus, Artificial Intelligence, Deepfakes, and Disinformation: A Primer, July 2022, Rand Corporation.

32 "This X Does Not Exist," https://thisxdoesnotexist.com/.

33 Davey Alba, "Facebook Discovers Fakes That Show Evolution of Disinformation," The New York Times, December 20, 2019, https://www.nytimes.com/2019/12/20/business/facebook-ai-generated-profiles.html.

34 Todd C. Helmus, Artificial Intelligence, Deepfakes, and Disinformation: A Primer, July 2022, Rand Corporation.

35 Tim Hwang, "Deepfakes: A Grounded Threat Assessment" (Center for Security and Emerging Technology, July 2020), https://cset.georgetown.edu/publication/deepfakes-a-grounded-threat-assessment/; Christiano Lima, "The Technology 202: As Senators Zero in on Deepfakes, Some Experts Fear Their Focus Is Misplaced," The Washington Post, August 6, 2021.

36 Joan E. Solsman, "YouTube's AI Is the Puppet Master Over Most of What You Watch," CNET, January 10, 2018, https://www.cnet.com/tech/services-and-software/youtube-ces-2018-neal-mohan/; Aaron Smith, Skye Toor, and Patrick Van Kessel, "Many Turn to YouTube for Children's Content, News, How—To Lessons," Pew Research Center, November 7, 2018, https://www.pewresearch.org/internet/2018/11/07/many-turn-to-youtube-for-childrens-content-news-how-to-lessons/#an-analysis-of-random-walksthrough-the-youtube-recommendation-engine; Zeynep Tufekci, "YouTube, the Great Radicalizer," The New York

Times, March 10, 2018, https://www.nytimes.com/2018/03/10/opinion/sunday/youtube-politics-radical.html; Galen Stocking et al., "Many Americans Get News on YouTube, Where News Organizations and Independent Producers Thrive Side by Side," Pew Research Center, September 28, 2020, https://www.pewresearch.org/journalism/2020/09/28/many-americans-get-news-on-youtube-where-news-organizations-and-independent-producers-thrive-side-by-side/.

37 "The Next Great Misinformation Superspreader: How ChatGPT Could Spread Toxic Misinformation at Unprecedented Scale," The Next Great Misinformation Superspreader: How ChatGPT Could Spread Toxic Misinformation at Unprecedented Scale—NewsGuard (newsguardtech.com).

38 "How to Check for Writing Made With ChatGPT (AI Detection)," March 28, 2023, Gold Penguin, How to Check for Writing Made With ChatGPT (AI Detection) | Gold Penguin.

39 "Arts and Humanities: Was This Written by a Human or AI?," Prabha Kannan, Stanford University Human—Centered Artificial Intelligence, March 16, 2023, Was This Written by a Human or AI? ¯_(ツ)_/¯ (stanford.edu).

40 "Arts and Humanities: Was This Written by a Human or AI?," Prabha Kannan, Stanford University Human—Centered Artificial Intelligence, March 16, 2023, Was This Written by a Human or AI? ¯_(ツ)_/¯ (stanford.edu).

41 Helmus, Todd C., Artificial Intelligence, Deepfakes, and Disinformation: A Primer. Santa Monica, CA: RAND Corporation, 2022, https://www.rand.org/pubs/perspectives/PEA1043-1.html.

42 Reflections (starlinglab.org).

43 Four Corners Project—An Initiative to Increase Authorship and Credibility in Visual Media.

44 SynthID—Google DeepMind.

45 Identifying AI—Generated Images with SynthID—Google DeepMind.

46 How to Differentiate a Real Person from an AI-Generated Image (msn.com).

47 How to Differentiate a Real Person from an AI-Generated Image (msn.com).

48 Generative or Genuine? My 5 Surefire Ways to Spot an AI Generated Image | Digital Camera World.

49 "Cheap Fakes vs. Deepfakes," Poynter, Cheap Fakes vs. Deepfakes—Poynter.

50 "Project: Detect DeepFakes: How to Counteract Misinformation Created by AI," Matt Groh, Overview ‹ Detect DeepFakes: How to Counteract Misinformation Created by AI—MIT Media Lab.

51 "Fact Sheets: How to Spot Manipulated Videos, including Deepfakes and Shallowfakes," Verify This, Brandon Lewi and Kelly Jones, June 22, 2022, How to fact—check deepfake, shallowfake videos | verifythis.com.

52 "Cheap Fakes vs. Deepfakes," Poynter, Cheap Fakes vs. Deepfakes—Poynter.

53 "Project: Detect DeepFakes: How to Counteract Misinformation Created by AI," Matt Groh, Overview ‹ Detect DeepFakes: How to Counteract Misinformation Created by AI—MIT Media Lab.

54 Terry Moran, Terezin... Children of the Holocaust 007 | The Royal Mile, E... | Flickr.

55 #morganfreeman #rihanna #superbowl i was thinking it but kept it to my... | TikTok.

56 An Intermediate Greek—English Lexicon. New York, Harper & Brothers. 1889. p. 349.

57 Robert.Audi_The.Cambridge.Dictionary.of.Philosophy.pdf (archive.org), p. 284.

58 Kidder, Rushworth (2003). How Good People Make Tough Choices: Resolving the Dilemmas of Ethical Living. New York: HarperCollins. p. 55.

59 Kidder, Rushworth (2003). How Good People Make Tough Choices: Resolving the Dilemmas of Ethical Living. New York: HarperCollins. pp. ix–x.

60 Kidder, Rushworth (2003). How Good People Make Tough Choices: Resolving the Dilemmas of Ethical Living. New York: HarperCollins. pp. 5 and 29–32.

61 Kidder, Rushworth (2003). How Good People Make Tough Choices: Resolving the Dilemmas of Ethical Living. New York: HarperCollins. p. 110.

62 Josephson Institute of Ethics Releases Study on High School Character and Adult Conduct – Josephson Institute of Ethics: Training, Consulting, Keynote Speaking.

63 Paradox Underscores Continued Need for Training in Ethical Decision—Making, https://www.hr.com/en/articles/paradox-underscores-continued-need-for-training-in_frbgprmw.html?s=14Eq7hn3Yocj9sx0t

64 Kidder, Rushworth (2003). How Good People Make Tough Choices: Resolving the Dilemmas of Ethical Living. New York: HarperCollins. p. 55.

65 Kidder, Rushworth (2003). How Good People Make Tough Choices: Resolving the Dilemmas of Ethical Living. New York: HarperCollins. p. 13.

66 Opinion | 5 Questions about Artificial Intelligence, Answered—*The Washington Post*, December 18, 2023.

67 Italy's Privacy Watchdog Bans ChatGPT over Data Breach Concerns | Artificial intelligence (AI) | *The Guardian*.

68 Opinion | 5 Questions about Artificial Intelligence, Answered—*The Washington Post*, December 18, 2023.

69 The-Challenger-Report-May23.pdf (https://omscgcinc.wpengine powered.com/wp-content/uploads/2023/06/The-Challenger-Report-May23.pdf).

70 Which US Workers Are Exposed to AI in Their Jobs? | Pew Research Center.

71 Global Economics Analyst the Potentially Large Effects of Artificial Intelligence on Economic Growth (BriggsKodnani) (key4biz.it).

72 FACT SHEET: President Biden Issues Executive Order on Safe, Secure, and Trustworthy Artificial Intelligence | The White House.

73 Helping People Understand When AI is Used In Political or Social Issue Ads (facebook.com).

74 New Labels for Disclosing AI-Generated Content | TikTok Newsroom.

75 Community Guidelines | TikTok.

76 Our Approach to Responsible AI Innovation—YouTube Blog—YouTube Blog.

77 These Social Media Platforms, Except for One, Have Added AI Protections—TheStreet.

Chapter 14

Spot
Disinformation
Game

14

In this chapter, I present two games that give students an opportunity to apply what they have learned so far by trying to spot common signs of disinformation, including deceptive use of AI. The games are based on those from the international nonprofit European Association for Viewers Interests (EAVI). They do not include all possible signs, and it is important to emphasize to students that a lack of any of the signs does not necessarily mean that the media they are evaluating is free of disinformation.

To illustrate the power of disinformation and engage students, have students play the games using media trending in pop culture. Since this is a wrap-up lesson plan for Part I, I suggest you quiz them for a grade.

Preparation

- Provide each student with hard copies or direct them to electronic versions of the Social Media News Evaluation Game[1] and the Is It Misleading News? identification game[2] sheets (Figures 14.1 and 14.2).
- Provide electronic examples of several types of pop culture media. To prevent students from simply looking up a report from a reputable fact-checking organization such as Snopes, provide your own examples or use the ones

DOI: 10.4324/9781003471301-16

that follow that have not been officially fact-checked as of this writing. Provide only the media itself and any claim the media may be making.

- Require the students to play the game individually using the game sheets.
- After each student has tallied their individual scores, bring them together in groups of three to four to compare scores and discuss differences.
- Give students the chance to adjust their individual scores if they desire.
- Ask each student to send their completed scoresheets to you.
- Reveal and discuss the "school solution" for each media example and the total score on both scoresheets.
- After the lesson, review the two submitted scoresheets for each group, determine the grade for each group, and assign that grade to each student in the group.

SOCIAL MEDIA NEWS EVALUATION GAME			
Directions: Start with zero and subtract or add points accordingly as you evaluate your media for authenticity and credibility. Compare your results with others.			
headlines	—the headline make use of ALL CAPS or excessive punctuation!!!??? —1 —the headline promises secret information, surprise, happiness, outrage —2	Images	—There are stock images or there are no captions on the images —1 —the images have been doctored or relate to different events —2
URL	—the publication does not have its own domain name or uses a free blog platform —1 —the domain is counterfeit, e.g. bbc.com.co or the social media handle is not verified —2	ads	—the post or linked media are sponsored by a company or organization —1 —there are many intrusive banner or pop—up ads or the ads look questionable and cheap —2
author	—there are no examples of their work elsewhere online —1 —there is no identifiable author or the author is using a pseudonym —2	text	—there are many spelling or grammar errors, or the appearance looks unprofessional —1 —the text frequently uses emotional, hyperbolic, or sensationalized language —2
date	—there is no date on the post or linked media —2 —the information in the post or linked media is no longer relevant or current —2	search	—there are no links or the links point to questionable sources —2 —there are no examples of this story elsewhere online —2
interviews & opinions	—the content quotes sources and names them +2 —the interviewee is qualified to speak with authority on the topic or more than one opinion was represented in the post or linked media +3	graphs & statistics	—refers to a study which is named and linked, or you can find the study online +2 —represents accurately the results of a study, or graphs and statistics are clear and precise +3

Figure 14.1 Social Media News Evaluation Game.

Roy Whitehurst.

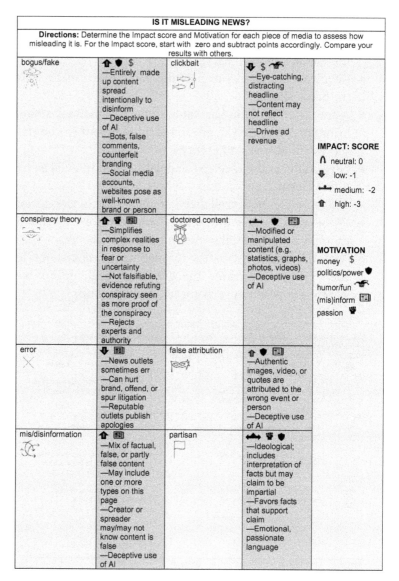

IS IT MISLEADING NEWS?				
Directions: Determine the Impact score and Motivation for each piece of media to assess how misleading it is. For the Impact score, start with zero and subtract points accordingly. Compare your results with others.				
bogus/fake	⬆ ● $ —Entirely made up content spread intentionally to disinform —Deceptive use of AI —Bots, false comments, counterfeit branding —Social media accounts, websites pose as well-known brand or person	clickbait	⬇ $ 🐎 —Eye-catching, distracting headline —Content may not reflect headline —Drives ad revenue	**IMPACT: SCORE** ∩ neutral: 0 ⬇ low: -1 ━ medium: -2 ⬆ high: -3
conspiracy theory	⬆ 👾 📱 —Simplifies complex realities in response to fear or uncertainty —Not falsifiable, evidence refuting conspiracy seen as more proof of the conspiracy —Rejects experts and authority	doctored content	━ ● 📱 —Modified or manipulated content (e.g. statistics, graphs, photos, videos) —Deceptive use of AI	**MOTIVATION** money $ politics/power ● humor/fun 🐎 (mis)inform 📱 passion 👾
error ✕	⬇ 📱 —News outlets sometimes err —Can hurt brand, offend, or spur litigation —Reputable outlets publish apologies	false attribution	⬆ ● 📱 —Authentic images, video, or quotes are attributed to the wrong event or person —Deceptive use of AI	
mis/disinformation	⬆ 📱 —Mix of factual, false, or partly false content —May include one or more types on this page —Creator or spreader may/may not know content is false —Deceptive use of AI	partisan	━ 👾 ● —Ideological; includes interpretation of facts but may claim to be impartial —Favors facts that support claim —Emotional, passionate language	

Figure 14.2 Is It Misleading News? Game.

Roy Whitehurst.

(Continued)

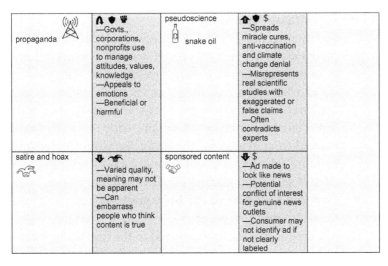

		pseudoscience	
propaganda	—Govts., corporations, nonprofits use to manage attitudes, values, knowledge —Appeals to emotions —Beneficial or harmful	snake oil	—Spreads miracle cures, anti-vaccination and climate change denial —Misrepresents real scientific studies with exaggerated or false claims —Often contradicts experts
satire and hoax	—Varied quality, meaning may not be apparent —Can embarrass people who think content is true	sponsored content	—Ad made to look like news —Potential conflict of interest for genuine news outlets —Consumer may not identify ad if not clearly labeled

Figure 14.2 (Continued)

EXAMPLES FOR STUDENT REVIEW

Image[3] (https://archive.ph/Vqgpl) QR Code 14.1

Claim: Buy weight-loss gummies because Oprah Winfrey says they work

Authenticity/credibility indicators: Headlines, images, ads, text (sensationalist language)

Misleading news types: Clickbait (headlines, images, and other media on the Internet that are intended to attract attention and encourage people to click on links to particular websites),[4] pseudoscience, disinformation, bogus, false attribution, doctored content

Analysis

➢ **Stop! Check for Biases and Mindset—the Author's and Your Own**.

The 'news article' is actually an ad presumably designed to appeal to readers who have a favorable view of Oprah Winfrey and want to lose weight. It will not catch the eye of readers who are apathetic about Winfrey, view her unfavorably, or have a keen eye for ads and are generally skeptical of them. The former group will be less likely to evaluate the ad dispassionately than the latter group.

> ➢ **Investigate the Source**
> For months in 2022 and 2023, ads and 'articles' on social media claimed celebrity Oprah Winfrey was selling and/or endorsing a line of weight-loss gummies. This particular 'article,' which is no longer active, took readers to what appeared to be the website of the respected news outlet *Time* but was actually a fake site with the URL "www.brownketoclub.us.com."[5] The fake site also included links to more fake pages about "Weight Loss Gummies" and "Keto Clean+ Gummies," all with changing URLs.

> ➢ **Can You Fact-Check the Information?** Yes

> ➢ **Find Trusted Coverage**
> No 'article' like the one pictured in the link had appeared on the *Time* website as of this writing.[6] The 'article' reads more like an ad than an actual news story. This is consistent for these kinds of ads, regardless of what the headline says.
>
> If you had clicked on any of the links within the article, it would have taken you to a page that used urgent and sensational language in an attempt to bait you into sharing your information.[7]
>
> While the pages aren't exactly the same, they use identical tactics. They promise a free bottle if you give them your information and try to pressure you into making a hasty decision by claiming that the time you have to get one is extremely limited. They also make sensational claims about the product's effectiveness and try to establish trust with apparent customer reviews. Neither page references Oprah, despite using her name in the ads.[8]

> ➢ **Trace Claims, Quotes, and Media to Their Original Context**
> For months, ads and fake articles on social media claimed Oprah Winfrey was selling or endorsing a line of weight-loss gummies. Oprah denied selling or endorsing weight-loss gummies in an October 2022 Instagram video.[9] The gummies were instead a version of a widespread scam that uses 'miracle' health and cosmetic products to persuade you to give your credit card information and then surprises you with the charges.[10]

➢ **Check for Deceptive Use of Artificial Intelligence**
None is apparent.
➢ **Summary**
The ad should not persuade your students. It has many signs of disinformation and uses clickbait, doctored content, false attribution, pseudoscience, and other tactics to try to persuade readers. The ad is typical of many that students will find in their social media feeds.

Tweet[11,12] (https://twitter.com/forbes/status/163566341022544 6912?s=46&t=zlhb4-8sfHMY27CILJgpAg) QR Code 14.2

The *Forbes* tweet links to a *Forbes* article[13] (https://pro. morningconsult.com/instant-intel/taylor-swift-fandom-demographic),[14] which has a link to the following chart (Figure 14.3):

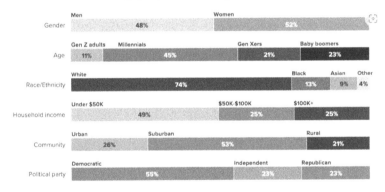

Figure 14.3 Demographic profile of avid Taylor Swift fans.

"The Taylor Swift Fandom Is White, Suburban and Leans Democratic," Ellyn Briggs & Saleah Blancaflor, Morning Consult, March 14, 2023, A Demographic Deep Dive Into the Taylor Swift Fandom (morningconsult.com).

Claim: More than half of US adults say they are Taylor Swift fans

Authenticity/credibility indicator: Graphs and statistics (chart)

Misleading news type: Misleading headline (headline of tweet does not accurately reflect the chart in linked report)

Analysis

- ➢ **Stop! Check for Biases—the Author's and Your Own**: Most viewers who are already Taylor Swift fans will have a bias toward believing the misleading tweet about Swift's fanbase. Many of the viewers who are ambivalent or critical of her will probably study the chart more, and some may pick up on the misleading tweet.
- ➢ **Investigate the Source**: The source is *Forbes*, which is a respected, standards-based news outlet.
- ➢ **Can You Fact-Check the Information?** Yes. We can fact-check the survey and the origins of the photo.
- ➢ **Find Trusted Coverage**
  The tweet (headline) is misleading because it suggests that a random group of adults was surveyed, and of those, more than half said they were Taylor Swift fans. The footnote of this chart, however, says that "self-identified avid Taylor Swift fans" were surveyed. In other words, the chart breaks down the demographics of those who are already avid fans, not random adults. So it's unclear which group was surveyed.
- ➢ **Trace Quotes and Media to Their Original Context**
  The tweet's photo of Taylor Swift first appeared on February 05, 2023, when Swift was attending the 65th Grammy Awards in Los Angeles, according to a reverse image search.
- ➢ **Check for Deceptive Use of Artificial Intelligence**: None is evident.
- ➢ **Summary**: The tweet should not persuade your students. Its title will probably mislead those who already have a positive view of Swift. However, the topic is relatively innocuous, so the spread of the misleading tweet will not do significant harm in terms of disinformation.

Infomercial[15,16] (https://web.archive.org/web/20221011142751/https:/lfyek.uk.com/zq11/) QR Code 14.3

Claim: The respected *Time* magazine reports that Reba McEntire endorses Nucentix KETO—GMY BHB GUMMIES because they "melt away" fat effortlessly, so you should try them too

Authenticity/credibility indicators: URL (fake), date (undated), search (questionable sources)

Misleading news types: Clickbait, sponsored content, false attribution, counterfeit (*Time* magazine website)

Analysis

➢ **Stop! Check for Biases and Mindset—the Author's and Your Own**.
   Viewers who view Reba favorably and struggle with weigh loss are the target of this 'infomercial.' These viewers may be duped by the official-looking *Time* magazine report, which supports Reba's endorsement by appearing to implicitly endorse the product. The infomercial also plays on viewers' fear of missing out with the language "Millions of Americans" in its headline.

➢ **Investigate the Source:** lfyek.uk.com, keto-gmygummies. com, Nucentix Nutrition[17]

➢ **Can You Fact-Check the Information?** Yes

➢ **Find Trusted Coverage**
   This is false advertising using a fake endorsement from celebrity Reba McEntire. There is no date on the website. It spoofs a website of a trusted news outlet—*Time*—and tries to get users to click on unknown and untraceable affiliate links. The spoofed *Time* magazine website even includes a "subscribe" button, fake article teasers in the sidebar, and *Time's* terms of use in small print at the bottom of the page.

   Clicking on any of these or on the hyperlinked text in the article that mentions "BioLyfe Keto" will take the user to the following website, try.keto-gmygummies. com[18] (https://web.archive.org/web/20221011144442/ https://try.keto-gmygummies.com/) QR Code 14.4

   The original version of this website is no longer available. Instead, it takes you to the website, https://keto-gmygummies. com/, which greets visitors with the statement, "Thanks for your interest in Keto BHB Gummies!" and asks them to call a toll-free phone number or send an email.

   The original website, try.keto-gmygummies.com, does not mention the "BioLyfe Keto" brand from the spoofed

Time website. The product offered is "Nucentix KETO-GMY BHB GUMMIES." The brand Nucentix is not written in text anywhere on the website, which makes it unsearchable.[19] The try.keto-gmygummies.com website has a prominent banner stating that the company has an A+ rating with the Better Business Bureau. The BBB website does not have records for a company called KETO-GMY BHB GUMMIES. While the company Nucentix Nutrition is not BBB accredited, it has an A+ rating, which the BBB notes is not calculated using customer reviews and "not a guarantee of a business's reliability or performance."[20]

As of October 11, 2022, the company's listing had seven customer reviews and six customer complaints. Many thought they were getting a reduced-price trial offer but were charged more than they expected without being able to review the charges at checkout.[21]

➤ **Trace Quotes and Media to Their Original Context**
The statements attributed to Reba McEntire are false. On August 3, 2022, the verified X account @reba published a thread that addressed in general terms some of the scams that have used her name. The only places where official Reba products are found are from her website, Dillard's, and Justin Boots. McEntire does not have a line of weight-loss products.[22]

This advertorial follows the same format as many other diet and CBD supplement products that use false attributions to celebrities as endorsements. In December 2021, fact-checkers debunked a similar claim for a CBD gummy pain relief product that was also not affiliated with Reba McEntire.[23]

➤ **Check for Deceptive Use of Artificial Intelligence**: No evidence.

➤ **Summary**: The ad should not persuade your students. It is a classic example of an ad that uses clickbait, false attribution, a counterfeit website, undated information, and questionable sources to appeal to viewers who view Reba favorably and struggle with weight loss. Viewers who lack the evaluation skills needed to realize the ad is misleading are particularly vulnerable.

Video[24] (https://www.tiktok.com/@mousetrapnews/video/7198 330131046305070) QR Code 14.5

Claim: Walt Disney Company is replacing Mickey Mouse as its mascot

Authenticity/credibility indicator: headline (all caps: "BREAKING!")

Misleading news type: Satire

Analysis

➢ **Stop! Check for Biases and Mindset—the Author's and Your Own**.

Nearly everyone has heard of Mickey Mouse, and most of those probably have a favorable impression of him, whether or not they have owned the character as a toy or visited a Disney theme park.

The title of the video will catch most viewers' attention. The video's creators and the site www.mousetrapnews.com are relying on viewers' **cognitive dissonance bias**, whereby we avoid having conflicting beliefs and attitudes because it makes us feel uncomfortable. They are also relying on viewers' **resistance bias**—the tendency to maintain our current judgments, even in the face of new evidence. We usually deal with these biases by rejecting or debunking the information that makes us feel uncomfortable, and we often fail to evaluate evidence dispassionately.

In this case, the video's creator and the website are hoping viewers will watch the video because they feel shocked, bewildered, and even skeptical that Disney would replace their beloved Mickey, and because they want to find out more so they can reject or debunk the video without dispassionately evaluating the evidence. Mousetrap News is not necessarily trying to hook viewers with a credible-sounding headline, as most standards-based news outlets do.

➢ **Investigate the Source**

The source, www.mousetrapnews.com, is a satirical news outlet. The site says so on its "About" page.[25] It also posts the statement "Real Disney News That Is 100%

Fake" on its social media pages. Students should discover this during their fact-check.

➤ **Can You Fact-Check the Information?** Yes, the video makes several claims that are presented as facts that we can check.

➤ **Find Trusted Coverage**
An Internet search uncovers reports from reputable fact-checking organizations that debunk the video. Walt Disney will not replace Mickey Mouse with Figment as its mascot. Snopes[26] indicates Mousetrap News is a satirical news site. If the story were true, it would be breaking news, and credible news outlets would have been reporting on it, which they were not.

   Although the video is satire and its overall claim is not true, we can still fact-check the specific subclaim that the copyright on Mickey Mouse will expire in 2024. The Snopes report[27] said the copyright to the animated version of Mickey in the 1928 cartoon Steamboat Willie expired on January 1, 2024, but that there is no sign Disney will stop using Mickey as a mascot, citing a statement from Disney.[28]

➤ **Trace Quotes and Media to Their Original Context**
Mousetrap News posted the video to social media on February 9, 2023. The full story appeared on its website by February 10. The copyright on the Steamboat Willie version of Mickey expired because the Copyright Act of 1976 and Copyright Term Extension Act of 1998 gave corporate copyright owners 95 years of protection for comic books, movies, television shows, and characters.[29] Of course, the image in the video of Walt Disney and Figment holding hands is fake. It is based on the actual *Partners* statue of Walt Disney and Mickey Mouse at Disneyland and Disney World.

➤ **Check for Deceptive Use of Artificial Intelligence**
None is evident.

➤ **Summary**: The video should not persuade your students. Mousetrap News uses a subject of almost universal appeal, Mickey Mouse, to get viewers to watch the video. As an outlet posting satirical news, the site's goal is to incite strong emotions in the reader so they will watch the video and visit the website, where they will see ads that help support the site financially. The TikTok video had more than 7.3 million views nearly a week after it was posted, suggesting that the video was effective.

▶ INSTAGRAM PHOTO

Instagram post[30] (https://www.instagram.com/p/B0M_iaJg-U4/?igshid=MDJmNzVkMjY%3D) QR Code 14.6

Claim: 2021 Scripps National Spelling Bee champion Zaila Avant-garde was in a commercial with NBA star Stephen Curry[31]

Authenticity/credibility indicator: Text (emotional, sensationalist language— "BIG," "insane," "grandmaster").

Misleading news type: Sponsored content. Zaila is wearing a stocking cap with the Under Armour logo.

Analysis

➤ **Stop! Check for Biases and Mindset—the Author's and Your Own**.
   Most students who are already familiar with Stephen Curry and/or Zaila Avant-garde will probably believe what the post is claiming without fact-checking. They will be biased toward believing the post. Some of those who are not familiar with them will fact-check the post with a more dispassionate approach.

➤ **Investigate the Source**
   The post appeared on the official Instagram account for Zaila. The blue checkmark means it is a verified account, which suggests that, among other things, it has no signs of being deceptive or misleading or engaging in manipulation. The account description indicates that Zaila Avant-garde is the 2021 Scripps National Spelling Bee champion. It has a balance of following and followers. This appears to be the account for the Zaila Avant-garde we're interested in.

➤ **Can You Fact-Check the Information?**
   We can fact-check the photo. The post's text is not checkable because its statements—including its emotional, sensationalist language—are judgments, not facts.

➤ **Find Trusted Coverage**
A reverse image search indicates the photo is authentic.

➤ **Trace Quotes and Media to Their Original Context**
A fact-check and Snopes[32] indicate the photo of Curry and Zaila was taken in 2018 during a photo shoot associated with Curry's commercial for athletic shoemaker Under Armour. The photo was taken no later than May 22.

➤ **Check for Deceptive Use of Artificial Intelligence**
None is evident.

➤ **Summary**
The post should persuade your students if they think the emotive language is reasonable. One could argue that the post does a good job of implicitly promoting the Under Armour shoes featured in the ad. Otherwise, the post will mostly resonate with readers who are already following Zaila.

Instagram Video (https://www.instagram.com/reel/Chh7Tb-lIpj/) QR Code 14.7

Claim: The (US) government has released photos of UFOs and aliens[33],[34]

Authenticity/credibility indicators: Headlines (promises secret information), images (doctored photos), search (photo or story not found elsewhere),

Misleading news types: Clickbait (title), conspiracy theory, bogus/fake photo and story

Analysis

➤ **Stop! Check for Biases and Mindset—the Author's and Your Own**.
The Instagram video (embedded photo collage and foreboding music) will catch the attention of most readers, even if the readers do not believe in UFOs or so-called aliens. Those predisposed to believe in them will find the post deeply engaging. The latter group is less likely to evaluate the information dispassionately, and many of them will come away believing more strongly in UFOs and aliens.

➤ **Investigate the Source**
The source of the photos is Douglas Pledger, a commercial and freelance designer who works in traditional and digital media. His work includes design, illustration, video, and writing. His artist watermark, douggy.com, appears on the photos.[35]

➤ **Can You Fact-Check the Information?** Yes

➤ **Find Other Sources**[36]
The video begins with some tense electronic music and a man shaking his head in a distressed way, as if he can't believe his eyes. The rest of the 53-second video shows a series of what appear to be old photographs. The images feature gory alien autopsies, UFO crash sites, and storage hangars. The black-and-white photos appear to be cracked and stained. Some have the mark of a paper clip, and they are stamped with official classified markings from what appears to be a government agency.

On closer inspection, the difficult-to-decipher stamps that frequently include the letters "US" are gibberish. They convey the importance and authority of official stamps but don't spell actual English words or stick to one alphabet. These are not real photos or stamps.

➤ **Trace Quotes and Media to Their Original Context**
The Instagram post appeared on August 21, 2022. The photos originally appeared in a TikTok video posted by @naturalismofyahweh2. The video has been removed as of this writing.

➤ **Check for Deceptive Use of Artificial Intelligence**
Lead Stories asked Pledger about the series titled "Classified UFO photos." He said the images appearing in the video were his and that he made them with an AI program.[37]

➤ **Summary**: The post should not persuade your students. It is a good example of the persuasive power of AI. But it will probably persuade some who already believe in the plausibility that UFOs and aliens exist.

Corrected error in a tweet (scroll down to item #4 on the linked page below):

Tweet[38]   (https://www.buzzfeednews.com/article/emerson
malone/news-corrections-errors-mistakes) QR Code 14.8

Claim: The *Los Angeles Times* corrects its misspelling of
Nicolas Cage's name and apologizes for the error

Authenticity/credibility indicators: None

Misleading news type: Error (corrected)

Analysis

➤ **Stop! Check for Biases and Mindset—the Author's
and Your Own**.
The tweet will engage readers who are familiar with
Nicolas Cage. Those who have a favorable view of him
will support the correction. Those who have an unfavorable view or are ambivalent about him will probably not
care one way or the other about the corrections. The former group will probably be more inclined to spot disinformation associated with the tweet.

➤ **Investigate the Source**
The Los Angeles Times

➤ **Can You Fact-Check the Information?** Yes

➤ **Find Trusted Coverage**
Nicolas Cage's name is easily found online. This is a
straightforward correction of the tweet.

➤ **Trace Quotes and Media to Their Original Context**
The original tweet misspelling Cage's first name was
posted on January 26, 2022, at 6 am on the *Los Angeles
Times's* website and X. By 10:42 am, the Times had corrected the error and apologized to Cage on X.

➤ **Check for Deceptive Use of Artificial Intelligence**
None is apparent.

➤ **Summary**: The prompt correction and apology illustrate
how reputable, respected media outlets preserve their
reputations. Your students should recognize and applaud
the *Los Angeles Times's* action.

▶ **TWEET WITH HYPERBOLIC, SENSATIONALIST
LANGUAGE:**

Tweet[39] (https://twitter.com/MarkOftheBEAS14/status/16350
01236704616448?s=20) QR Code 14.9

Note: Teachers of middle and high schoolers may need to explain what hyperbolic, sensationalist language is and the term 'market share' used in the tweet about the banking industry

Claim: Bank owners, investors, and customers operate in a risky industry. The recent problems in the banking industry indicate these owners, investors, and customers are going to lose all or much of their money

Authenticity/credibility indicator: Text (sensationalist, hyperbolic language)

Misleading news types: Clickbait (sensationalist, hyperbolic language), opinion

Analysis

➤ **Stop! Check for Biases and Mindset—the Author's and Your Own**.
   The use of sensationalist, hyperbolic language such as "swimming in a sea of sharks" and "bloodbath" will draw in many readers. Readers who follow financial news will be particularly interested. Many of these latter readers will be unable to detect disinformation.

➤ **Investigate the Source**
   X account @MarkOftheBEAS14 posted the tweet. A person behind the account says they "walk by faith! Esoteric knowledge! My heart is in the right place and my intentions are good." Its pinned tweet indicates the account "admires" the #unvaccinated "for withstanding the greatest pressure I have ever seen." Another tweet discusses how "global powers" and the US government were involved in the Nord Stream 2 gas pipeline sabotage, suggesting the individual is suspicious of US government activities. The account is unverified because it does not have a blue checkmark, which could mean there were recent changes to the profile photo, display name, or username or because X determined it posted misleading or deceptive information.

➤ **Can You Fact-Check the Information?** We cannot fact-check the tweet because it expresses an opinion without evidence.

➤ **Find Trusted Coverage**

Sensationalism is a type of media bias in which information is presented in a way that shocks or makes a deep impression. Often, it gives readers a false sense of conclusion that all prior reporting has led to this finale of a story.

Sensationalist language is often dramatic yet vague. It often involves hyperbole—at the expense of accuracy—or warping reality to mislead or provoke a strong reaction in the reader.

In recent years, some media outlets have been criticized for overusing the term 'breaking' or 'breaking news,' which historically was reserved for stories of deep impact or importance.

With this type of media bias, reporters often increase the readability of their pieces using vivid words and phrases. But many of these are heavy with implications that can't be objectively corroborated.

Here are some examples of sensationalist words and phrases media makers use that are designed to provoke strong emotions:

- Abuse
- Blast
- Bury
- Chaotic
- Desperate
- Destroy
- Embroiled in...
- Explosive
- Forcing
- Lashed out
- Onslaught
- Remarkable
- Rips
- Scathing
- Shocking
- Showdown
- Slams

- Torrent of tweets
- Warning
- Worry

➢ **Trace Quotes and Media to Their Original Context**
The tweet appears to be the original.

➢ **Check for Deceptive Use of Artificial Intelligence**
None is apparent.

➢ **Summary**: The tweet should not persuade your students. It expresses an opinion without supporting evidence, so we cannot fact-check it. Yet we can say that it uses sensationalist, hyperbolic language to catch our eye.

▶ TWEET WITH POSITIVE PROPAGANDA:

Tweet[40] (https://twitter.com/SJCS_MariettaGA/status/1130514814936244225?s=20) QR Code 14.10

Claim: SJCS students should vote for candidates for the 2019–2020 SJCS student council because the advertising is great and because it's their civic duty

Authenticity/credibility indicator: Ad

Misleading news type: (Positive) propaganda

Analysis

➢ **Stop! Check for Biases and Mindset—the Author's and Your Own**.
Most members of the target audience for this book, middle and high school students, will see this tweet as relevant because it reflects an event that occurs regularly at their school. The post also reflects students' civic responsibilities. However, many students will not be disposed to detect questionable sources, disinformation, or deceptive use of AI, if any, associated with the tweet.

➢ **Investigate the Source**
An Internet search indicates the source of the tweet is St. Joseph Catholic School, located in Marietta, Georgia. The school's X profile indicates the school is a "twice recognized, 2003 & 2016 National Blue Ribbon School

of Excellence, AdvancED accredited for students in" K–grade 8.

➤ **Can You Fact-Check the Information?** We could fact-check that the names on the posters are the actual names of the candidates. However, this is unnecessary because the information on the campaign posters is opinions from the candidates about their qualifications and future performance, and we cannot fact-check opinions.

➤ **Find Trusted Coverage**
Since we do not need to fact check, we do not need to find other sources.

➤ **Trace Media to Their Original Context**
Since we do not need to fact-check, there is no need to trace the tweet's information to its original context.

➤ **Check for Deceptive Use of Artificial Intelligence**
There are no signs of deceptive use of AI associated with the tweet.

➤ **Summary**
The tweet is an example of positive propaganda because it sends a message to students that voting is an important civic duty. Although we cannot fact-check the tweet, your students should have no reason to think there is disinformation or deceptive AI associated with it.

Instagram Video[41] (https://www.instagram.com/reel/Cb8YBkZAh9f/?igshid=MDJmNzVkMjY%3D) QR Code 14.11

Claim: Tom Cruise jumps over fellow actor Keegan-Michael Key[42]

Authenticity/credibility indicators: Search (leads to questionable source), image/video (created by AI)

Misleading news types: Bogus/fake, doctored content, parody

Analysis

➤ **Stop! Check for Biases and Mindset—the Author's and Your Own**.
The tweet will catch the eye of most viewers, whether they are Tom Cruise fans or not. The appearance of someone jumping over another draws the eye. Most Tom

Cruise fans who notice the "DeepTomCruise" label on the video will find the video deeply engaging. However, these fan viewers will be less likely to scrutinize the video to determine if it is authentic.

➢ **Investigate the Source**

The video was created by Tom Cruise impersonator Miles Fisher and video creator Chris Ume, according to the fact-check site Verify. As of this writing, Fisher had 220,000 followers on Instagram and had posted various Cruise videos on the account. He went viral on TikTok, where his @deeptomcruise account had amassed more than 3.4 million followers.[43]

➢ **Can You Fact-Check the Information?** Yes

➢ **Find Trusted Coverage**

The video appears to show Tom Cruise jumping over actor Keegan-Michael Key. Cruise seems to say, "Just want to jump in here and wish you luck! Congrats on the American Film Institute (AFI) Awards. Congrats on life. Congrats on the look. Work on the humor a little bit."[44]

The video with the tweet had nearly three million views as of this writing. Many viewers wondered how the 59-year-old *Top Gun* star was able to jump over the six-foot Key. Cruise is 5 feet 7 inches tall. One tweet said: "Tom Cruise is 59 doing sh** like this, HOW????"[45]

But the video is a deepfake. Miles Fisher has been creating Tom Cruise deepfake videos for years.[46]

➢ **Trace Quotes and Media to Their Original Context**

This video was recorded during the AFI Awards luncheon on March 11, 2022 in Beverly Hills, California. Verify tracked the clip back to accounts known for making deepfake videos with an actor digitally altered to look like Tom Cruise.[47]

Ume said he and Fisher created the video to educate viewers using parody. He said that they label every video with a watermark, "parody," and "DeepTomCruise." They also make Cruise's face look younger. They do this work to raise awareness about deepfakes in an engaging way.[48]

➤ **Check for Deceptive Use of Artificial Intelligence**
As noted earlier, Ume and Fisher used AI to create the deepfake video. Signs it is a deepfake include the following:

- **Source**. This deepfake was created by video creator Chris Ume and Cruise impersonator Miles Fisher, according to Verify. Ume creates deepfake videos and posts them to social media.[49]
- **Facial hair**. At the 4-second mark, the five o'clock shadow on the face of "Tom Cruise" has a linear look that sharply contrasts with the skin on his right cheek.
- **Lip movements**. "Tom's" lip movements look unnatural, particularly during the 4–6 minute segment.
- **Face**. At the 6-second mark, there is an odd, linear shadow from "Tom's" nose down to his mouth.

➤ **Summary**: The video should not persuade your students. Cruise did not perform that stunt. The video is a deepfake created by an impersonator and a video creator.[50]

▶ RECOMMENDED NEXT STEPS

In the second semester, have your students use their skills to spot disinformation in media supporting the social studies, civics, and ELA curriculum and the learning standards. Go to my website, medialiteracysleuth.com, for examples.

▶ NOTES

1 Beyond The Headlines—The Online News Verification Game—EAVI.
2 Infographic: Beyond Fake News – 10 Types of Misleading News – Seventeen Languages—EAVI.
3 Time (archive.ph).
4 CLICKBAIT | definition in the Cambridge English Dictionary.
5 Time (archive.ph).
6 "No, Oprah Isn't Selling or Endorsing Weight Loss Gummies," Emery Winter, Verifythis.com, March 10, 2023, Oprah Isn't Selling Weight Loss Gummies, or Any Kind of Gummy | verifythis.com.
7 "No, Oprah Isn't Selling or Endorsing Weight Loss Gummies," Emery Winter, Verifythis.com, March 10, 2023, Oprah Isn't Selling Weight Loss Gummies, or Any Kind of Gummy | verifythis.com.

 8 "No, Oprah Isn't Selling or Endorsing Weight Loss Gummies," Emery Winter, Verifythis.com, March 10, 2023, Oprah Isn't Selling Weight Loss Gummies, or Any Kind of Gummy | verifythis.com.

 9 Instagram, Oprah on Instagram: "Fraud alert! Please don't buy any weight loss gummies with my picture or name on them. There have been social media ads, emails, and fake...".

10 "No, Oprah Isn't Selling or Endorsing Weight Loss Gummies," Emery Winter, Verifythis.com, March 10, 2023, Oprah Isn't Selling Weight Loss Gummies, or Any Kind of Gummy | verifythis.com.

11 Tweet Citing A Taylor Swift Survey: *Forbes*: Free Download, Borrow, and Streaming: Internet Archive.

12 (20) *Forbes* on X: "More Than Half of US Adults Say They're Taylor Swift Fans, Survey Finds https://t.co/Flsvq1CHVY https://t.co/oUdrPlZn1d"/X (twitter.com).

13 More Than Half of US Adults Say They're Taylor Swift Fans, Survey Finds (forbes.com), Marisa Dellatto, March 14, 2023.

14 "The Taylor Swift Fandom Is White, Suburban and Leans Democratic," Ellyn Briggs & Saleah Blancaflor, Morning Consult, March 14, 2023, A Demographic Deep Dive Into the Taylor Swift Fandom (morningconsult.com).

15 Fact-Check: Fake Website Uses Fake Celebrity Interviews To Flog Keto Weight Loss Products | Lead Stories.

16 Fact-Check: Fake Website Uses Fake Celebrity Interviews to Flog Keto Weight Loss Products | Lead Stories (archive.org).

17 Fact-Check: Fake Website Uses Fake Celebrity Interviews to Flog Keto Weight Loss Products | Lead Stories (archive.org).

18 Keto—GMY BHB Gummies (archive.org).

19 Fact-Check: Fake Website Uses Fake Celebrity Interviews to Flog Keto Weight Loss Products | Lead Stories (archive.org).

20 Fact-Check: Fake Website Uses Fake Celebrity Interviews to Flog Keto Weight Loss Products | Lead Stories (archive.org).

21 Fact-Check: Fake Website Uses Fake Celebrity Interviews to Flog Keto Weight Loss Products | Lead Stories (archive.org).

22 Fact-Check: Fake Website Uses Fake Celebrity Interviews to Flog Keto Weight Loss Products | Lead Stories (archive.org).

23 Fact-Check: Fake Website Uses Fake Celebrity Interviews to Flog Keto Weight Loss Products | Lead Stories (archive.org).

24 https://www.tiktok.com/@mousetrapnews/video/7198330131046305070.

25 About (mousetrapnews.com).

26 "No, Mickey Mouse Isn't Being Replaced as Disney's Mascot," Izz Scott LaMagdeleine, Snopes, February 16, 2023, No, Mickey Mouse Isn't Being Replaced as Disney's Mascot | Snopes.com.

27 "No, Mickey Mouse Isn't Being Replaced as Disney's Mascot," Izz Scott LaMagdeleine, Snopes, February 16, 2023, No, Mickey Mouse Isn't Being Replaced as Disney's Mascot | Snopes.com.

28 "So Mickey Mouse Is About to Enter the Public Domain. Can Anyone Actually Make Money Off Him?," Erik Sherman, Observer, February 6, 2023, Mickey Mouse Enters Public Domain, But Profit Is Not Obvious. | Observer.

29 "So Mickey Mouse Is About to Enter the Public Domain. Can Anyone Actually Make Money Off Him?," Erik Sherman, Observer, February 6, 2023, Mickey Mouse Enters Public Domain, But Profit Is Not Obvious. | Observer.

30 Instagram, https://www.instagram.com/p/B0M_iaJg-U4/?igshid=MDJmNzVkMjY%3D.

31 "Was Zaila Avant-garde in a Steph Curry Commercial?," Dan Evon, Snopes, July 9, 2021, Was Zaila Avant—garde in a Steph Curry Commercial? | Snopes.com.

32 "Was Zaila Avant-garde in a Steph Curry Commercial?," Dan Evon, Snopes, July 9, 2021, Was Zaila Avant—garde in a Steph Curry Commercial? | Snopes.com.

33 Instagram: https://www.instagram.com/reel/Chh7Tb-lIpj/.

34 "Fact-Check: Government Did NOT Release Photos of UFOs And Aliens — Images Created With AI—Powered Tool," Sarah Thompson, Lead Stories, August 23, 2022, Fact check: Government Did NOT Release Photos Of UFOs And Aliens — Images Created With AI—Powered Tool | Lead Stories.

35 "Fact-Check: Government Did NOT Release Photos of UFOs And Aliens — Images Created With AI—Powered Tool," Sarah Thompson, Lead Stories, August 23, 2022, Fact check: Government Did NOT Release Photos Of UFOs And Aliens — Images Created With AI—Powered Tool | Lead Stories.

36 "Fact-Check: Government Did NOT Release Photos Of UFOs And Aliens — Images Created With AI—Powered Tool," Sarah Thompson, Lead Stories, August 23, 2022, Fact check: Government Did NOT Release Photos of UFOs And Aliens — Images Created With AI—Powered Tool | Lead Stories.

37 "Fact check: Government Did NOT Release Photos Of UFOs And Aliens — Images Created With AI—Powered Tool," Sarah Thompson, Lead Stories, August 23, 2022, Fact check: Government Did NOT Release Photos of UFOs And Aliens — Images Created With AI—Powered Tool | Lead Stories.

38 "18 Cringey and Hilarious Corrections From News Outlets In 2022," Emerson Malone, Buzz Feed News, December 16, 2022, The Best News Corrections In 2022 (buzzfeednews.com).

39 https://twitter.com/MarkOftheBEAS14/status/163500123670461 6448?s=20.

40 https://twitter.com/SJCS_MariettaGA/status/1130514814936244 225?s=20.

41 Instagram, Chris Ume on Instagram: "#deeptomcruise jumps are inhuman. @keeganmichaelkey @milesfisher".

42 "No, a video of Tom Cruise jumping over Keegan—Michael Key isn't real. It's a deepfake," Kelly Jones, Verify, April 28, 2022, Tom Cruise deepfake video goes viral | verifythis.com.

43 "No, a video of Tom Cruise jumping over Keegan—Michael Key isn't real. It's a deepfake," Kelly Jones, Verify, April 28, 2022, Tom Cruise deepfake video goes viral | verifythis.com.

44 "No, a video of Tom Cruise jumping over Keegan—Michael Key isn't real. It's a deepfake," Kelly Jones, Verify, April 28, 2022, Tom Cruise deepfake video goes viral | verifythis.com.

45 "No, a video of Tom Cruise jumping over Keegan—Michael Key isn't real. It's a deepfake," Kelly Jones, Verify, April 28, 2022, Tom Cruise deepfake video goes viral | verifythis.com.

46 "No, a video of Tom Cruise jumping over Keegan—Michael Key isn't real. It's a deepfake," Kelly Jones, Verify, April 28, 2022, Tom Cruise deepfake video goes viral | verifythis.com.

47 "No, a video of Tom Cruise jumping over Keegan—Michael Key isn't real. It's a deepfake," Kelly Jones, Verify, April 28, 2022, Tom Cruise deepfake video goes viral | verifythis.com.

48 "No, a video of Tom Cruise jumping over Keegan—Michael Key isn't real. It's a deepfake," Kelly Jones, Verify, April 28, 2022, Tom Cruise deepfake video goes viral | verifythis.com.

49 "No, a video of Tom Cruise jumping over Keegan—Michael Key isn't real. It's a deepfake," Kelly Jones, Verify, April 28, 2022, Tom Cruise deepfake video goes viral | verifythis.com.

50 "No, a video of Tom Cruise jumping over Keegan—Michael Key isn't real. It's a deepfake," Kelly Jones, Verify, April 28, 2022, Tom Cruise deepfake video goes viral | verifythis.com.

Go Deeper

Evaluate Text-Based Arguments

15

When I was training to be a CIA analyst, one thing that was drilled into me was learning to write well by making a logical argument that included a clear, precise premise supported by evidence from credible sources. Years later, when I became a CIA instructor, I taught these same core skills to new analysts. US diplomats, military officers, and other US government officials relied on CIA analysts to make clear, accurate assessments using strong arguments backed by logic. After all, CIA analysis—in addition to being timely, accurate, and relevant—is supposed to be objective. Good argumentation helps CIA analysts do that. By making solid analytic arguments, CIA analysts have earned the reputation of appealing to readers' ethos—their respect for the author.

Middle and high school students should expect the same from social media posts, so we're going to dig deeper and talk about arguments on social media in the context of formal logic. The tendency for social media users to debate each other—and even engage in hostile online confrontation—makes it critical for students to identify these arguments. But there is often little room for detailed argumentation because social media posts are typically brief, especially on sites like X, where brevity is enforced. Instead, many users—and many examples of

NLG-based AI, for that matter—make arguments that are simplistic, lack evidence, or are based on faulty reasoning.

In the context of formal logic, an **argument** is a set of explicit or implicit messages—often called statements—that can be true or false, but not both. One of the statements is meant to be the **conclusion** (or claim), and the remaining statements are meant to be the **premises**. The premises are supposed to offer **reasons** to believe or accept the conclusion. The reasons are often linked to premises with the word 'because.'[1,2]

▶ DEFINITIONS

Evidence: Data or information that support a premise.

Premise: What the claimant wants you to agree with—to persuade you of. The explicit or implicit statement that the claimant wants you to accept. The premise must be supported by other statements. Some sources call it a claim or proposition.

Reasoning: A stated or unstated link between the evidence and the premise. Often based on assumptions. Reasoning can be rational and persuasive or irrational and unpersuasive.

In the context of formal logic, an argument does not connote conflict or confrontation. Rather, it tries to persuade with evidence and reason and appeal to a student's logos more than their ethos or pathos.[3,4]

Strong arguments seek to persuade **for good reasons**. The logic of the argument is probably faulty if the reasons do not make sense as an answer to the hypothetical challenge or when they follow the word 'because.'[5,6] An argument may enhance its message with visual media—e.g., photos, videos, charts—but it cannot be an argument if it relies exclusively on them. (See the next chapter on visual-based arguments).

Many credible sources consider premises to be the evidence for an argument's conclusion. For example, the University of Massachusetts, in its Introduction to Philosophy course, says, "The premises of an argument are those statements or propositions in it that are intended to provide the support or evidence."[7]

Study.com says, "A premise is the foundational evidence of a conclusion."[8]

In this book, we expect premises in social media posts—including those created by NLG-based AI such as ChatGPT—to offer evidence for a conclusion, and we evaluate an argument in part on how well its premises do so. Many social media posts do not include explicit sources that would comprise a premise, and as a result, many are purely opinion and not arguments at all. It is up to the student to identify and evaluate the credibility of the sources as part of the fact-checking process.

Picking up where we left off in Chapter 2 about the relationship between information, news, entertainment, persuasion, and propaganda, let's discuss the relationship to arguments.

I depict the relationship this way (Figure 15.1):

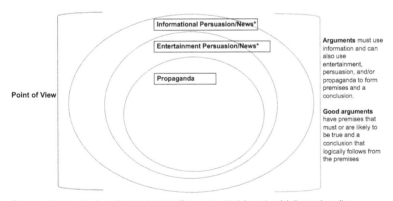

Tweens and teens view 'news' to include topics like sports, entertainment, celebrity gossip, culture, and science. They see 'the news' as the narrow, traditional agenda of politics and current affairs, according to a 2022 study by the Reuters Institute for the Study of Journalism.

Figure 15.1 Arguments and the social media ecosystem.[9]

Author's rendering of what he calls the "social media ecosystem."

▶ TEXT-BASED ARGUMENTS

Note: I base much of the information about text-based arguments on the work of Kevin DeLaplante, who maintains the Critical Thinker Academy (https://www.youtube.com/watch?v=B2WWeWUBhKU).[10]

For ease of analyzing a text-based argument, we can put it in what is called the **standard form**.

Here's a simple one:

1. All dogs wag their tails.
2. Lassie is a dog.
Therefore, Lassie wags her tail.

We put each premise on separate numbered lines, with the conclusion at the end, preceded with indicator words such as 'therefore,' 'so,' 'hence,' 'thus,' 'it follows that,' 'as a result,' and 'consequently.' Premises 1 and 2 are offered as reasons to accept the conclusion that Lassie wags her tail.[11]

In real life and on social media, spoken and written arguments are more informal. This one might appear as, "Does Lassie wag her tail? Of course, she's a dog, isn't she?"[12]

It's much easier to see the structure of the argument when it's written in standard form. In this informal version, you have to infer the conclusion, "Lassie wags her tail" from the question and the "of course" part. And you have to fill in a missing premise. What you're given is "Lassie is a dog," but the conclusion only follows if you assume that all or most dogs wag their tails. This is not a given; it's an assumption. So the argument only makes sense because you're filling in the background premise automatically.[13]

Not all sentences can function as premises for argumentative purposes. For example, questions don't count as premises since they don't assert anything that can be true or false. Neither can a command like, "Don't use your cell phone in class!" That's a request to do or not do something, and it makes no sense to ask if the action or the command is true or false.[14]

However, in the context of logic and argumentation, for a sentence to act as an argument's premise or a conclusion, there has to be a common understanding of what the sentence is stating. The person making the argument and the argument's target audience must share an understanding of the conditions in which the sentence is true from the conditions in which it is false. If the sentence is too vague given its context or its meaning is unclear, it cannot be an argument's premise because there is no mutual understanding.[15]

As social media consumers, students have two options: (1) ask the creator or poster for clarification, or (2) evaluate the argument as they interpret it and wait for clarification later. This book has students practice the latter approach.[16]

▶ WHAT IS A GOOD ARGUMENT?

In formal logic, the most basic definition of a good argument is pretty simple: It's an argument that gives us good reasons to believe the conclusion. Mere persuasion is not the ultimate goal of argumentation, at least as this term is used in philosophy and rhetoric.[17]

In the real world of social media, however, the ultimate goal of an argument is usually to persuade, for good or bad reasons. In other words, posts on social media are usually used to try to persuade students to believe something or act on something. Such posts often use fallacies and manipulative tactics to do so, especially when they are pure opinion with no supporting facts.[18] We'll cover those in later chapters.

An important goal of this book is to teach students how to spot bad arguments. Let's first look at ways text-based arguments can fail to be "good," and from these, we'll extract two essential conditions for a text-based argument to be "good."

Here's an argument:

1. All school buses are blue.
2. My school has school buses.
Therefore, my school's school buses are blue.[19]

It's a bad argument, as you may see. The problem is that the first premise is false—all school buses are not blue. But that's the only problem with this argument. The logic of this argument is good. When we say that the logic is good, we mean that the premises logically support or imply the conclusion or that the conclusion follows from the premises.[20]

In this case, it should be clear that if the premises of this argument were all true, then the conclusion would have to be true. If all school buses were blue, and if my school has school buses, then it would follow that my school's buses would have to be blue. The conclusion follows from the premises.[21]

Now let's look at another argument:

1. All teenagers are mammals.
2. Peter is a mammal.
Therefore, Peter is a teenager.[22]

Are all the premises true? Well, are all teenagers mammals? Credible evidence says they are. Is Peter a mammal? We have no reason to question the premise—the premise is demonstrably or at least plausibly true—so we can say that it is true. Therefore, in this argument, all the premises are true.[23]

Now how about the logic? This is where we have a problem. Just because all teenagers are mammals and Peter is a mammal, it does not mean that Peter has to be a teenager. Peter could be a dog or a cat or a mouse. Even if we grant that all the premises are true, those premises don't give us good reason to accept that conclusion.[24]

This argument has the opposite problem of the first one. The first argument has good logic but a false premise. In this argument, all the premises are true, but the logic is bad. They're both bad arguments but bad in different ways.[25]

An argument must satisfy a pair of conditions if it is going to be good:[26]

▶ THE TRUTH CONDITION

All premises must be true or plausible, based on evaluating them using SIFT.[27] To streamline the prose, from here on in this book, I will often simply refer to premises as being true, but what I really mean is that they are true or plausible.

▶ THE LOGIC CONDITION

If all the premises were true, then the conclusion must or would plausibly follow.[28]

When we're evaluating the logic of an argument, we don't care if the premises are actually true or false. The premises might all be false, but that's irrelevant to whether the logic is good or bad. What matters to the logic is only the hypothetical "if." If all the premises were true, would the conclusion follow?[29] When evaluating the logic of an argument, we assume all the premises are true, and we ask what follows from them.[30]

The Truth and Logic Conditions are the two necessary conditions for an argument to be good, but they may not be sufficient conditions. They do not by themselves guarantee that an argument is going to be good. An argument can satisfy both conditions but still fail to be good for other reasons.[31]

Take this argument, for example: "Why, of course Carlos loves to eat earthworms! He loves to eat spaghetti because he loves how it tastes, and he thinks spaghetti tastes like earthworms!"[32]

Putting it in standard form:

1) Carlos loves to eat spaghetti because he loves how it tastes.
2) Carlos thinks spaghetti tastes like earthworms.
Therefore, Carlos loves to eat earthworms.[33]

This argument satisfies the Logic and Truth Conditions, but it is likely to be false, nonetheless. Carlos may gag at the thought of eating earthworms, even if he thinks they taste like spaghetti. Even so, these are the two most important conditions to remember when you're doing argument analysis.

A good argument satisfies the Logic Condition in two ways. One is if the argument is **valid**. Another is if it is **strong**. "Validity" and "strength" are the logical 'glue' that binds premises and conclusions together.[34]

A valid argument has the following hypothetical or conditional property: If all its premises are true, its conclusion cannot be false.[35]

Here's a **valid** argument:

1. All cats play with dogs.
2. Felix is a cat.
Therefore, Felix plays with dogs.[36]

In this case, we know the first premise is false (not all cats play with dogs), but the argument is still valid because if all the premises were true, it would be logically impossible for the conclusion to be false. Validity is the strongest logical glue between an argument's premises and conclusion.[37]

Here's an invalid argument:

1. All cats play with dogs.
2. Felix plays with dogs.
Therefore, Felix is a cat.[38]

The first premise is the same, 'All cats play with dogs'. But the second premise is different. Instead of assuming that Felix is a cat, we're assuming that Felix plays with dogs.[39]

If these premises are both true, does it mean that Felix must be a cat? No, it does not follow. It would follow if we said that only cats play with dogs, but the first premise doesn't say that. All we can assume is that in this hypothetical world, all cats play with dogs, but that lots of other animals besides cats might also play with dogs, and Felix might be one of those other animals.[40]

Invalid arguments can still be good arguments. Even if they don't guarantee the conclusion, they can still give us good reasons to believe the conclusion, so they can still satisfy the Logic Condition.[41] In other words, they can be **strong** arguments.

Let's take a look at this argument:

1. About 90% of humans live in the northern hemisphere.
2. Aaliyah is human.
Therefore, Aaliyah lives in the northern hemisphere.[42]

In this case, the premises make it very likely—90% likely—that the conclusion is true. They don't guarantee that Aaliyah lives in the northern hemisphere, but they provide good reasons to think that she does.[43]

So this argument satisfies the Logic Condition because if all the premises are true, they give us good reason to believe the conclusion. This is what we call a **strong** argument, in contrast to a **weak** argument.[44]

The argument with a premise that Felix plays with dogs is logically **weak**. It does not satisfy the Logic Condition, so it can't be a good argument. But the second argument about Aaliyah is a logically **strong** argument. It satisfies the Logic Condition, so it can be a good argument.

Note what both arguments have in common. They're both logically **invalid** because neither has premises that, if true, guarantee the conclusion.[45]

Every argument is either valid or invalid. There are no 'degrees' of validity. Validity is like an electric light. It is either on or off, but not both.[46]

The distinction between strong and weak arguments, however, is a matter of degree. We might say an argument is very strong, or moderately strong, or moderately weak, or very weak. But we as social media consumers decide when the premises provide enough evidence or reason to accept the conclusion.[47]

Here are some simple argument forms that are recognized as valid, strong, or weak, respectively.

VALID

1. ALL A's are B's.
2. X is an A.
Therefore, X is a B.

Here is another example of a valid argument:

1. All teenagers are mammals.
2. Peter is a teenager.
Therefore, Peter is a mammal.[48]

STRONG

If we change 'all' to 'most' we get an invalid but strong argument:

1. Most A's are B's.
2. X is an A.
Therefore, X is a B.

Here's an example of this argument form:

1. Most teenagers are mammals.
2. Peter is a teenager.
Therefore, Peter is a mammal.[49]

The conclusion doesn't follow with certainty, but we're specifying that 'most' means 'enough to make it reasonable to accept the conclusion.'[50]

WEAK

If we switch from 'most' to 'some' we get a weak argument:

1. Some A's are B's.
2. X is an A.
Therefore, X is a B.[51]

Here's an example of this argument form:

1. Some teenagers are mammals.
2. Peter is a teenager.
Therefore, Peter is a mammal.[52]

"Some teenagers are mammals" does not even guarantee 50–50 odds. The way this term is commonly used in logic, "some" just means that at least one teenager is a mammal.[53]

Summary

These definitions summarize what we've learned so far about arguments:

VALID: If all the premises are true, the conclusion follows with certainty.[54]

STRONG: If all the premises are true, the conclusion follows with high probability.[55]

WEAK: If all the premises are true, the conclusion follows neither with certainty nor with high probability.[56]

Validity, strength, and weakness in the context of logic and argumentation describe the logical relationship between the premises and the conclusion. Both valid and strong arguments are good because they satisfy the Logic Condition. Weak arguments are considered bad because they do not satisfy the Logic Condition.[57]

Some social media posts meet the Logic Condition, but many do not meet the Truth Condition because their premises are unsourced claims, not explicit evidence.

Argument analysis is a two-stage process, and students should do it as part of their evaluation of the social media post. First, they should evaluate the logic. Then they should determine if the premises (the offered evidence) are true or plausible[58] as part of the fact-checking process.

▶ LESSON PLAN

Note: Teachers may need to explain the intricacies of the filibuster so students can understand this lesson.

This lesson requires all students to recall the definition of an argument and an argument's relationship to the social media ecosystem, how to determine if an argument exists, and what makes a good argument. They must also apply their skills to evaluate if a text makes an argument and if it is a good one. Higher achieving students must also evaluate an argument more deeply by asking questions like the following:

- Does the argument contain implicit or explicit messages? What are they?
- What is the creator or poster of the argument trying to achieve? Why?

In-Class Activity 1: Evaluate a Text-Based Argument
Direct students to the following text-based tweet (Figure 15.2) from Jeff Jacoby, *Boston Globe* columnist (or to a trending text-based tweet from pop culture). Divide students into groups of two to three and have each group evaluate the tweet using the skills they have learned, including applying SIFT and the steps to evaluate argumentation.

Jeff Jacoby
@Jeff_Jacoby

Thanks to the toxic partisanship and polarization that now dominate American politics, the modern #filibuster's impact has been to make the Senate more dysfunctional & less deliberative. But blowing it up would make Congress even worse.

My new column: bostonglobe.com/2022/01/09/opi...
1/9/22, 10:37 AM

Figure 15.2 Text-based tweet from Jeff Jacoby, **Boston Globe** columnist, from September 9, 2022.

https://twitter.com/Jeff_Jacoby/status/1480186904360501249?s=20

Stop! Check for Biases and Mindset—the Author's and Your Own.

Before doing anything else, pause and take a deep breath.

There is no link to open for more information, just a string of comments. Don't read them.

How do you feel when reading the tweet? How might your preexisting views of Congress affect your reaction? How might mindset and biases influence your reaction? Try to keep an open mind about the topic.

Investigate the source: This tweet is a snippet from an op-ed piece, meaning it expresses the opinion of the author. The tweet's author is *Boston Globe* columnist Jeff Jacoby. He says on his verified X account, @Jeff_Jacoby, that he is "an op-ed columnist at the Boston Globe, a purveyor of refreshing conservative cheer in the midst of a dusty liberal wilderness." So his tweet is not neutral.

This does not mean his tweet should be dismissed out of hand as simply representing an automatic rejection of the views of those who oppose his beliefs. But it does mean we need to keep an eye out for blind spots someone with strong beliefs can have.[59]

Similarly, we need to be careful not to accept or reject Jacoby's tweet automatically based on how much his political beliefs align with our own. As critical thinkers, we must control for our biases.[60] And we must dispassionately analyze his tweet to determine whether we should be persuaded by it.

▶ CHECK FOR AN ARGUMENT

Ask students to try to put the tweet into an argument's standard form to help them see if the tweet makes an argument at all.

After students respond, show the "school solution" for the standard form:

1. Toxic partisanship and polarization dominate American politics.
2. The filibuster, as used in this toxic environment today, has made the Senate more dysfunctional and less deliberative.

Therefore, getting rid of the filibuster would make Congress more dysfunctional and less deliberative.

Now ask the students if the tweet makes an argument and why or why not.

After students respond, tell them the "school solution" is that the tweet does not make an argument. The standard form here contains the necessary parts of an argument, including two statements and a conclusion, and the statements are not commands or questions.

However, the statements are too vague, given the context, to function as premises that an actual argument needs. We can't reasonably expect all relevant parties, including Jacoby and his intended audience (*Boston Globe* readers on X), to have a shared understanding of the meaning of the statements and whether they are true or false. The audience may have different interpretations of what "toxic partisanship," "polarization," "more dysfunctional," and "less deliberative" mean in this context.

▶ DETERMINE IF THE ARGUMENT SATISFIES THE LOGIC CONDITION

Ask the students to discuss in groups whether the tweet would satisfy the Logic Condition if it were an argument and contained sufficiently clear premises.

After they answer, give them the school solution that the tweet would not satisfy the Logic Condition because the conclusion would not logically follow from the statements if they were premises. If toxicity and polarization have used the filibuster to make the Senate more dysfunctional and less deliberative, this would not necessarily mean getting rid of the filibuster would make Congress more so.

▶ CAN YOU FACT-CHECK IT?

Ask the students to discuss in groups if they can fact-check the two statements.

After they answer, give them the school solution that we cannot fact-check them because they are vague and subject to interpretation. The fact-check results would probably vary from source to source.

Find Trusted Coverage
Not applicable.

Trace Claims, Quotes, and Media to Their Original Contexts
Students do not need to trace the statements to their original contexts because Jacoby is not claiming they are original.

Check for Deceptive Use of Artificial Intelligence
None is apparent.

Determine If the Argument Satisfies the Truth Condition
After they answer, give them the school solution that the tweet would not satisfy the Truth Condition because the statements are too vague to be premises.

Overall Evaluation of the Tweet

Jacoby could probably have made his statements clearer so
that he could make an argument with his tweet that would
pass the Logic and Truth Conditions. Twitter's restrictions on length make that task challenging, however.

Let's see if Jacoby does better in his linked full article on the
topic, which provides more details. Have students examine
it using the same evaluation steps they used for his tweet.

In-Class Activity 2: Evaluate the Article the Tweet Links To

Direct students to an electronic version of Jacoby's accompanying op-ed article (or provide a news article from pop
culture). Keep students in their three groups and have
each group evaluate the article using the skills they used
for the tweet, including applying SIFT and the steps to
check for an argument.

   Quote (Jeff Jacoby Op-Ed Article) (https://www.
bostonglobe.com/2022/01/09/opinion/filibuster-has-
been-bad-repealing-it-would-be-worse/?p1=StaffPage)[61]
QR Code 15.1

▶ STOP! CHECK FOR BIASES AND MINDSET—THE AUTHOR'S AND YOUR OWN

How do you feel when reading the article? What do you think of
the article's title? How does it make you feel? How might your
preexisting views of Congress affect your reaction? How might
your mindset and biases influence your thoughts?

   Take a deep breath. Try to keep an open mind about the topic.

Investigate the Source

We have already done this for the tweet, so no need to do so
again.

Check for an Argument

Ask the students to identify statements and the conclusion of a
potential argument and put them in standard form. Ask
them to identify any reasoning using words such as 'because.'

After students respond, display the 'school solution':

1. Before 1970, Senate rules made the filibuster—a parliamentary tactic meant to ensure debate and encourage compromise—powerful and rare because they permitted a senator or group of senators in the minority to forestall a vote on any measure by speaking on the Senate floor and refusing to sit down until the majority agrees to compromise.
2. Since 1970, however, the filibuster has made the Senate more dysfunctional and less deliberative because it has become an artificial gimmick to prevent debate.
3. Eliminating the filibuster would inevitably hand power to opponents of those who got rid of it because it has done so before.

Therefore, the filibuster ought to be reformed by returning to the rules before 1970 that would make it an effective way to prevent a majority from making sweeping controversial changes at the expense of a minority.

Ask: Does the article make an argument?

Ask: Are the statements too vague, given the context, to function as premises? Can we reasonably expect all relevant parties, including Jacoby and his intended audience (*Boston Globe* readers on X), to have a shared understanding of the meaning of the statements and whether they are true or false? Might the audience have different interpretations of what "more dysfunctional and less deliberative" in the second statement means in this context?

School solution: The article makes an argument because it has premises that are sufficiently clear and are not questions or commands. Premise 2 includes vague language, but the additional reasoning (indicated by the word "because") and details of the article give enough clarity that most readers will have a shared understanding of them.

Another premise not included above is tangential to the others and does not strengthen the argument: Democrats and Republicans have shown hypocrisy by seeking to eliminate the filibuster when they are in the majority and preserving it when they are in the minority. Students can make a strong case to omit this one from the argument.

▶ DETERMINE IF THE ARGUMENT SATISFIES THE LOGIC CONDITION

Ask the students to discuss in their groups whether the article satisfies the Logic Condition.

After they answer, give them the school solution. The article satisfies the Logic Condition because its premises, if true or plausible, make it "very likely" that the conclusion is true.

▶ CAN YOU FACT-CHECK IT?

Ask the students to discuss in their groups if they can fact-check the premises.

After they answer, give them the school solution:

Premise 1: We can fact-check it using evidence, hyperlinks in the article, and smart searching, allowing for potential differing interpretations of "powerful and rare."

Premise 2: We can fact-check it using evidence in the article, hyperlinks to more information, and smart searching, allowing for potential differing interpretations of "dysfunctional and less deliberative."

Premise 3: We can fact-check it using evidence in the article, hyperlinks to more information, and smart searching. However, in keeping with the informal nature of social media posts, we must interpret "inevitably" to mean "frequently" or "often."

▶ FIND TRUSTED COVERAGE

Assign each group one of the three premises and ask them to fact-check it. Have them report their findings to the class.

Then provide evidence students should have used to fact-check the premises:

Premise 1: Hyperlinks to *Mr. Smith Goes to Washington* YouTube clip, *Time* article on the number of filibusters in the 19th century.

Premise 2: Hyperlinks to the *Atlantic* article on rules change, Schumer's letter, *Boston Globe* article on Schumer, Manchin's statements in *WSJ* report, Sinema's statements in Axios and National Review reports, CNN report on Senate's bipartisan letter, Politico article on the number of Senate Democrats' filibusters under Trump, Hill report on Trump's tweet.

Premise 3: Hyperlinks to Obama's quote, NPR article on Obama's quote, Politico report on the Weich essay.

Ask each group: Do the premises pass the fact checks? Are they based on evidence from standards-based news outlets or fact-checking organizations that are members of the IFCN?

School Solution:

Premise 1 passes the fact-check. Stewart's filibuster in the movie is all over YouTube from different sources, and *Time*, the hyperlinked source for the history of the filibuster, is a credible news outlet.

Premise 2 passes the fact-check. The hyperlinked *Atlantic* article is behind a paywall, but the other hyperlinked sources[62,63] are credible and corroborate the premise.

Premise 3 passes the fact-check. The hyperlinked sources are all credible news outlets.

We can move on to the next step.

Trace Claims, Quotes, and Media to Their Original Contexts

We can trace the quotes and other evidence in the article to their original contexts using the hyperlinks and additional searching.

Check for Deceptive Use of Artificial Intelligence
None is apparent.

Determine If the Argument Satisfies the Truth Condition
Ask students how they can determine if the argument satisfies the Truth Condition.

They should answer that they can determine this by checking if each premise is true or plausible.

The First Premise Satisfies the Truth Condition
Ask students how many pieces of evidence support it. Answer: There are at least two pieces of evidence to support this straightforward, factual premise.

No additional reasoning is needed or provided; this is a straightforward fact-check.

The Second Premise Satisfies the Truth Condition
Ask students how many pieces of evidence there are to support it. Answer: There are nine pieces of evidence to support this straightforward, factual premise.

No additional reasoning is needed or provided; this is a straightforward fact-check.

The Third Premise Satisfies the Truth Condition
Ask students how many pieces of evidence there are to support it. Answer: There are three pieces of evidence to support this premise.

The author provides reasoning to support this premise, which is appropriate here. One might debate the meaning of "inevitably hand power to opponents," but citing a long history as a reason that eliminating the filibuster would "inevitably hand power to opponents of those who got rid of it, because it has done so before" provides the additional support this premise might need in the view of some readers.

Explain that this premise taps into our general aversion to contradictions. Arguments that can be shown to end in a contradiction are weak, but even outside of logic, we tend to feel and act negatively toward people who say one thing and do another, according to Jonathan Haber.[64]

Jacoby is arguing that Democrats might regret killing the filibuster because they will inevitably find themselves in the minority again at some point in the future.[65]

Rhetorically, Jacoby taps a common tactic of **quoting a figure beloved by the opposition** (in this case, former US president Barack Obama) to make the writer's point for him, according to Haber: Eliminating the filibuster carries a big downside to whatever party gets rid of it as a temporary means to achieve a short-term goal.[66]

▶ OVERALL EVALUATION OF THE ARTICLE

Jacoby makes an argument. However, effective persuasion techniques are also necessary to make the argument compelling. Haber says that two things could have made Jacoby's piece more persuasive:

- Letting examples illustrate what Jacoby perceives as Democratic hypocrisy rather than actually using the word himself. Calling someone a hypocrite tends to make the accuser look mean-spirited and shrill, limiting the effectiveness of an argument. It might be considered a **manipulation tactic** (see Chapter 18). It is better to let your opponent's words and deeds speak for themselves rather than telling readers how to interpret them.[67]
- Presenting a future-oriented argument at the end of your presentation, allowing you to present yourself as offering a future-oriented solution to a dilemma you previously described.[68]

▶ WRAP UP

Ask students some or all the following questions about what they discovered when evaluating the tweet and then the entire article:

- How did your emotions influence your reaction to the tweet? Did they change after you read the full article, and if so, how?

- How did your biases and mindset influence your reaction to the tweet? Did they change after you read the full article, and if so, how?
- Could you fact-check the tweet? How about the full article?
- What was different about fact-checking the tweet versus the full article?
- Did you find disinformation in the tweet? In the article? If just in the article, why do you think that was the case?
- Could you trace claims, quotes, and media to their original contexts in the tweet? If so, how hard was it? Compare your experience with tracing them for the full article.
- Does the tweet make an argument? If so, how good is the argument? What makes it good or bad?
- What does your experience tell you about getting your news only from a tweet or other snippet of information in a social media post?

▶ NOTES

1 Structure of an Argument—Critical Thinking | Intelligent Speculation.
2 What Is a Good Argument? | The Critical Thinker Academy, Kevin Delaplante.
3 What Is a Good Argument? | The Critical Thinker Academy, Kevin Delaplante.
4 Structure of an Argument—Critical Thinking | Intelligent Speculation.
5 What Is a Good Argument? | The Critical Thinker Academy, Kevin Delaplante.
6 Structure of an Argument—Critical Thinking | Intelligent Speculation.
7 "Introduction to Logic," University of Massachusetts, Introduction to Logic (umass.edu), Fall 2001.
8 "What Is a Premise?: Overview, Identification and Usage," Premise Overview, Identification & Usage | What Is a Premise?—Video & Lesson Transcript | Study.com.
9 Author's rendering of what he calls the "social media ecosystem".
10 What Is a Good Argument? | The Critical Thinker Academy, Kevin Delaplante.

11 What Is a Good Argument? | The Critical Thinker Academy, Kevin Delaplante.

12 What Is a Good Argument? | The Critical Thinker Academy, Kevin Delaplante.

13 What Is a Good Argument? | The Critical Thinker Academy, Kevin Delaplante.

14 What Is a Good Argument? | The Critical Thinker Academy, Kevin Delaplante.

15 What Is a Good Argument? | The Critical Thinker Academy, Kevin Delaplante.

16 What Is a Good Argument? | The Critical Thinker Academy, Kevin Delaplante.

17 What Is a Good Argument? | The Critical Thinker Academy, Kevin Delaplante.

18 What Is a Good Argument? | The Critical Thinker Academy, Kevin Delaplante.

19 What Is a Good Argument? | The Critical Thinker Academy, Kevin Delaplante.

20 What Is a Good Argument? | The Critical Thinker Academy, Kevin Delaplante.

21 What Is a Good Argument? | The Critical Thinker Academy, Kevin Delaplante.

22 What Is a Good Argument? | The Critical Thinker Academy, Kevin Delaplante.

23 What Is a Good Argument? | The Critical Thinker Academy, Kevin Delaplante.

24 What Is a Good Argument? | The Critical Thinker Academy, Kevin Delaplante.

25 What Is a Good Argument? | The Critical Thinker Academy, Kevin Delaplante.

26 What Is a Good Argument? | The Critical Thinker Academy, Kevin Delaplante.

27 What Is a Good Argument? | The Critical Thinker Academy, Kevin Delaplante.

28 What Is a Good Argument? | The Critical Thinker Academy, Kevin Delaplante.

29 What Is a Good Argument? | The Critical Thinker Academy, Kevin Delaplante.

30 What Is a Good Argument? | The Critical Thinker Academy, Kevin Delaplante.

31 What Is a Good Argument? | The Critical Thinker Academy, Kevin Delaplante.

32 What Is a Good Argument? | The Critical Thinker Academy, Kevin Delaplante.

33 What Is a Good Argument? | The Critical Thinker Academy, Kevin Delaplante.

34 What Is a Good Argument? | The Critical Thinker Academy, Kevin Delaplante.

35 What Is a Good Argument? | The Critical Thinker Academy, Kevin Delaplante.

36 What Is a Good Argument? | The Critical Thinker Academy, Kevin Delaplante.

37 What Is a Good Argument? | The Critical Thinker Academy, Kevin Delaplante.

38 What Is a Good Argument? | The Critical Thinker Academy, Kevin Delaplante.

39 What Is a Good Argument? | The Critical Thinker Academy, Kevin Delaplante.

40 What Is a Good Argument? | The Critical Thinker Academy, Kevin Delaplante.

41 What Is a Good Argument? | The Critical Thinker Academy, Kevin Delaplante.

42 What Is a Good Argument? | The Critical Thinker Academy, Kevin Delaplante.

43 What Is a Good Argument? | The Critical Thinker Academy, Kevin Delaplante.

44 What Is a Good Argument? | The Critical Thinker Academy, Kevin Delaplante.

45 What Is a Good Argument? | The Critical Thinker Academy, Kevin Delaplante.

46 What Is a Good Argument? | The Critical Thinker Academy, Kevin Delaplante.

47 What Is a Good Argument? | The Critical Thinker Academy, Kevin Delaplante.

48 What Is a Good Argument? | The Critical Thinker Academy, Kevin Delaplante.

49 What Is a Good Argument? | The Critical Thinker Academy, Kevin Delaplante.

50 What Is a Good Argument? | The Critical Thinker Academy, Kevin Delaplante.

51 What Is a Good Argument? | The Critical Thinker Academy, Kevin Delaplante.

52 What Is a Good Argument? | The Critical Thinker Academy, Kevin Delaplante.

53 What Is a Good Argument? | The Critical Thinker Academy, Kevin Delaplante.

54 What Is a Good Argument? | The Critical Thinker Academy, Kevin Delaplante.

55 What Is a Good Argument? | The Critical Thinker Academy, Kevin Delaplante.

56 What Is a Good Argument? | The Critical Thinker Academy, Kevin Delaplante.

57 What Is a Good Argument? | The Critical Thinker Academy, Kevin Delaplante.

58 What Is a Good Argument? | The Critical Thinker Academy, Kevin Delaplante.

59 "Arguing Over the Filibuster," Jonathan Haber, LogicCheck, January 14, 2022.

60 "Arguing Over the Filibuster," Jonathan Haber, LogicCheck, January 14, 2022.

61 The filibuster has been bad, but repealing it would be worse—*The Boston Globe*, Jeff Jacoby Globe Columnist, Updated January 9, 2022.

62 "Filibustering in the Modern Senate," Scott Bomboy, Filibustering in the Modern Senate | Constitution Center, December 9, 2022.

63 "No, senators do not have to talk to filibuster a bill," Emery Winter, January 21, 2022, Silent filibuster: Senators don't have to talk to filibuster | verifythis.com.

64 "Arguing Over the Filibuster," Jonathan Haber, LogicCheck, January 14, 2022.

65 "Arguing Over the Filibuster," Jonathan Haber, LogicCheck, January 14, 2022.

66 "Arguing Over the Filibuster," Jonathan Haber, LogicCheck, January 14, 2022.

67 "Arguing Over the Filibuster," Jonathan Haber, LogicCheck, January 14, 2022.

68 "Arguing Over the Filibuster," Jonathan Haber, LogicCheck, January 14, 2022.

Evaluate Visual-Based Arguments

16

Adding visual elements to a persuasive text-based argument can often strengthen its persuasive effect. In my career as a CIA analyst, I routinely used satellite images in my analytic reports and briefings to policymakers because, at a minimum, the images helped them understand the analytic insights—the argument—I was conveying.

Sometimes the images were the only media that would truly drive my argument home. My analysis and briefings on the devastation caused by the 2004 earthquake and tsunami in the Indian Ocean region depended on my making a persuasive visual-based argument that the destruction was widespread and unprecedented.

But there is debate over whether visuals by themselves can make good arguments, or arguments at all. Kneupper (1978) claims that nonverbal elements such as pictures, etc., can be used *in* an argument, but they cannot function *as* an argument unless "linguistically translated."[1] Albert Cairo says charts *are* visual arguments but that they are easy to misunderstand if we do not pay close attention.[2] On the other hand, Jonathan Haber questions whether we should consider memes as capable of making valid, strong arguments. Should we instead dismiss them as childlike, given how they lack the sophistication of

DOI: 10.4324/9781003471301-19

other forms of visual argumentation, much less verbal ones like campaign speeches and editorials?[3] And what about text-to-image media that AI tools such as DALL-E produce? Can they make arguments?

This book takes the position that visuals such as photos and videos—including those created by AI—as well as charts, memes, etc., can provide key *support for* an argument, but they must have text or spoken words to form *an* argument. We will call arguments that rely heavily on visual media visual-based arguments.

There are two main types of visuals: quantitative visuals and qualitative visuals. Quantitative visuals seek to present data graphically and clearly so the audience can see the data spatially. Quantitative visuals seek to persuade the reader by appealing to the reader's logos and using reasoning. For example, sometimes it is easier to understand the disparity in certain statistics if you can see the disparity graphically. Bar graphs, pie charts, Venn diagrams, histograms, and line graphs are common ways to present quantitative data spatially.[4]

On the other hand, qualitative visuals such as photos, videos, and memes appeal to our pathos. Such images often try to tell a story, which can be more persuasive than hearing or reading about the information. For example, one image of a middle school student crying after a school shooting would probably have a greater emotional impact than pages of text describing the shooting or a chart with statistics about it.[5]

First, let's review. The most basic definition of a good argument is one that gives us good reasons to believe the conclusion. On social media, the ultimate goal of an argument is usually to persuade, for good or bad reasons.

A good argument, even one on social media, must satisfy the Logic Condition—its if all its premises are true or plausible, its conclusion must follow with certainty or high probability—and the Truth Condition—all its premises must be true or plausible. Recall that a good argument satisfies the Logic Condition if it is valid or strong. A valid argument has a conclusion that cannot be false if all its premises are true or plausible. A strong argument gives us good reason to believe the conclusion if all the premises are true or plausible.

▶ LESSON PLAN

This lesson requires all students to recall the definition of an argument and an argument's relationship to the social media ecosystem, determine if an argument exists, and what makes a good argument. They must apply their skills to evaluate if a visual with text makes an argument and if it is a good one. Higher achieving students must also evaluate a visual-based argument more deeply by asking questions like the following:

- What is the creator or poster of the argument trying to achieve?

▶ IN-CLASS ACTIVITY 1: EVALUATE A PHOTO

First, we will examine a photo to see how the photo itself fails to make an argument. Second, we will look at an associated tweet to see if it makes an argument without the photo. Third, we will evaluate whether the same tweet makes an argument with the support of the photo, and if it does, if it is a good argument and why or why not. Finally, we will look at two memes to see if we can evaluate them for an argument.

Divide students into groups of three to four.

Display the Photo Below with No Caption. Ask Students to Evaluate It

Photo (https://www.gettyimages.com/detail/news-photo/united-states-border-patrol-agent-on-horseback-tries-to-news-photo/1235366682)[6] QR Code 16.1

Stop! Check for Biases and Mindset—the Author's and Your Own

Each student should say to themselves:

- What do I think is happening in this photo? What evidence do I see that leads me to that conclusion?
- How do I feel when viewing the photo? What strong reactions, if any, do I feel?

- How might confirmation bias and other biases influence my thoughts?
- What mindset do I bring? Fixed or flexible?
- I am going to take a deep breath.
- I am going to try to keep an open mind about the topic.

Investigate the Source

The photo appears on the account of Waikinya J. S. Clanton @WJSClanton, who joined X in January 2012, had about 2,000 followers at the time of this writing, and describes herself as "fighting hate across the South." She says on her X account and linked personal website that she is the "MS Director at the Southern Poverty Law Center." This indicates her potential argument is probably not neutral but draws from that belief system. We need to watch for blind spots that someone with strong beliefs can express. We should also be careful not to accept or reject Clanton's post automatically based on how much her political beliefs align with ours. Rather, we need to control our biases as we engage with her post.

There are no signs that Ms. Clanton's X account is an automated (bot) account. It has detailed personal information, an unambiguous profile photo, no excessively divisive words or hashtags, and a realistic volume and pattern of tweets and retweets and of followers and following.

But who took the photo? A reverse image search indicates that Paul Ratje/AFP via Getty Images did.

Check for an Argument

Ask each group to identify any implicit statements and implicit conclusions, if any, and put them in standard form.

After students respond, show the school solution's implicit statements and implicit conclusion. The statements and conclusion students identify should resemble the following:

1. The scene is a dry, gentle hill.
2. A lighter-skinned man in a cowboy hat is high up on a horse. He is wearing a vest with small holsters for knives or other tools.

3. The horse has the number '5' and the white outline of a star on its flank.
4. The man on the horse has an intense expression on his face.
5. Two darker-skinned men are standing on the ground near him.
6. The lighter-skinned man is grabbing one of the darker-skinned men by the shirt and is holding a cord or strap near the man's back.
7. The man he is grabbing, whose face is visible, is grimacing or smiling.
8. The other darker-skinned man is facing away from the camera and appears to be running away from the lighter-skinned man.
9. The two darker-skinned men are carrying what looks like food and drinks in plastic bags for more than two people.

Hence, the lighter-skinned man is in a law enforcement role and is trying to keep the two darker-skinned men from traveling and doing something that he and/or perhaps an organization he represents consider wrong or illegal.

Ask the class what evidence supports the statements. Students should say that the photo itself provides the evidence for the nine statements.

Ask the students if the photo alone can make an argument and why or why not.

Students should answer that a visual such as a photo implies too many statements with too many interpretations and too many different conclusions to make an argument.

We can skip the steps "Determine If the Argument Satisfies the Logic Condition" and "Determine if the Argument Satisfies the Truth Condition."

Can You Fact-Check the Photo?

We can fact-check the photo by determining who took it and when, where, and why the photographer took it.

Find Trusted Coverage

Using reverse image search, students should find that the photo is one of numerous images of US Border Patrol agents riding horses, shouting, and, according to many viewers, becoming "aggressive" toward Haitian migrants that appeared on social media in the fall of 2021. Many commentators and social media posters who saw the photo said or implied that the agents were whipping the migrants.

Trace Photo to Its Original Context

Ratje took the photo on September 19, 2021. A paraphrase of its caption is that the photo shows a Border Patrol agent on a horse trying to stop a Haitian migrant from going into an encampment next to the Rio Grande River near the Acuna Del Rio International Bridge in Del Rio, Texas.[7]

Check for Deceptive Use of Artificial Intelligence

None is evident.

Overall Evaluation of the Photo and Its Implicit Message

The photo itself, without the tweet, is eye-catching, and its implicit message elicits strong emotions in most viewers. But it does not make an argument.

> **Now display the associated tweet and have students evaluate it.**
>
> The year: 2021. The location: United States of America. The agency: US Customs and Border Patrol...and YES, that is a WHIP and a US Customs and Border Patrol agent on horseback! What you are witnessing is a humanitarian crisis and an attack on Haitian migrants fleeing 4 their lives.[8]

Stop! Check for Biases—the Author's and Your Own

Each student should say to themselves:

- How do I feel when viewing the tweet? What strong reactions, if any, do I feel?

- How might confirmation bias and other biases influence my thoughts?
- What mindset do I bring? Fixed or flexible?
- I am going to take a deep breath.
- I am going to try to keep an open mind about the topic.

Investigate the Source

We have already determined that the source of the tweet is Waikinya J.S. Clanton @WJSClanton.

Check for an Argument

Students should determine how many explicit or implied statements are in the tweet. Have students put the statements in standard form to see if the tweet makes an argument.

After students give answers, click slide to show the school solution:

1. A US Border Patrol agent uses whips to control Haitians at the US border. (Explicit)
2. These Haitian migrants are trying to flee a humanitarian crisis that threatens their lives. (Explicit)

Therefore, US Border Patrol agents are physically abusing vulnerable Haitian migrants.

Ask the students if the tweet alone makes an argument and why or why not. If it does, is it a good argument? Why or why not?

Students should say that the tweet alone does make an argument because the statements are premises that are either true or false but not both, are sufficiently clear and unambiguous, and are not questions or commands and because the conclusion must follow with high probability if the premises are true or plausible. We can determine if premise two is true or plausible by determining if the United Nations has declared a humanitarian crisis in Haiti.

Determine If the Argument Satisfies the Logic Condition

To make this a good argument, the argument has to satisfy the Logic Condition. It can do so if it is valid—if all its premises are true or plausible, the conclusion cannot be false. Or it can do so if it is strong—if all its premises are true or plausible, they give us good reason to believe the conclusion.

The tweet's argument is not valid because the conclusion could still be false even if both premises are true or plausible; some readers may not believe the US Border Patrol agents are necessarily abusing Haitian migrants. But the argument is strong because many readers would think the premises give them good reason to believe the agents are doing so.

Can You Fact-Check the Information?

We can fact-check the two premises because we can determine if they are true or false.

Find Trusted Coverage

Have each group fact-check premise one. First, they should look for reports from reputable fact-checking organizations using the site https://bit.ly/fact—search. If they find no results, they should use their Internet search skills to look for reports from credible news outlets.

In this case, Snopes reported[9] that although agents were found to have used excessive force against the Haitians, there's no evidence they had whips or struck anyone with reins during an incident in Del Rio, Texas, on September 19, 2021. Snopes said that journalists who saw the incident appeared to have mistaken long reins that one agent was swinging at migrants for an actual whip.

Snopes indicated that one Border Patrol agent used his horse rein to menace migrants by spinning it in a lasso-like motion. It described the photo we are evaluating as "a white, cowboy hat-wearing border agent on horseback [who]…reaches with his right hand to grab the back of a man's shirt. As he does so, a long, leather rein flies out freely, appearing to make contact with the migrant."[10] Snopes reported that long reins are used to control the horse.[11]

Snopes also reported[12] that Ratje, the photographer, indicated he did not see any Border Patrol agents use whips on anyone. Ratje described how the agent in this photo was swinging the rein and that such movement can be misinterpreted when looking at the photo.

Students should also find evidence from reputable news outlets[13,14] supporting premise two, that Haitian migrants are seeking refugee status and trying to flee reinforcing calamities in Haiti, including two earthquakes, a tropical storm, and gang violence.

Using both EAVI charts, students should find that the tweet and associated account show no signs of disinformation. We have already checked for signs of an automated account/bot and found none.

Trace the Premises to Their Original Context

Premise one has appeared in various forms on social media and on reputable news sites, according to an Internet search. Premise two has also surfaced online in various forms, though much less than premise one.

Check for Deceptive Use of Artificial Intelligence

None is apparent.

Determine If the Tweet's Argument Satisfies the Truth Condition

The tweet's argument does not satisfy the Truth Condition because our fact-check indicates premise one is not true.

Overall Evaluation of the Tweet

The tweet's argument without support from the photo is not a good one because it does not satisfy the Truth Condition.

Now ask the students to evaluate the tweet with the photo as support.

Stop! Check for Biases and Mindset—the Author's and Your Own

Each student should ask themselves:

- How do I feel when viewing the tweet and photo together? What strong reactions, if any, do I feel?
- What mindset do I bring? Fixed or flexible?
- What do I think of the tweet's language and word choice? What words, if any, cause me to feel strong emotion? What emotions?
- How might confirmation bias and other biases influence my thoughts?
- I am going to take a deep breath.
- I am going to try to keep an open mind about the topic.

Investigate the Source

We have already determined the sources of the photo and the tweet.

Check for an Argument

Students should evaluate the image and tweet to see if they form a visual-based argument and, if so, whether it is a good argument.

Ask the students if the tweet with the photo makes different statements and/or a different conclusion. If so, have them list them in standard form.

In this case, the standard form has a different first statement and a stronger conclusion:

1. A US Border Patrol agent uses whips (or whip-like devices) to whip Haitians at the US border. (Explicit)
2. These Haitian migrants are trying to flee a humanitarian crisis that threatens their lives. (Explicit)

US border control practices represent the same kind of racism and brutality seen during the era of slavery in the United States.

Ask the students if the tweet with the photo makes an argument and why or why not.

Students should say that the tweet with photo does make an argument because the statements are premises that are either true or false but not both, are sufficiently clear and unambiguous, and are not questions or commands and because the conclusion must at least reasonably follow from the premises if the premises are true. We can determine if premise two is true by determining if the United Nations has declared a humanitarian crisis in Haiti.

Ask the students why we mention in the conclusion the broader themes of racism and brutality seen during the slavery era in the United States.

After students answer, discuss what role the photo actually played as the post went viral in the media.

- In the photo, a horseback-riding border patrolman is holding a long cord and appeared to many viewers to be using it to control crowds of would-be migrants.
- Context: Many viewers thought the overall treatment of the migrants at the time was disturbing as border agents were trying to deal with an influx of thousands of Haitians trying to get into the country.
- First, X, some mainstream media, and, finally, some members of the US government initially said that the cords were whips used by agents to beat the Haitians.
- However, it became clear that these were reins used by anyone riding a horse to control their mount.
- The photo has been fact-checked numerous times, and the photographer says the photos were misrepresented as depicting agents violently whipping migrants.
- But the corrections did not calm public anger, and accusations continued to fly for weeks that the reins were being used "like whips" against the crowd. There were official calls for investigations and possible punishment for the US Border Patrol agents in the photos.

So why did images like this one spur such an outcry about whips? Largely because they recall memories of historic scenes

FLOGGING A SLAVE FASTENED TO THE GROUND.

Figure 16.1[16] Engraving by Walter George Mason entitled *Flogging a Slave Fastened to the Ground* (1853).

like the one in Figure 16.1 (an engraving) in which Black slaves are being whipped by white masters during the period of slavery in much of the United States.[15]

In this context, the photo implies, but does not state, the conclusion of the argument—that US border control practices represent the same kind of racism and brutality seen during the era of slavery in the United States.[17]

Determine If the Visual Argument Satisfies the Logic Condition

The visual argument passes the Logic Condition because it is strong. This broader, more provocative argument is strong because many readers would think the premises give them good reason to think US border control practices represent the same kind of racism and brutality seen during the era of slavery in the United States.

The argument is not valid, however. The conclusion does not necessarily follow from the premises, whether the premises turn out to be true or false. If the US Border Patrol agent was in fact whipping two Haitian migrants trying to cross the border, it does not necessarily follow that US border control practices represent the same kind of racism and brutality seen during the era of slavery in the United States. They may or may not, but in the context of logic, the conclusion does not necessarily follow.

For the conclusion to necessarily follow, you would need to establish how the race and motivation of today's Border Patrol agents are similar to those of historic slave owners. You would also need one or more evidence-backed statements that Haitian migrants trying to enter the country illegally are morally equivalent to Africans kidnapped from their own countries and brought to the United States in bondage. You would need evidence that establishes that the goals of border agents trying to manage a crowd were the same or similar to the goals of those holding the whips over slaves in the US South.

Can You Fact-Check the Information?

Yes.

Find Trusted Coverage

Students have already fact-checked the photo and the premises.

Trace the Premises to Their Original Context

Students have already determined the original context for the photo and premises.

Check for Deceptive Use of Artificial Intelligence

None is evident.

Determine if the Argument Satisfies the Truth Condition

The visual argument does not satisfy the Truth Condition because premise one is not true. Our fact-checking of reputable sources indicates the US Border Patrol agents were not whipping the migrants.

However, the argument was convincing to many because it seemed plausible, aided in part by the photo. Recall that a plausible premise is a statement. where the audience believes it has good reason to think it's true, and so is willing to grant it as a premise.

Overall Evaluation of the Media

Students should hesitate to be persuaded by the visual argument (text-based tweet with photo). It does not meet the Truth Condition because premise one is not true.

It is also not a valid argument, only a strong one. The connection between the premises and broader conclusion does not have explicit evidence to support it, so few people have made this argument explicitly. Instead, they have relied on the emotional impact of the image to appeal to the viewers' pathos and ethos and bolster a relationship between current border control procedures and the historic practice of slavery.[18]

This is the power of images. It can distort our ability to evaluate media, having us rely too much on our pathos and ethos and not enough on our logos.

▶ IN-CLASS ACTIVITY 2: EVALUATE MEMES

Divide students into groups of three to four.

Have each group evaluate two memes. They are going to determine if the memes make visual-based arguments and, if so, whether they make good ones. For a refresher on memes, see Chapter 7.

This lesson requires all students to recall the definition of an argument and an argument's relationship to the social media ecosystem, how to determine if an argument exists, and what makes a good argument. They must apply their skills to evaluate if a meme with text makes a visual-based argument and if it is a good one. Higher achieving students must also evaluate the meme more deeply by asking questions like the following:

- What is the creator or poster of the meme trying to achieve? Why?

Display the first meme, Figure 16.2, without the title or caption. Ask students to evaluate it.

Figure 16.2[19] Student hearing about news literacy for the first time.

Stop! Check for Biases and Mindset—the Author's and Your Own

Depending on their own mindset and biases and how they feel about learning news literacy, some students might interpret this image behind the meme as conveying the sense that the child is resisting learning news literacy. It all depends on whether they think the student is covering their ear to avoid hearing about it or cupping it to hear better. The teacher may want to draw this out in discussion, including what students think the creator intended to convey. As the creator of this meme, I intend to convey that some students initially resist learning news literacy skills.

Investigate the Source

A reverse image search indicates that the Flicker account woodleywonderworks created the image behind the meme on April 5, 2007, and uploaded it on July 21, 2007.

 Students should find that the meme itself first appeared on my website, Selected Media from My Book – Media Literacy Sleuth (https://medialiteracysleuth.com/figure-16-2/) QR Code 16.2

Check for an Argument

Recall from Chapter 7 that viewers who recognize the core component of a meme—such as an image of a movie actor or an idiosyncratic expression in the meme's text, will often be quick to reinterpret it as it spreads. As a result, the meme could be persuasive to them, usually with implicit premises. To these insiders, a meme can often make a good argument.

With this in mind, assign students to groups of three to four. Ask each group to identify any statements and the conclusion, if any, and put them in standard form.

After students respond, provide the school solution. The statements and conclusion that students identify should resemble the following:

1. A preteen is standing next to a giant loudspeaker.
2. The student is covering (or cupping) their ear closest to the loudspeaker.
3. The student has an unpleasant (or pleasant) expression on their face.
4. The student appears to resist (or welcome) learning news literacy skills.

5. The student is similar to me; I can relate to them.
Therefore, I resist (or welcome) learning news literacy skills.

Ask the class what evidence supports the statements. Students should say that the meme itself provides the evidence for the five statements, depending on how they interpret it.

Ask the students if the meme itself makes an argument and why or why not.

Most students should discover that group members disagree on what statements two to five are saying. As a group, then, they should answer that the meme has four unclear statements that are not necessarily true, and therefore there is an unclear conclusion. As a result, the meme does not make an argument for most of the students.

We can skip the steps "Determine if the Argument Satisfies the Logic Condition" and "Determine if the Argument Satisfies the Truth Condition."

Can You Fact-Check the Information?

We can only fact-check statement one. We cannot fact-check the other statements because they are unclear and subject to interpretation.

Find Trusted Coverage

Statement one: A reverse image source indicates that numerous other sources have published the photo behind the meme, suggesting, but not guaranteeing, that the preteen actually is standing next to a giant loudspeaker.

Trace the Meme to Its Original Context

The image as originally posted appears to be a composite. The edges of the student's body are distorted, suggesting they have been added later, straight lines appear in several places, and the wall molding at the floor is uneven, indicating the edges of several images. This constitutes disinformation because the creator/poster does not indicate this.

Check for Deceptive Use of Artificial Intelligence

None is evident.

Determine If the Argument Satisfies the Truth Condition

Not applicable. More specifically, statements two, three, four, and perhaps five (depending on the reader's age), would not be plausible to much of the target audience.

Overall Evaluation of the Meme: The meme does not make an argument for most students, mainly because several of its statements are subject to interpretation and because the image is probably conveying disinformation; the student is probably not standing next to the loudspeaker.

Next, Have Students Evaluate the Second Meme[20]

Display the meme in Figure 16.3 without its title or caption. Ask students to evaluate it.

Student after learning news literacy skills.

Figure 16.3[21] Student after learning news literacy skills.

Stop! Check for Biases and Mindset—the Author's and Your Own

Unlike the first meme, most students, regardless of their mindset and biases toward news, are likely to interpret the image behind the meme as conveying that students become more curious and better evaluators of news. A few may interpret the student's expression as conveying a dislike of using news literacy skills, perhaps revealing their resistance to using the skills even after learning them. The teacher may want to draw that out in discussion. Students should also share what they think the creator intended to convey. As the creator of this meme, I intend to convey that most students will become more curious about the news and will more closely evaluate news posts using the skills; I intend to say nothing about whether they like using the skills.

Investigate the Source

A reverse image search indicates that the Flicker account woodleywonderworks created the image behind the meme on September 23, 2007, and uploaded it the next day. The image appears to be a single photo. Students should find that the meme itself first appeared on my website, Selected Media from My Book – Media Literacy Sleuth (https://medialiteracysleuth. com/figure-16-3/) QR Code 16.3

Check for an Argument

Assign students to groups of three to four. Ask each group to identify any statements and the conclusion, if any, and put them in standard form.

After students respond, click the slide to show the school solution. The statements and conclusion that students identify should resemble the following:

1. A preteen is outdoors and squinting through a magnifying glass over their left eye.
2. The student has an unpleasant (or pleasant) expression on their face.
3. The student appears to resist (or welcome) investigating a news post using news literacy skills.
4. The student is similar to me; I can relate to them.

Therefore, I resist (or welcome) learning news literacy skills.

Ask the class what evidence supports the statements. Students should say that the meme itself provides the evidence for the four statements, depending on how they interpret it.

Ask the students if the meme makes an argument and why or why not.

Most students should discover that group members disagree on what statements two and three are saying. As a group, then, they should answer that the meme has two unclear premises statements that are not necessarily true, and therefore there is an unclear conclusion. As a result, the meme does not make an argument for most of the students.

We can skip the steps to "Determine if the Argument Satisfies the Logic Condition" and "Determine if the Argument Satisfies the Truth Condition."

Can You Fact-Check the Information?

We can only fact-check statement one. We cannot fact-check the others because they are unclear and subject to interpretation.

Find Trusted Coverage

Statement one: A reverse image search indicates that numerous other sources have published the photo behind the meme, suggesting, but not guaranteeing, that the preteen actually is outside and squinting through a magnifying glass over their left eye.

Trace the Meme to Its Original Context

The image as originally posted appears to be a single photo. The meme does not appear to contain disinformation.

Check for Deceptive Use of Artificial Intelligence

None is evident.

Determine if the Argument Satisfies the Truth Condition

Not applicable. More specifically, premises statements two, three, and perhaps four (depending on the reader's age), would not be plausible to much of the target audience.

Overall Evaluation of the Meme: The meme does not make an argument for most students, mainly because statements two, three, and perhaps four, are subject to interpretation.

Many memes are less sophisticated than other forms of visual argumentation, and much less so than verbal arguments in campaign speeches and editorials.[22] Students should approach memes not as conventional logical arguments that appeal to our logos but as a form of persuasive communication appealing more to our pathos, according to Haber.[23]

Still, students can evaluate memes to determine if they make an argument, just as they do for other media. They should recall that we cannot evaluate an argument using the superficial, incomplete form we usually see them in on social media. These arguments often rely on implicit or assumed premises, so we must reconstruct them before we can evaluate them. This goes especially for memes.[24]

▶ NEXT STEPS

- Use the calendar-based pop culture and social studies, civics, and ELA events as examples for your students to practice evaluating text- and visual-based arguments. These can support your learning objectives.

Go to my website, https://medialiteracysleuth.com/, for more evaluations of visual-based arguments.

▶ NOTES

1 Kneupper, C.W. (1978), "On argument and diagrams," *Journal of the American Forensic Association*, 14, 181–186.
2 Graphics That Seem Clear Can Easily Be Misread: Misreading Data Visualizations Can Reinforce Biased Perceptions, Albert Cairo, Graphics That Seem Clear Can Easily Be Misread—Scientific American, September 1, 2019.
3 Memes, Memes (logiccheck.net), December 1, 2021.
4 Crowther, Kathryn, Lauren Curtright, Nancy Gilbert, Barbara Hall, Tracienne Ravita, and Kirk Swenson. "Successful College Composition." 2nd edition. Book 8. Georgia: English Open Textbooks, 2016. https://oer.galileo.usg.edu/english-textbooks/8/.

5 Crowther, Kathryn, Lauren Curtright, Nancy Gilbert, Barbara Hall, Tracienne Ravita, and Kirk Swenson. "Successful College Composition." 2nd edition. Book 8. Georgia: English Open Textbooks, 2016. https://oer.galileo.usg.edu/english-textbooks/8/.

6 United States Border Patrol Agent on Horseback Tries to Stop a… News Photo—Getty Images.

7 United States Border Patrol Agent on Horseback Tries to Stop a… News Photo—Getty Images.

8 (17) Waikinya J.S. Clanton on X: "The year: 2021 The location: United States of America The agency: US Customs and Border Patrol… and YES, that is a WHIP and a US Customs and Border Patrol agent on horseback! What you are witnessing is a humanitarian crisis and an attack on Haitian migrants fleeing 4 their lives https://t.co/gpRjFXC2iG"/X (twitter.com). https://twitter.com/WJSClanton/status/1440032349714931725?s=20.

9 "Photos Spark Flurry of Rhetoric About 'Whips' at the Border," Bethania Palma, Snopes, July 8, 2022, Photos Spark Flurry of Rhetoric About 'Whips' at the Border | Snopes.com.

10 "Photos Spark Flurry of Rhetoric About 'Whips' at the Border," Bethania Palma, Snopes, July 8, 2022, Photos Spark Flurry of Rhetoric About 'Whips' at the Border | Snopes.com.

11 "Photos Spark Flurry of Rhetoric About 'Whips' at the Border," Bethania Palma, Snopes, July 8, 2022, Photos Spark Flurry of Rhetoric About 'Whips' at the Border | Snopes.com.

12 "Photos Spark Flurry of Rhetoric About 'Whips' at the Border," Bethania Palma, Snopes, July 8, 2022, Photos Spark Flurry of Rhetoric About 'Whips' at the Border | Snopes.com.

13 "Fact-Check—How Haitian Migrants Make Their Way to the US Border," Reuters, September 24, 2021, Fact-Check—How Haitian Migrants Make Their Way to the US Border | Reuters.

14 "Why Are so Many Haitians at the US—Mexico Border?," BBC News, Bernd Debusmann Jr., September 24, 2021, Why Are so Many Haitians at the US—Mexico Border?—BBC News.

15 "Photos Spark Flurry of Rhetoric About 'Whips' at the Border," Bethania Palma, Snopes, July 8, 2022, Photos Spark Flurry of Rhetoric About 'Whips' at the Border | Snopes.com.

16 Schomburg Center for Research in Black Culture, Manuscripts, Archives and Rare Books Division, The New York Public Library. "Flogging a Slave Fastened to the Ground" The New York Public Library Digital Collections. 1853. https://digitalcollections.nypl.org/items/510d47da-7643-a3d9-e040-e00a18064a99.

17 "Photos Spark Flurry of Rhetoric About 'Whips' at the Border," Bethania Palma, Snopes, July 8, 2022, Photos Spark Flurry of Rhetoric About 'Whips' at the Border | Snopes.com.

18 That Looks Terrible! (logiccheck.net).

19 Selected Media from My Book – News Literacy Sleuth.

20 News Literacy Sleuth. Image behind the meme holds a Creative Commons 2.0 license.

21 Selected Media from My Book – News Literacy Sleuth.

22 Memes, Memes (logiccheck.net), December 1, 2021.

23 Memes, Memes (logiccheck.net), December 1, 2021.

24 The Critical Thinker Academy: What Is a Fallacy?, https://youtu.be/EJp4bZhhYfw.

Spot Fallacies

17

I was out in the yard with my friends, running and playing with a ball, as a typical little kid does. When the ball rolled into the doghouse where my friend's German Shepherd guarded her pups, I happily ran to get it. The pups' mom would have none of it. She charged at me, growling, barking, and bearing her sharp teeth. Before I realized that getting that ball was a bad idea and I should run, her teeth ripped into my left calf. I screamed, wriggled free, and ran home, bleeding and crying.

My physical injuries healed over time, leaving a scar I hardly notice. But my emotional scars remain to this day. My heart skips a beat whenever I see a German Shepherd out for a walk with its owner. I can't help but assume that the dog is mean and wants to attack me, and I keep my distance. I commit the **fallacy of composition**, projecting the properties of the individual—in this case, that German Shepherd mom protecting her pups years ago—onto the whole, assuming that all German Shepherds are mean and want to sink their teeth into me.

This fallacy, like many others, is irrational. Although I'm aware of mine after all these years, many people posting on social media are not. Fallacies (defined next) are usually unintentional. But they can undermine the argument the poster is trying to make. The good news is that students can learn to spot fallacies in arguments, including in their own posts.

 DOI: 10.4324/9781003471301-20

A **fallacy** is an argument. But it's a bad argument because it contains one or more errors in reasoning.[1,2,3]

An argument can have two categories of fallacies. An argument with a **formal fallacy** has an invalid structure or 'form,' which renders the argument invalid and causes it to fail the Logic Condition. An argument with an **informal fallacy** may meet the Logic Condition but fail the Truth Condition because it has incorrect, implausible, or irrelevant premises.[4,5,6,7,8,9] There are many types of formal and informal fallacies; I list common ones in this chapter and in the Resources section.

A fallacious argument may appear to be well-reasoned.[10,11] We often mistake fallacious arguments for good ones and end up believing their misleading claims and disinformation.[12]

Fallacies may be committed intentionally to manipulate or persuade one or more people (see Common Manipulation Tactics), unintentionally because of human limitations such as carelessness, cognitive or social biases and ignorance, or limitations of language.[13] Therefore, some of the fallacies I discuss in this chapter can be used as manipulation tactics.

Teachers and students should understand this overlap and not be too concerned with whether a fallacy listed below falls more under the category of a manipulation tactic.

▶ COMMON FALLACIES

- **Ad hominem**—the speaker attacks the character, motive, or some other attribute of the person making an argument rather than attacking the substance of the argument itself. *Example*: Criticizing a person's appearance instead of addressing his/her statement or complaint.

- **Bandwagon**—when someone claims that something is true or correct because many people believe it to be so. *Example*: All my friends are using this diet to lose weight, so it must work for everyone.

- **Cherry-picking or fallacy of omission**—when someone chooses evidence that supports their point of view while ignoring evidence that contradicts it. *Example*: A drug company promotes its new medication to combat high cholesterol without revealing possible side effects unless required by law.

- **False dilemma**—also referred as the **either/or fallacy, false dichotomy**, or **false binary**. It asserts that there are only two options, and only one is true. *Example*: If you do not fly the American flag at home, then you are unpatriotic.

- **Hasty generalization**—reaching a conclusion about an entire category while ignoring or downplaying distinctions with it. *Example*: Employers would rather hire older generations than Gen Xers. Gen Xers are not trustworthy.

- **Authority**—supporting a claim by citing someone who is not an authority in the field or who is likely to be biased. *Example*: The voter cited the Democrat, who says his Republican rival for the election is corrupt.

- **Scapegoating**—singling out a person or group for unmerited blame and consequent negative treatment. *Example*: The team lost because of the goalie.

- **Scare tactic or fear-mongering**—a form of manipulation that causes fear by using exaggerated rumors of impending danger to get others to accept a point. *Example*: You should not vaccinate kids. Vaccines cause autism.

- **Sweeping generalization**—applying a general rule to a particular case that may be an exception. *Example*: School supplies always go on sale right before the school year starts, so we can count on them going on sale this year.

Here's an example of a **formal fallacy**:

"If I cast my lure accurately, then I will catch fish. I caught fish, so I am casting my lure accurately." This argument basically says:

1. If A, then B.
2. B.
Therefore, A.

This argument commits the **fallacy of affirming the consequent**.[14] It affirms that B (I caught fish) occurred because of A (I cast my lure accurately). It is also sometimes called the **post hoc (ergo propter hoc) fallacy**, which means "after this, therefore because of this." It implies a cause and effect when there might not be one.[15]

Here's an example of an **informal fallacy**:

"It's ok to bully that student. All your classmates do it."

This argument is bad because it relies on an implicit premise that most of us would reject.[16]

Let's reconstruct the argument and put it into standard form to see this more clearly.

1. If all your classmates do something, it's ok to do it. (Implicit premise)
2. All your classmates bully that student.

Therefore, it's ok to bully that student.

Note that the structure of the argument is fine; this is a valid argument. The problem is that the implicit first premise is not plausible; most of us would reject the view that an action is moral if everyone does it. This is sometimes called the **bandwagon fallacy**: An argument is considered sound and true because it is popular.[17,18] The second premise is also probably implausible; it's unlikely that all the classmates bully the student.[19]

As you recall from Chapter 15, "Evaluate Text-Based Arguments," we cannot determine if an argument is fallacious by using the shallow, partial form we usually see on social media. This form of an argument often relies on implicit or assumed premises, so we must reconstruct it before we can determine if it is fallacious.[20]

Consider this argument: "Snowmen can't survive above-freezing temperatures; they are made of ice." It would be unfair to say this argument is bad (because its logic is weak) by looking only at this superficial version:

1. Snowmen are made of ice.

Therefore, snowmen cannot survive above-freezing temperatures.

This version has an implicit premise, "Ice cannot survive above-freezing temperatures," that would provide the connection between being made of ice and being a snowman:

1. Snowmen are made of ice.
2. Ice cannot survive above-freezing temperatures. (Implicit premise)

Therefore, snowmen cannot survive above-freezing temperatures.

We can evaluate the argument and determine if it is fallacious only after we add the implicit premise. We now see that the argument is not fallacious.

▶ WHY STUDENTS SHOULD LEARN ABOUT FALLACIES

The quality of an argument on social media—the credibility and balance of the evidence, its relevance and logical strength, and its level of bias—varies.[21] Generally, those who create the post will try to persuade you to see their side of the argument. There is nothing wrong with trying to persuade someone to look at a topic from your perspective, particularly if you present credible evidence. Often, however, creators will not have credible evidence and will often use fallacies to try to sway your thinking.

Fallacies are successful and persistent mainly because students fail to recognize them. Students often let their biases, not facts, influence their decision-making. This can lead them to believe lies or partial truths and make poor decisions.

Teaching your students how to spot fallacies in social media will help them recognize poor arguments, think in a more reasoned way, and be less vulnerable to unwarranted media persuasion in and out of the classroom.

▶ LESSON PLAN

In-Class Group Activity: Identify Common Fallacies in Pop Culture Media

This lesson requires all students to recall what a fallacy is, the two categories of fallacies, and specific types of fallacies. They must also evaluate several types of social media to determine which, if any, contains a fallacy and what type of fallacy it demonstrates. Higher achieving students must also explain how students can be easily persuaded by fallacies on social media.

Divide students into groups of three to four. Direct each group to different electronic examples from social media, each with a different category of fallacy.

Have each group answer the following questions.

- Does the creator/poster make an argument? Is it a good one? Why or why not?
- What fallacy does the media use?
- How does the fallacy affect the persuasiveness of the argument?

▶ FORMAL FALLACY

Tweet

On June 9, 2022, US Rep. Jim Jordan, R-Ohio, tweeted a response to public hearings held by the House Select Committee to Investigate the January 6 Attack on the US Capitol. He asked when Congress would hold a hearing in primetime on what he claimed was unprecedented crime in cities governed by Democrats.

Tweet (https://twitter.com/Jim_Jordan/status/153497471649 0006528)[22] QR Code 17.1

Students should provide responses like the following:

Does the Author/Poster Make an Argument? Is It a Good One? Why or Why Not?

Identify the explicit and implicit statements and a conclusion and put them in standard form:

1. The House Select Committee to Investigate the January 6 Attack on the United States Capitol is holding public hearings (in primetime). (Implicit)
2. There is no primetime hearing on (alleged) record crime in US cities run by Democrats. (Explicit)

Therefore, there should be a primetime hearing on record crime in US cities run by Democrats.

Rep. Jordan makes an implicit argument because there are two premises (one implicit) that are clear and are not questions or commands and a conclusion (implicit). However, his argument is not a good one. It meets the Truth Condition because both premises are true or plausible. But it does not meet the Logic Condition because the conclusion does not necessarily or plausibly follow from the premises. Just because there was (at the time of the tweet) a primetime hearing on the January 6 attack and not one targeting Democratic leaders of US cities does not mean there should be a hearing about Democrats who run US cities and the (alleged) record crime in them. The logic of the argument falls apart because of its structure. The argument relies on a **structural fallacy**.

What Fallacy Does the Media Use?

Jordan is using the **red herring fallacy**.[23] This is a fallacy by which someone presents irrelevant information to try to distract others from a topic that's being discussed, often to avoid a question or shift the discussion to something else. In this example, Jordan is attempting to distract attention from the January 6 hearings and toward the irrelevant issue of alleged record crime in Democrat-controlled US cities.

How Does the Fallacy Affect the Persuasiveness of the Argument?

The **red herring fallacy** gives the argument poor structure and causes the logic of the argument to crumble.

▶ INFORMAL FALLACY

A TikTok video clip with background music suggested that it shows Dr. Anthony Fauci in 1984 describing to an audience at the US National Institutes of Health a malicious plan to create the AIDS pandemic, according to PolitiFact.[24] But in the clip from a lecture Fauci gave on AIDS at the NIH on November 4, 1984, Fauci was actually discussing how the disease emerged in the United States in 1979 and how it was recognized as a new disease in 1981.[25]

In the TikTok video clip, Fauci says,

"You take an infectious agent and you introduce it into a population in which the spread among those individuals—if it's sexual—contact spread—it's a perfect set—up to spread." (AIDS/Dr. Anthony Fauci, NIH, 1984)

An Instagram user who shared the clip (now removed from the platform) wrote, "This maniac" needs to go to prison, but that prison was not nearly sufficient punishment for his "#crimesagainsthumanity."[26]

The following is the relevant part of what Fauci said. The portion that was shared in the Instagram post is in italics:

"I'll get to in some of the later slides how this disease, which we surmised early on, started off in the male homosexual population in this country. *Not that there was anything intrinsically different or wrong or what—have—you about homosexuality. It was very simple; it's straightforward epidemiology. You take an infectious agent and you introduce it into a population in which the spread among those individuals—if it's sexual—contact spread—it's a perfect set—up to spread.*"[27,28]

The entire video of Fauci is here:

Video (https://collections.nlm.nih.gov/catalog/nlm:nlmuid-101674642-vid)[29] QR Code 17.2

Have Each Group Present Their Evaluation of the Instagram Post to the Class

Groups evaluate the post. They can search online to verify evidence and reasoning if needed. Then each group should discuss for no more than 5 minutes the following questions:

1. Does the author/poster make an argument? Is it a good one? Why or why not?
2. What fallacy does the media use?
3. How does fallacy affect the persuasiveness of the argument?

Students should give answers similar to these:

Does the Instagram Post Make an Argument? Is It a Good One? Why or Why Not?

Identify the explicit and implicit statements and a conclusion and put them in standard form:

1. Dr. Anthony Fauci gave a lecture on AIDS at the NIH on November 4, 1984. (Implicit statement)
2. Fauci's comments in the lecture are evidence that he plotted to spread AIDS in the United States. (Implicit statement)
3. Fauci committed crimes against humanity for plotting to spread AIDS in the United States. (Explicit statement)

Therefore, this maniac needs to serve multiple lives behind prison bars, but that's not nearly enough of a punishment for his #crimesagainsthumanity.

The post makes an argument because it contains statements that are premises because they are reasonably clear and are not questions or commands, and a conclusion that could plausibly follow from the premises if all the premises are true or plausible. However, it is not a good argument because premises two and three lack evidence to support them and are incorrect; it does not meet the Truth Condition. If we assume all three premises are true or plausible, however, many readers will think the conclusion is logical and reasonable. So the argument is valid and meets the Logic Condition because the structure of the argument is fine.

What Fallacy Does the Media Use?

The Instagram post commits the **ad hominem fallacy**—attacking the person or group rather than the point he or she is trying to make. In this example, the post attacks the person (Fauci), calling him a "maniac" rather than the point he is trying to make in the lecture. Fauci is trying to explain how AIDS first emerged in the United States in 1979, how it started off in the male homosexual population in the United States, and how it was recognized as a new disease in 1981.

How Does the Fallacy Affect the Persuasiveness of the Argument?

On the surface, the argument would seem persuasive to some readers because it appeals to their ethos (many readers' tendency to believe what a scientist says, no matter what) but also their pathos (taking advantage of most readers' emotional recoil at the thought that Fauci might have plotted to bring AIDS to the United States). Calling Fauci a "maniac" would stoke their emotions further and inhibit their rational evaluation of the argument using their logos.

In fact, the suggestion is false that Fauci's comments in 1984 are evidence he plotted AIDS. The disease emerged in the United States several years earlier and originated decades before that.

▶ NEXT STEPS

- Have your students use their skills to identify fallacies in pop culture and social media posts supporting the social studies, civics, or ELA curriculum throughout the school year.

Go to my website, **medialiteracysleuth.com**, for more recent media evaluations and lesson plans, which I update regularly.

▶ NOTES

1 The Critical Thinker Academy: What Is a Fallacy?, https://youtu.be/EJp4bZhhYfw.
2 News Literacy Project, "Arguments & Evidence," Lesson (checkology.org).
3 Purdue Online Writing Lab, Fallacies // Purdue Writing Lab.
4 The Critical Thinker Academy Podcast, #006: Introduction to Fallacies, https://youtu.be/_ij0xVDEdTQ.
5 The Critical Thinker Academy: What Is a Fallacy?, https://youtu.be/EJp4bZhhYfw.
6 News Literacy Project, "Arguments & Evidence," Lesson (checkology.org).

7 Purdue Online Writing Lab, Fallacies // Purdue Writing Lab.

8 The Critical Thinker Academy: What Is a Fallacy?, https://youtu. be/EJp4bZhhYfw.

9 Gibbs NM. Formal and Informal Fallacies in Anesthesia. *Anaesth Intensive Care.* 2010 Jul;38(4):639—46. doi: 10.1177/0310057X 1003800405. PMID: 20715725.

10 The Critical Thinker Academy: What Is a Fallacy?, https://youtu. be/EJp4bZhhYfw.

11 Fallacies | Internet Encyclopedia of Philosophy (utm.edu).

12 The Critical Thinker Academy Podcast, #006: Introduction to Fallacies, https://youtu.be/_ij0xVDEdTQ.

13 Fallacies | Internet Encyclopedia of Philosophy (utm.edu).

14 The Critical Thinker Academy: What Is a Fallacy?, https://youtu. be/EJp4bZhhYfw.

15 The Critical Thinker Academy: What Is a Fallacy?, https://youtu. be/EJp4bZhhYfw.

16 The Critical Thinker Academy Podcast, #006: Introduction to Fallacies, https://youtu.be/_ij0xVDEdTQ.

17 Common Logical Fallacies, Erika Thorsen, English teacher at Squa-licum High School in Washington State, Email: Erika.thorsen@ bellinghamschools.org.

18 The Critical Thinker Academy: What Is a Fallacy?, https://youtu. be/EJp4bZhhYfw.

19 The Critical Thinker Academy: What Is a Fallacy?, https://youtu. be/EJp4bZhhYfw.

20 The Critical Thinker Academy: What Is a Fallacy?, https://youtu. be/EJp4bZhhYfw.

21 Bias | *Psychology Today.*

22 Rep. Jim Jordan on Twitter: "When's the primetime hearing on record crime in Democrat—run cities?" / Twitter.

23 "Snopestionary: The 'Red Herring' Fallacy," Bethania Palmer, Snopes, June 10, 2022, Snopestionary: The 'Red Herring' Fallacy | Snopes.com.

24 "A Video Clip Shows Fauci Plotted AIDS Pandemic? Pants on Fire!," Tom Kertscher, PolitiFactd, October 28, 2021, PolitiFact | A video clip shows Fauci plotted AIDS pandemic? Pants on Fire!

25 AIDS: acquired immunodeficiency syndrome—Digital Collec-tions—National Library of Medicine (nih.gov).

26 "A Video Clip Shows Fauci Plotted AIDS Pandemic? Pants On Fire!," Tom Kertscher, PolitiFactd, October 28, 2021, PolitiFact | A video clip shows Fauci plotted AIDS pandemic? Pants on Fire!

27 "A Video Clip Shows Fauci Plotted AIDS Pandemic? Pants on Fire!,"
Tom Kertscher, PolitiFact, October 28, 2021, PolitiFact | A video
clip shows Fauci plotted AIDS pandemic? Pants on Fire!

28 AIDS: Acquired Immunodeficiency Syndrome—Digital Collec-
tions—National Library of Medicine (nih.gov).

29 AIDS: Acquired Immunodeficiency Syndrome—Digital Collec-
tions – National Library of Medicine (nih.gov).

Spot Manipulation Tactics

Chapter

18

Remember the story I told you in Chapter 12 about the email threat to cut off my home's power supply? That was a manipulation tactic commonly called **intimidation**: "Do or think this, or there will be consequences." Fortunately, I did not fall for it— this time.

▶ DEFINITION

Manipulation tactic: An *act*, often intentional, vice an argument per se, that tries to influence, persuade, or control one or more people, often for unethical or self-serving reasons. Some may use an argument and one or more fallacies (see common fallacies) to achieve their effect.

As with fallacies, teachers and students should understand this overlap and not be too concerned with whether one of the following manipulation tactics falls more under the category of a fallacy.

▶ WHY SPOTTING MANIPULATION TACTICS IS IMPORTANT

Manipulation tactics are all over students' social media feeds. Many posters who use them do so on purpose to persuade us to believe or do something. Although manipulation tactics can be

DOI: 10.4324/9781003471301-21

used to make an argument without committing an error in reasoning (a fallacy),[1] they are usually used when manipulators
have no logical, rational argument they want you to accept.

Consider this scenario based on one from the *Stanford Encyclopedia of Philosophy*[2]:

Mei plans to do Y, but Jorge wants her to do X. Jorge has tried
unsuccessfully to provide Mei with reasons for doing X rather
than Y. If Jorge is unwilling to resort to coercion or force, he
might deploy any of the following tactics to try to influence
Mei's choice. For example, Jorge might:

1. Charm Mei into wanting to please him by doing X.
2. Exaggerate the advantages of doing X and the disadvantages of doing Y, and/or understate the disadvantages of
   doing X and the advantages of doing Y.
3. Make Mei feel guilty for preferring to do Y.
4. Induce Mei into an emotional state that makes doing X
   seem more appropriate than it really is.
5. Point out that doing Y will make Mei seem less worthy
   and appealing to her friends.
6. Make Mei feel bad about herself and portray Y as a choice
   that will confirm or exacerbate this feeling, and/or portray X as a choice that will disconfirm or combat it.
7. Do a small favor for Mei before asking her to do X, so
   that she feels obligated to comply.
8. Make Mei doubt her own judgment so that she will rely
   on Jorge's advice to do X.
9. Make it clear to Mei that if she does Y rather than X,
   Jorge will withdraw his friendship, sulk, or become irri-
   table and generally unpleasant.
10. Focus Mei's attention on some part of doing Y that Mei
    fears and then increase her fear to dissuade her from do-
    ing Y.

We could reasonably call each of these a manipulation tactic.
Many of them also have more specific, familiar names, such
as 'guilt trip' (tactic 3), 'peer pressure' (tactic 5), 'negging'
(tactic 6), 'gaslighting' (tactic 8), and 'emotional blackmail'
(tactic 9).[3]

Not everyone will agree that every tactic on this list is manipulation. In some cases, whether the tactic seems manipulative may depend on unspecified details. For example, if Y is dishonest, it may not be manipulative for Jorge to get Mei to feel guilty about planning to do Y.[4]

One or more fallacies often accompany manipulation tactics. For example, a social media post that relies exclusively or overly on an appeal to pathos and ethos vice logos to support its otherwise good argument is a sign of possible manipulation, according to Haber.[5]

Manipulation tactics are successful and persistent because they appeal to our pathos and ethos to establish their credibility, making it hard to recognize them. In those cases, we may let our mindset and biases, not facts, influence us. We end up believing disinformation and making poor decisions.

People who are particularly uneasy, scared, emotionally on edge, or feel their lives are out of control are most susceptible to manipulation, according to an article by Whitson and Galinsky in the journal *Science*.[6] They are more likely to perceive conspiracies and feel superstitious, and they often seek to gain a sense of control by perceiving patterns or correlations where none exist or to simplify the reasons for the chaos they feel.

But there's good news. Teaching students how to spot manipulation tactics will make them less vulnerable to manipulation in and out of the classroom.

▶ LESSON PLAN

In-class activity: Spot manipulation tactics in social media

This lesson requires all students to recall what a manipulation tactic is and understand common types. They must also evaluate several types of social media to determine which, if any, contains a manipulation tactic and which type(s) it demonstrates. Higher achieving students must also explain how students can be easily persuaded by manipulation tactics on social media.

Give each student the following list of common manipulation tactics with definitions and examples.

Common Manipulation Tactics

- **Distract and Drown**: overwhelming the target (individuals) by inundating them with a tremendous amount of information or demands, making it difficult for them to focus on anything else and diverting them from facts or other information. Usually done by bringing up outrageous or divisive points of view. *Example*: A politician consistently interrupts a reporter, avoiding questions and bringing a nonrelated issue to the conversation.

- **Fake News Claim**: false or misleading information presented as news used to damage the reputation of a person or entity. In recent years, it has been applied by high-profile people to any news unfavorable to them (whether true or not). Fake news can reduce the impact of real news by competing with it and making real news doubtful. It particularly has the potential to undermine trust in serious media coverage. *Example*: A former US president has been credited with popularizing the term by using it to describe any negative press coverage of himself.

- **False Dichotomy**: two alternatives are presented as the only choices and mutually exclusive. *Example*: The parents said to their child, "You must go to college or get a job." In reality, a third option might be for the student to go to college part time and get a part-time job.

- **Fearmongering**: throughout their evolutionary history, humans have paid attention to danger in order to survive. Fearmongering exploits those feelings by making people perceive the world as more dangerous than it really is and placing emphasis on unlikely situations to captivate people's attention. Fearmongering can increase support for a position or individual by fear of perceived danger. *Example*: A US congressperson tries to increase support for their bill in Congress to put a hold on AI development by instilling fear in everyone at a town hall meeting in their home district, saying that AI "will put everyone here out of work."

- **Fear of Missing Out (FOMO)**: worrying about being absent from or overlooking a rewarding social experience.[7] *Example*: The student decided to practice the backflip and post a video of it on TikTok after seeing what seemed like most of their friends doing it.

- **Hyperbole**: a way of speaking or writing that makes someone or something sound much larger, smaller, better, worse, more unusual, etc., than they are. It is commonly used to exaggerate issues or circumstances that benefit the user of the hyperbole or put their opponent in a poor light. *Example*: Advertising uses hyperbole to exaggerate the benefits of products to boost sales. Politicians use it to exaggerate their accomplishments while diminishing those of their opponents.

- **Populism**: emphasizes the idea of "the people" and often contrasts this group with the "elite." It is frequently associated with anti-establishment and anti-political sentiment. In the United States, one type focuses on culture and intellectual elitism and the other on economics and financial elites. When used as a disingenuous tactic, it makes the opponent harder to relate to or seem "not part of us." See "Us versus Them." *Example*: The populist US political candidate, in an appeal to poor rural voters, promised to raise the minimum wage.

- **Pretending to Be the Hero**: a person who seeks recognition for "heroism," especially by creating a harmful situation that they can resolve. It is a way to feel in control and invincible. Some people believe they are the smartest and "best person for the job" and the "hero" of the story (even when not true). They convince others to follow them even when, clearly, they are not who they say they are. Those followers look the other way to justify their choice instead of questioning their judgment. *Example*: The firefighter seeking a promotion committed arson and then put the fire out to enhance their reputation.

- **Trigger Words**: terms viewed as derogatory or unpleasant and used to activate people's reactions. Some terms may hold a different meaning in another culture and would not elicit a reaction. *Examples in the United States*: alien (undocumented immigrant), 'Karen' (a person who exhibits behavior arising from privilege), tree hugger.

- **Us vs. Them**: oversimplifying and distorting complex problems by dividing the world into us and them and scapegoating and vilifying the latter. When we perceive that our group is in direct competition with another, especially over a limited resource, we are likely to experience hostility toward members of that group. The mere categorization of people into us and them is enough to produce hostilities. One reason for this is that our self-esteem comes partly from our group membership. *Example*: Immigrants coming into the United States are perceived to take American jobs, creating a hostile (us versus them) attitude against the immigrants.

- **Victimhood**: a mindset in which a person or group of people considers themselves a victim of the negative actions of others. Someone who acts from a place of victimhood claims that things that happen to them are the fault of someone or something other than themselves when their circumstances are mostly or completely their own fault. They want people to feel sorry for them or use it as an excuse for something, to do something negative against the other party, or to get people to follow them, creating a sense of purpose. *Example*: The teen was staring at their cell phone, walked past a warning sign, fell into a deep hole, and claimed the construction company was at fault.

- **Vilification**: saying or writing unpleasant things about someone or something to cause other people to have a bad opinion of them and to damage their reputation. Usually done by exaggerating and spreading false information. Even if proven wrong, damage has been done. *Example*: all Mexicans coming into the United States are murderers and rapists.

Divide students into groups of three to four. Direct each group to different electronic examples from social media, each demonstrating a different manipulation tactic. I include several examples in this lesson.

Have each group answer the following questions about the examples and report their findings to the class.

- Does the creator/poster make an argument? Is it a good one? Why or why not?
- What manipulation tactic(s) does the media use?
- How does the manipulation tactic(s) affect the persuasiveness of the argument?

YouTube video clip from *Star Wars Episode 3: Revenge of the Sith*:

 On the page in the link below, search in the Video section for the clip entitled *Anakin Confronts Obi-Wan*.

Video[8] (https://www.starwars.com/databank/anakin-skywalker) QR Code 18.1

Students should give answers similar to these:

Does the Post Make an Argument? Is It a Good One? Why or Why Not?

Identify the explicit and implicit statements and conclusion and put them in standard form. Students can present Anakin's potential argument or Obi-Wan's potential argument. Let's lay out Anakin's:

1. Obi-Wan has pledged allegiance to the Republic. (Explicit statement)
2. Obi-Wan is not with me because he has not pledged allegiance to me. (Implicit statement with reasoning "because...")

Therefore, Obi-Wan is my enemy.

Anakin makes an argument because his statements are premises because they are clear, have yes/no answers, and are not questions or commands. Fact-checking (perhaps by watching the movie to get broader context) indicates his premises are true, so his argument meets the Truth Condition. But it is a bad argument because it does not meet the Logic Condition. Even if we can say his premises are true or plausible, his conclusion does not necessarily follow that Obi-Wan is Anakin's enemy. Obi-Wan could work with Anakin in other ways. Anakin's logic fails because his argument relies on a manipulation tactic to reach its conclusion.

What Manipulation Tactic Does Anakin Use?

Anakin claims that if Obi-Wan is not with him, then Obi-Wan is his enemy. This is a manipulation tactic called a **false dichotomy**.[9] Obi-Wan is trying to keep Anakin from joining the "Dark Side."

How Does the Manipulation Tactic Affect the Persuasiveness of Anakin's Argument?

Just because Obi-Wan disagrees with Anakin does not automatically make them enemies.[10] Obi-Wan's reply, "Only a Sith deals in absolutes," shatters Anakin's manipulation tactic, so his argument is probably not persuasive to most viewers.

Ad

Scroll to section #7 in the linked page below to see the ad.
   Ad[11] (https://www.drip.com/blog/fomo-marketing) QR code 18.2 Students should give answers similar to these:

Does the Post Make an Argument? Is It a Good One? Why or Why Not?

Identify the explicit and implicit statements and a conclusion and put them in standard form:

1. Shakur Shades has a money-back guarantee. (Explicit statement)
2. Shakur Shades has free shipping. (Explicit statement)
3. People like me like Shakur Shades. (Implicit statement)

Therefore, I should buy Shakur Shades.

The ad is for "Shakur Shades," created in the style that the late rapper and actor Tupac Shakur wore.[12] The ad makes an argument because it contains three premises that are clear and are not questions or commands.

But it is a bad argument. First, it does not satisfy the Logic Condition. Even if we assume all the premises are true or plausible, the conclusion does not necessarily follow that you should buy Shakur Shades. You may have different tastes and preferences about sunglasses than the three reviewers featured on the website have. Second, the argument does not satisfy the Truth Condition. The first and second premises are true, but the third is not, because there are almost certainly at least a few purchasers whom you consider similar to you (however you define "similar") that do not like the sunglasses; after all, the website only displays reviews from three people. It is also possible that the three featured reviews are fake.

The argument fails because it relies on a manipulation tactic to reach its conclusion.

What Manipulation Tactic Does the Media Use?

The argument relies on the **FOMO** manipulation tactic. In this case, the ad tries to get you to experience FOMO anxiety by relying on current customers "like you" to validate the product. Customer testimonials are one of the most tried and true marketing techniques. They let prospects know that other people are already using your product, and they are super happy about it. Therefore, prospects should act so they don't miss out on the benefits.[13]

How Does the Manipulation Tactic Affect the Persuasiveness of the Argument?

The argument is probably persuasive to many viewers because it exploits our emotions by appealing to our pathos, clouding our ability to rely more on our logos to evaluate the product before deciding whether to buy it.

▶ NEXT STEPS

- Have your students use their skills to identify manipulation tactics that occur on social media throughout the school year. These can be from pop culture or support the civics, social studies, and ELA curriculum and learning standards.

Go to my website, medialiteracysleuth.com, for more recent examples and lesson plans, which I update periodically.

▶ NOTES

1 "Ethical Realism: Manipulative Tactics," August 30, 2013, Manipulative Tactics | Ethical Realism (wordpress.com).
2 "The Ethics of Manipulation," *Stanford Encyclopedia of Philosophy*, April 21, 2022, The Ethics of Manipulation (Stanford Encyclopedia of Philosophy).
3 "The Ethics of Manipulation," *Stanford Encyclopedia of Philosophy*, April 21, 2022, The Ethics of Manipulation (Stanford Encyclopedia of Philosophy).
4 "The Ethics of Manipulation," *Stanford Encyclopedia of Philosophy*, April 21, 2022, The Ethics of Manipulation (Stanford Encyclopedia of Philosophy).
5 Pathos (logiccheck.net).
6 Jennifer A. Whitson and Adam D. Galinsky, "Lacking Control Increases Illusory Pattern Perception." *Science* 322, 115—117 (2008). DOI:10.1126/Science.1159845.
7 Fear of Missing Out (FOMO): Some Causes and Solutions | Psychology Today.
8 Scene from Star Wars: Episode III—Revenge of the Sith, "If you are not with me, then you are my enemy!" Anakin Skywalker | StarWars.com.
9 "Q: Is fact—checking enough to stop the spread of misinformation on the Internet?," Sissel McCarthy, September 13, 2022, News Literacy Matters, Q: Is fact—checking enough to stop the spread of misinformation on the Internet?—News Literacy Matters.
10 "Q: Is fact—checking enough to stop the spread of misinformation on the Internet?," Sissel McCarthy, September 13, 2022, News Literacy Matters, Q: Is fact—checking enough to stop the spread of misinformation on the Internet?—News Literacy Matters.

11 "8 of the Best FOMO Marketing Examples You Must See," Emil Kristensen, Drip, May 24, 2022, 8 of the Best FOMO Marketing Examples You Must See (drip.com).
12 "8 of the Best FOMO Marketing Examples You Must See," Emil Kristensen, Drip, May 24, 2022, 8 of the Best FOMO Marketing Examples You Must See (drip.com).
13 "8 of the Best FOMO Marketing Examples You Must See," Emil Kristensen, Drip, May 24, 2022, 8 of the Best FOMO Marketing Examples You Must See (drip.com).

Apply the Skills Throughout the School Year

Chapter 19

Evaluate Pop Culture, Civics, ELA, and Social Studies Events

In Part III, I provide a short chapter to reinforce student understanding of my recommended steps to evaluate any type of social media. I also offer two sample lesson plans teachers can use with their students to practice applying the skills in this book. In the first lesson, I evaluate a post on a pop culture event, and in the second, I evaluate a post supporting the civics, ELA, and social studies curriculum. On my website, medialiteracysleuth.com, I periodically post more evaluations with lesson plans, divided according to each month of the school year, typically September–May.

Teachers can use these evaluations in several ways. If they have not yet taught their students the evaluation skills from Parts I and II (Chapters 1–18) of this book, I recommend using the first part of the school year, September–December, to do so using the information and lesson plans in these chapters. I encourage teachers to start out using examples of social media on trending pop culture topics to pique students' interest and keep them engaged, gradually weaving in media supporting the social studies, civics, and ELA curriculum as the year goes on. In this way, students learn both media literacy skills and the social studies, civics, and ELA curriculum at the same time.

If teachers have already covered the skills in Parts I and II when the school year begins, I recommend using the calendar-based media evaluations in Part III to keep students' skills fresh.

DOI: 10.4324/9781003471301-23

These evaluations cover a mix of pop culture and social studies, civics, and ELA-related examples from social media. Teachers can also use more recent evaluations from my website.

The following are my recommended steps to evaluate any type of social media. **Note**: I have tweaked the order of the steps from what I presented in Parts I and II. Now that students should understand each step, I think this new sequence is the most streamlined and time-efficient approach.

Here are the steps:

1. **Stop! Check for Biases and Mindset—the Author's and Your Own**
2. **Investigate the Source**
3. **Check for an Argument**
4. **Determine If the Argument Satisfies the Logic Condition**
5. **Check for Fallacies**
6. **Can You Fact-Check It?**
7. **Find Trusted Coverage**
8. **Trace Claims, Quotes, and Media to Their Original Context**
9. **Check for Manipulation Tactics**
10. **Check for Deceptive Use of Artificial Intelligence**
11. **Determine If the Argument Satisfies the Truth Condition**
12. **Overall Evaluation of the Media**

▶ FINAL LESSON PLAN: APPLY ALL THE SKILLS

This lesson reinforces students' prior knowledge of the 12 evaluation steps but also reshapes their knowledge by asking them to consider the steps in a new order. It asks all students to recall and apply each of the steps to two social media posts and evaluate each post using the steps. Higher achieving students should also ask questions such as the following:

- What is the context?
- What is the setting? What are the clues about the setting?

- What may be missing from the post? For images and video, what may be just out of the frame?
- What was the producer/poster of the post trying to capture?
- What story do you think is behind the post?
- Is this an example of propaganda?
- How does the propaganda appeal to my biases?

▶ ACTIVITY 1

Pop Culture: Video on Elon Musk

Media Type: **Video**[1] (https://www.tiktok.com/@b.t.s. hearmeout/video/7134885879520202030?is_from_webapp= 1&web_id=7132056045975979562) QR Code 19.1

Media Platform: TikTok

Let's apply the steps we have learned to evaluate this video.

Stop! Check for Biases and Mindset—the Author's and Your Own

Before sharing, pause and take a deep breath. Ask yourself:

- How does the video make me feel?
- What emotions am I feeling? Anger? Disbelief? Meh?

Let your emotions subside before you evaluate the media.

- What cognitive biases may be causing me to feel this way?
- Is confirmation bias causing you to ignore or discount evidence that could prove or disprove a premise?
- Is resistance bias causing you to maintain your current judgments about Elon Musk, even in the face of new evidence?
- Is groupthink causing your uncritical acceptance of a popular viewpoint?

Investigate the Source

We probably don't know the person in the video who is trying to make an argument, so we should not automatically trust them. Using our Internet search skills, leave TikTok and investigate the source.

Check for an Argument

The creator/poster of the video makes three statements: that Elon Musk's father, Errol, had a baby with his stepdaughter or "step-niece"; Errol said that his "point on the planet is to make more babies"; Errol said he is "proud" of it.

First, we need to ask: Is it an argument? Let's try to put it in standard form and see what we come up with.

1. Elon Musk's father, Errol, had a baby with his stepdaughter/ step-niece.
2. Errol said his purpose in life is to make more babies.
3. Errol said he is proud of his purpose.
Conclusion:?

There is no statement to serve as a conclusion. So the three other statements are not premises because they can't offer reasons to believe a conclusion that is not present. This is not an argument.

Determine If the Argument Satisfies the Logic Condition

We cannot determine this because we do not have an argument to evaluate.

Identify Fallacies

Since there is no argument, there are no fallacies to evaluate.

Can You Fact-Check It?

Can we still fact-check the three statements? Let's start with the first statement, that Musk's father had a baby with his step-daughter or step-niece.

The person makes this statement as though it's fact based, not opinion or conjecture without evidence, so we can fact-check it. The person cites no evidence to evaluate, so we need to use our Internet search skills and see what we find.

Find Trusted Coverage

We can first see if any reputable fact-checking sites have reported on this. The URL https://bit.ly/fact—search allows searches of several fact-checking sites at once. Using click restraint, our search results over several pages do not include a fact-check from an IFCN member.

However, a variety of credible media outlets, including *Newsweek* (a longtime US news weekly periodical), report that Musk's father, Errol Musk, did in fact father a child with his stepdaughter, Jana, in 2018. So, we can confidently say that statement one is true.

In this case, we're done. But if your students were doing research for a school research paper, they would want to pick the most reliable, authoritative source in the search results to back up the statement. In our search results, *Newsweek* would arguably be the most reliable source to support this statement.

Following these steps for the second statement, that Musk's father *said* his "point on the planet is to make more babies," we find several reasonably reputable news sources that corroborate it, in slightly different words, including the *Guardian*, the *Sun*, and the Huffington Post.[2] According to these sources, Errol said, "The only thing we are on Earth for is to reproduce."[3,4]

Following these steps for the third statement, that Errol is "proud" of fathering more babies, we only find the quotes, "I can't see any reason not to," and that it is his God-given duty." This is not the same as being "proud." In sum, the first and second statements are true, but the third is not.

We can check for disinformation to determine the motivation of the creator or poster of the video. Because we have determined that the first and second statements are true, we can focus on the motivation behind the third statement, that Errol Musk was "proud" to father the child. Let's check for disinformation using the Social Media Evaluation Game and the Common Types of Misleading News Identification Game sheets.

There is no headline per se to draw us in, because the poster/creator is relying on the "automatic play" feature of TikTok, the video and images that appear, and the captions on the images to catch our attention. The video and images do not appear to be stock or doctored, other than having captions.

The author claims to have a TikTok account, @b.t.shearmeout, a podcast, and a Gmail address, and these have a sizable following. As of this writing, there are no banner or pop-up ads, but the originator/poster does have a statement on their account page, "Road to 1 million," that suggests they seek more engagement, either for simple fame or perhaps for revenue from TikTok.

The captioned text and accompanying audio dialogue are informal, as would be expected from many social media posts, but not especially emotional, hyperbolic, or sensationalized language. There is no readily apparent date on the post. There are no source quotes or links to sources, but there are versions of this story elsewhere online. We can presume the two people in the video are as qualified as anyone to speak about the topic. There is no need for graphs or statistics in this example.

The video does not appear to be from an automated (bot) account. The account has detailed personal information, an unambiguous profile photo, no excessively divisive words or hashtags, and a realistic volume and pattern of tweets and retweets and of followers and following.

Overall, there are not enough red flags to suggest disinformation. Of course, the author would like to reach one million likes and may receive compensation if their video likes reach that threshold.

We can conclude that this TikTok video contains Clickbait, and the third statement is mild misinformation.

Trace Claims, Quotes, and Media to Their Original Contexts

In this case, there is no need to trace the statement to its original context because this is a straight, unambiguous fact-check with no context to verify.

Check for Manipulation Tactics

We could say the person is using a mild form of the **discredit** manipulation tactic—perhaps trying to delegitimize Errol Musk by saying his act was "some crazy sh*t," that "he did not regret that sh*t at all," and "that's f*ked." The person may use this tactic because they have no logical, rational argument to back up their three statements. They are relying mostly on appealing to the viewer's pathos—i.e., the viewer follows the TikTok account primarily to be entertained.

The video probably relies less on our ethos because fewer viewers (hopefully) would trust the TikTok account as a source of information the way they would a standards-based news site.

Check for Deceptive Artificial Intelligence

Is there deceptive AI involved—e.g., is the video a shallow fake or a deepfake? We have no reason to think so. The account @b.t.s.hearmeout posts lots of videos of two people talking inside a vehicle; the main thrust is the discussion via captions. These videos do not feature celebrities, the most common target of deepfakes. The mouth movements of both people match the audio dialogue. There is no mismatched skin tone between the face and the neck. The video also has vehicles moving in the background, something a deepfake creator would probably not devote time and effort to include.

Determine If the Argument Satisfies the Truth Condition

Not applicable because there is no argument to evaluate.

Overall Evaluation of the Video

The video does not make an argument. It does give two facts about Errol Musk.

▶ ACTIVITY 2

Social studies topic: Video on Biden's student loan forgiveness program
   Media type: Video[5] (https://www.instagram.com/tv/ChtLrZ dAAAS/?igshid=YmMyMTA2M2Y%3D) QR Code 19.2
   Media platform: Instagram

Note: Teachers who have not yet taught students about basic economic principles such as inflation may need to explain the concepts in order for students to participate effectively in this lesson.

Summary: @rationalboomer (rationalboomer) makes several statements in this video posted on August 25, 2022. He says something like this:

- Republicans are being hypocritical by accusing the student loan forgiveness program of giving away free money and causing inflation because their forgiven Paycheck Protection Program (PPP) loans do the same things.

Before we go further, we need to put ourselves in critical thinking mode. We can do that by applying the first step of the SIFT method.

Stop! Check for Biases and Mindset—the Author's and Your Own

Before sharing, ask yourself:

- How does the video make me feel?
- What emotions am I feeling? Anger? Disbelief? Meh?
- How does the speaker's word choice affect my emotions?

Take a deep breath to let your emotions settle. Prepare to evaluate the media dispassionately.

Check your biases and mindset:

- What cognitive biases may cause you to feel this way?
- Could confirmation bias cause you to believe a premise and ignore or discount evidence that could disprove a premise?
- Could resistance bias cause you to maintain your current judgments about the program, even in the face of new evidence?
- What mindset might you have toward the program? Do you tend to approve/disapprove of government aid programs?

Investigate the Source

Leave Instagram and use your Internet search skills. Since rational-boomer is not a mainstream, standards-based news source, this step is important. We quickly find that he has a decent following and does a podcast in which he discusses his opinions on a wide variety of issues. Many topics center on criticizing Donald Trump.

Check for an Argument

Now that we're in critical thinking mode and thinking rationally, remember that most posts on social media seek to persuade us to believe or do something. But many posts don't offer sufficient reasons for us to be persuaded, often because they rest on nonexistent or weak arguments or on fallacies or manipulation tactics to convince us.

First, we need to ask, Is rationalboomer making an argument? Let's try to identify premises and a conclusion by putting his statements in standard form:

1. Forgiven student loans give away free money. (Implied statement)
2. Forgiven PPP loans give away free money.
3. Forgiven student loans cause inflation. (Implied statement)
4. Forgiven PPP loans cause inflation.

Therefore, Republicans with forgiven PPP loans who deny that their forgiven loans give away free money and cause inflation and criticize student loan forgiveness for doing both are hypocritical.

We can see that there are four statements. We could quarrel a bit that the first two statements are too vague in this context because rationalboomer and viewers of his video may have different interpretations of what "free money" is. Ideally, we should ask rationalboomer to clarify what he means before continuing. Since we can't do that easily, let's assume that "free money" means free for the recipients, not necessarily for the taxpayer. Let's continue to evaluate his statements.

We could say each of the statements is true or false, but not both. There is a conclusion, and the statements offer reasons for the conclusion, so we can say the statements are premises. Therefore, rationalboomer is making an argument.

Does he make a good argument that is persuasive for good reasons, i.e., one offering premises that his audience is willing to accept and demonstrating how the conclusion follows logically from those premises? Or does he make a bad argument that does not have one or both of these things and should not persuade us?

Determine If the Argument Satisfies the Logic Condition

To help answer that, let's see if his argument satisfies the **Logic Condition**. Does the conclusion follow from the premises? Here is his argument again:

1. Forgiven student loans give away free money.
2. Forgiven PPP loans give away free money.
3. Forgiven student loans cause inflation.
4. Forgiven PPP loans cause inflation.

Therefore, Republicans with forgiven PPP loans who deny that their forgiven loans give away free money and cause inflation and criticize student loan forgiveness for doing both are hypocritical.

Setting aside whether each premise is true or false, we can say the conclusion follows from the premises. His argument satisfies the Logic Condition.

How does his argument satisfy the Logic Condition? Is it valid or strong?

Remember, a valid argument is one with the condition that if all its premises are true, the conclusion cannot be false. It's the strongest possible logical glue between premises and conclusion.[6] In rationalboomer's argument, the conclusion cannot be false, assuming all four premises are true. His argument is valid. In sum, his argument satisfies the Logic Condition because it is a valid argument.

Check for Fallacies

The premise that Republicans are hypocritical suffers from the **fallacy of composition**—projecting the properties of the individual onto the whole. Even if one could argue that the specific Republicans mentioned are hypocritical, not all Republicans had PPP loans forgiven or even supported forgiveness for those who did.

Can You Fact-Check It?

Yes. We can fact-check all four premises.

Find Trusted Coverage

Premise One: Student loan forgiveness gives away free money.

Using our Internet search skills, we find many reputable media outlets that lean left, right, or center (according to the AllSides Media Bias Chart) were reporting on this at the time of this writing. For example, according to *Time*, the program allowed borrowers who earn under $125,000 to cancel $10,000 in federal school loan debt, while married couples qualified for $10,000 per person in debt cancellation if their joint income was under $250,000. Borrowers with Pell Grants, which primarily target low-income students, qualified for an additional $10,000 in loan cancellation, or a total of $20,000, if they met the income requirements.[7] According to Reuters, the nonpartisan Congressional Budget Office in September calculated that debt forgiveness would cost the government about $400 billion.[8] **Is student loan forgiveness free money? Yes, although only partially for those who qualified**.

Premise Two: PPP loan forgiveness gives away free money.

Rationalboomer only cited the White House X account, which at the time of this writing did not say whether PPP forgiveness is free money. The White House only tweeted, and rationalboomer generally repeated, *how much* PPP forgiveness seven Republicans received.

For example, rationalboomer said that Matt Gaetz (R-FL) received $476,000 in forgiven PPP loans. The White House tweeted that Gaetz received about $482,000. Using the search string *"Matt Gaetz" AND "Payment Protection Program,"* we find a report from PolitiFact[9], which generally corroborates rationalboomer's figure.

Rationalboomer claimed that Marjorie Taylor-Greene (R-GA) had $180,000 forgiven. The White House tweeted that she received $183,500. Searching on "Marjorie Taylor-Greene" and "Payment Protection Program" again surfaces the PolitiFact report, which put the amount at about $182,000.

Rationalboomer said that Greg Pence (R-IN) had $79,441 forgiven. PolitiFact reported that the figure was spot on.

Rationalboomer claimed that Rep. Vern Buchanan (R-FL) had $2.8 million forgiven. The White House tweeted he had $2.3 million forgiven. PolitiFact reported that he had $2.6 billion forgiven—pretty close.

Rationalboomer said that Ralph Norman (R-SC) had $306,000 forgiven. PolitiFact indicated that he actually received almost double the relief—$608,500.

Rationaleboomer claimed that Mark Wayne Mullin (R-OK) had $988,000 forgiven. The White House tweeted that he had $1.4 million forgiven. PolitiFact reported that he had 1.4 million forgiven, matching the tweet.

Finally, rationaleboomer said Carol Miller (R-WV) had $3.1 million forgiven; PolitiFact indicated that Miller's husband received that amount.

Is PPP loan forgiveness free money? Yes, for the recipients (including the Republican business owners cited above).[10]

Premise Three: Student loan forgiveness increases inflation. Using the search string "student loan forgiveness" AND inflation, clicking the News tab, and using click restraint, we find that many media outlets leaning left, right, or center were reporting on the issue. For example, Forbes, a "lean center" outlet, indicated that the inflation impact will be "relatively small," or about 0.15%.[11] **Does the student loan forgiveness program increase inflation? Technically, yes, but essentially, no.**

Premise Four: PPP loan forgiveness increases inflation. Rationalboomer only cited the White House X account, which did not say whether PPP forgiveness increases inflation. Using Internet searching, we found no reporting on the issue. **It is unclear if PPP loan forgiveness increases inflation**.

Trace Claims, Quotes, and Media to Their Original Contexts

The student loan forgiveness program, announced in August 2022, was to forgive up to $10,000 per borrower. The US Small Business Administration and Treasury Department started the PPP to provide forgivable loans to help small businesses and nonprofit institutions impacted by the COVID-19 pandemic and economic downturn make payroll and cover other expenses. The program was authorized initially by the Coronavirus Aid, Relief and Economic Security Act (CARES) of 2020, modified by subsequent legislation, and reauthorized by the Coronavirus Response and Relief Supplemental Appropriations Act of 2021. Lawmakers were not barred from taking advantage of the PPP, and Democratic and Republican politicians both received loans for their businesses.[12]

Check for Manipulation Tactics

One could argue that the White House premise of Republican hypocrisy uses the **projection** manipulation tactic,[13] whereby a person is accused of something and simply turns it around on the accusers. The premise might also be an example of **whataboutism**[14]—immediately redirecting the conversation away from the alleged "wrongdoing" of the manipulator to another person or group. In this case, the manipulator is the White House, and the other group is the White House Republican critics. In this case, the White House and some Democrats responded to the Republican premises that the student loan forgiveness was giving away free money and increasing inflation by saying the same thing about Republicans whose PPP loans were forgiven.

Some Republican responses to the White House tweets essentially claimed that the White House and Democrats were using the **false equivalency** manipulation tactic[15]—i.e., trying to make people think that student loan forgiveness and PPP loan forgiveness were equivalent in their effects when they were not. Some Republicans who claimed the student loan forgiveness would increase inflation were also engaging in **fearmongering**[16]—i.e., stoking fear among American taxpayers during a time of high inflation that may have inhibited their ability to question and think logically and rationally, including by seeking out reliable information on the issue. Finally, some Republican responses used the tactic of **misrepresentation**[17]—intentional distortion of a fact or idea to make it seem better or worse than it really is. In this case, some Republicans exaggerated the effects of student loan forgiveness on inflation.

Check for Deceptive Artificial Intelligence

The video does not appear to contain manipulation or other deceptive use of AI. It does not have indicators of a deepfake, voice cloning, or generative text such as ChatGPT.

Determine If the Argument Satisfies the Truth Condition

Are all the premises true or plausible? To find out, let's lay out each premise and the evidence and reasoning for each.

> **Premise One: Student loan forgiveness gives away free money**.
> - Rationalboomer is using reasoning to imply the program gives away free money, and his reasoning is pretty sound. Although the evidence he explicitly cites—the White House X account—does not say the program provides "free" money, the evidence I found generally supports the premise that qualified recipients receive partial forgiveness. A reasonable person would conclude that the evidence supports the premise.
> **Conclusion: This premise satisfies the Truth Condition**.

Premise Two: PPP loan forgiveness gives away free money.

- Rationalboomer is using reasoning to say the PPP amounts to "free money." His reasoning is pretty sound. The evidence we found generally support the premise. A reasonable person would conclude that the evidence supports the premise.

Conclusion: This premise satisfies the Truth Condition.

Premise Three: Student loan forgiveness will increase inflation.

- Rationalboomer is using reasoning to say the student loan forgiveness program will increase inflation. The *Forbes* piece indicates there will be an increase but that it will be insignificant.

Conclusion: This premise satisfies the Truth Condition, barely.

Premise Four: PPP loan forgiveness will increase inflation.

- Rationalboomer is using reasoning to say that the PPP will increase inflation. But his reasoning is unsound because we don't have evidence to reason from.

Conclusion: This premise does not satisfy the Truth Condition.

Overall, rationalboomer's argument does not satisfy the Truth Condition because premise four is not true or plausible. Recall that an argument can only meet the Truth Condition if all its premises are true or plausible.

▶ OVERALL EVALUATION OF THE MEDIA

Rationalboomer's argument is not a good argument. It satisfies the Logic Condition because it is valid, but it does not satisfy the Truth Condition because one of its premises is not true or plausible.

His argument would probably be persuasive to viewers who already have a mindset and biases that cause them to view these Republicans unfavorably.

▶ **NOTES**

1 WHAT…#hearmeout_cast #btshearmeout #viral #fyp #podcast #conspirancyth… | TikTok.

2 Elon Musk's Father Confirms Second Secret Child With Step-daughter, Marco Margaritoff, July 15, 2022.

3 "FAMILY TIES Elon Musk's Shock Reaction to Father Errol's Kid with STEPDAUGHTER Revealed as CEO's Dad Says He's Ready for MORE Babies," Alex Diaz, July 15, 2022, updated August 1, 2022.

4 "Elon Musk's Father Says He Isn't Proud of His Son," Gloria Oladipo, @gaoladipo, August 1, 2022.

5 WELL THAT DIDN'T AGE WELL | Instagram.

6 What Is a Good Argument? | The Critical Thinker Academy, Kevin Delaplante.

7 The Student Loan Forgiveness Application Is Online. Join Our Free Webinar on Nov. 15 to Apply | NextAdvisor with TIME, The Student Loan Forgiveness Application Is Online. Join Our Free Webinar on November 15 to Apply, Alex Gailey, senior reporter at NextAdvisor, November 10, 2022.

8 US Appeals Court Temporarily Blocks Biden's Student Loan Forgiveness Plan | Reuters. US Appeals Court Temporarily Blocks Biden's Student Loan Forgiveness Plan, Eric Beech and Steve Gorman, October 22, 2022.

9 PolitiFact | Businesses Associated with These GOP Politicians Had Pandemic Loan Program Borrowings Forgiven, www.PolitiFact.com/factchecks/2022/aug/30/instagram—posts/businesses—associated—these—gop—politicians—had—pa/.

10 David Autor, David Cho, Leland D. Crane, Mita Goldar, Byron Lutz, Joshua Montes, William B. Peterman, David Ratner, Daniel Villar and Ahu Yildirmaz, "The $800 Billion Paycheck Protection Program: Where Did the Money Go and Why Did It Go There?" *Journal of Economic Perspectives*, Spring 2022, Vol. 36, No. 2, pp. 55—80.

11 How Loan Forgiveness Will Impact Inflation – Forbes Advisor, Kelly Anne Smith, August 25, 2022.

12 How Does the Paycheck Protection Program Impact the National Income and Product Accounts (NIPAs)? | US Bureau of Economic Analysis (BEA).

13 Common Manipulation Tactics, Erika Thorsen, English Teacher at Squalicum High School, Bellingham, WA.

14 Common Manipulation Tactics, Erika Thorsen, English Teacher at Squalicum High School, Bellingham, WA.

15 Common Manipulation Tactics, Erika Thorsen, English Teacher at Squalicum High School, Bellingham, WA.

16 Common Manipulation Tactics, Erika Thorsen, English Teacher at Squalicum High School, Bellingham, WA.

17 Common Manipulation Tactics, Erika Thorsen, English Teacher at Squalicum High School, Bellingham, WA.

Afterword

My passion for news and media literacy grew naturally from my work as a CIA analyst and instructor of CIA analysts. Of all the topics I taught new CIA analysts, evaluating the credibility of intelligence reports was my favorite. After the rampant disinformation surrounding the 2016 US presidential election, I realized this same skill was critical for people outside the CIA if the United States wanted to preserve and strengthen its democracy.

I quickly recognized that preteens and teens are at a ripe age to learn news literacy skills. They are fascinated with social media, and their minds are sufficiently open to learn the skills. That's why I focused this book on the teachers who teach them.

And there are other reasons. These students' ability to make informed, rational, and logical evaluations of media will help them perform better in school. More importantly, the skills will help them make better decisions in life and engage confidently and effectively in the civil discourse necessary for a healthy democracy.

The lesson plans in this book are intended to make teaching news literacy easier for you, their teachers, to weave into your curriculum. I hope the book's heavy focus on trending pop culture on social media will make it easier for you to "hook" students on news literacy and that the lessons on social studies-civics-ELA topics will be a natural segue for you to ensure you cover the curriculum.

I periodically evaluate news on social media and post my evaluations on my website, **medialiteracysleuth.com**. I encourage you to visit the site frequently to find lessons you can easily incorporate into your curriculum. In the meantime, I would love to hear your thoughts on the book, how I might improve it, whether you have tried the activities with your students, and how it went. You can reach me via email:

roywhitehurst4@gmail.com, Instagram: royw9293, LinkedIn: www.linkedin.com/in/roy-whitehurst-7170353b, or X: https://twitter.com/RoyWhitehurst2.

▶ TOOLS

Fact-Checking

- Google Fact Check Tools (https://toolbox.google.com/factcheck/explorer)
- Media Smarts' Programmable Search Engine (https://cse.google.com/cse?cx=009843066196008418578:5c4h08rfa8q#gsc.tab=0)

Image and Video Analysis

- **Google reverse image search** (https://images.google.com/)

- **Tineye** (https://tineye.com/)

- **FotoForensics** (https://fotoforensics.com/): Can identify elements in a photo that have been added.

- **Forensically** (https://29a.ch/photo-forensics/#level-sweep): Provides several tools, including clone detection, noise analysis, and metadata analysis, to aid in forensic analysis of images in content.

- **Image Verification Assistant** (https://mever.iti.gr/forensics/): Claims to build a "comprehensive tool for media verification." It offers several tools, including image tampering–detection algorithms, reverse image search, and metadata analysis.

- **Ghiro** (https://getghiro.org/): Claims to be a "fully automated tool designed to run forensics analysis over a massive amount of images, just using a user-friendly and fancy web application" (Tanasi and Buoncristiano, 2017).

- **InVid WeVerify browser plug-in (for videos)** (extension://mhccpoafgdgbhnjfhkcmgknndkeenfhe/popup.html#/app/tools/all):

Provides a web extension that allows users to freeze-frame videos, perform reverse image searches on video frames, magnify frozen video images, and more (InVID and WeVerify, 2022).

- **Content Credentials** (https://contentcredentials.org/verify): A tool from the Content Authenticity Initiative that content creators can use to transparently share the details of how they created an image. When content, e.g., an image, is uploaded to the tool, the tool displays available metadata about the content. This can include who created the content, when the content was created or edited, whether AI generated at least part of the content, and which applications and devices were used to create the content. The CAI is a group of creators, technologists, journalists, and activists leading the global effort to address digital misinformation and content authenticity.[1]

▶ **RESOURCES**

Steps to Evaluate News on Social Media

1. Stop! Check for Biases and Mindset—the Author's and Your Own
2. Investigate the Source
3. Check for an Argument
4. Determine If the Argument Satisfies the Logic Condition
5. Check for Fallacies
6. Can You Fact-Check the Information?
7. Find Trusted Coverage
8. Trace Claims, Quotes, and Media to Their Original Context
9. Check for Manipulation Tactics
10. Check for Deceptive Use of Artificial Intelligence
11. Determine If the Argument Satisfies the Truth Condition
12. Evaluate the Media Overall

Recurring Events for News Literacy Instruction		
Date	Pop Culture	Social Studies/Civics/ELA
September	Choose your event from the prior summer (e.g., World UFO Day, Book Lovers Day, National Rock 'N Roll Day, etc.), Back to School Ads, Labor Day	Labor Day (workers' rights)
September 11	9/11, Patriot Day #911truth, #911wasaninsidejob, #bushdid911	9/11, Patriot Day
September 16	Batman Day	
September 17		Constitution Day
September 22	National Ice Cream Cone Day	
September 26	National Comic Book Day	
September	Yom Kippur	
September–October	Rosh Hashanah	
September–October	Hispanic Heritage Month	Hispanic Heritage Month
October	Indigenous Peoples' Day (2nd Monday in October)	Indigenous Peoples' Day (2nd Monday in October)
October	National Bullying Prevention Month, National Anti—Bullying (Pink Shirt) Day	
October	Halloween (scary movies, popular characters)	Halloween (media making, cinematography, parody, caricatures)
October	Political campaigns (ads, caricatures, etc.)	Political campaigns (ads, caricatures, etc.) Media Literacy Week

(Continued)

Recurring Events for News Literacy Instruction		
Date	*Pop Culture*	*Social Studies/Civics/ ELA*
November	Political campaigns (ads, caricatures, etc.)	Political campaigns (ads, caricatures, etc.)
November	Diwali	
November	Veterans Day	Veterans Day (US history)
November	Thanksgiving (Black Friday shopping)	Thanksgiving (US history)
November	Hanukkah	
December	Christmas (ads)	
December	Kwanzaa	
December	New Year's Eve (parties)	
January	New Year's Day (resolutions)	
January	Martin Luther King Jr. Day (Civil Rights)	Martin Luther King, Jr. Day (Civil Rights)
January		National (US) Slavery and Human Trafficking Prevention Month, International Human Trafficking Month
January	Golden Globe Awards	
January 27	International Holocaust Remembrance Day	International Holocaust Remembrance Day
February	Super Bowl (ads)	Super Bowl (ads)
February	Groundhog Day	
February	Grammy Awards	
February	Valentine's Day (ads)	Valentine's Day (ads)
February	Presidents' Day (ads)	Presidents' Day (US history, ads)
February	Black History Month	Black History Month
March	Women's History Month	Women's History Month
March	Ash Wednesday	
March	Academy Awards (Oscars)	

(Continued)

	Recurring Events for News Literacy Instruction	
Date	**_Pop Culture_**	**_Social Studies/Civics/ ELA_**
March	St. Patrick's Day (drinking)	
March	Holi	Holi (diversity and inclusion)
March	March Madness (sports)	
April	April Fool's Day (pranks)	
April 2	International Fact-Checking Day	International Fact-Checking Day
April	Beginning of Ramadan	Beginning of Ramadan (diversity and inclusion)
April	Earth Day (celeb involvement)	Earth Day
April	Palm Sunday/Good Friday/Easter	Palm Sunday/Good Friday/Easter (diversity and inclusion)
May	Eid al—Fitr	Eid al—Fitr (diversity and inclusion)
May 4	Star Wars: "May the Fourth Be With You"	
May	Cinco de Mayo	Cinco de Mayo
May	Memorial Day (official start of "summer")	Memorial Day (US history)
May	National Teen Self-Esteem Month	
June	LGBTQ Pride Month	
June	Juneteenth	Juneteenth (human rights, diversity and inclusion)
June		Flag Day

Note

1 FAQ—Content Authenticity Initiative.

Index

Pages in *italics* refer to figures.